THE LIGHT IN THE WILDERNESS

How Religion Has Led the World Astray

Norman Martin Wolk, M.D.

Bloomington, IN  Milton Keynes, UK

authorHOUSE®

AuthorHouse™
1663 Liberty Drive, Suite 200
Bloomington, IN 47403
www.authorhouse.com
Phone: 1-800-839-8640

AuthorHouse™ *UK Ltd.*
500 Avebury Boulevard
Central Milton Keynes, MK9 2BE
www.authorhouse.co.uk
Phone: 08001974150

First published by AuthorHouse 2/12/2007

ISBN: 978-1-4259-5792-6 (sc)

Printed in the United States of America
Bloomington, Indiana

This book is printed on acid-free paper.

This Book is dedicated to:

YAHUWEH Elohim, and

His Revealed and Written Word, the TORAH, and
His Revealed and Living WORD, the Messiah of Israel,
YAHOSHUA

"Thy WORD is a lamp unto my feet,
and a light unto my path."
[Psalm 119:105]

"I know, O Yahuweh, that a man's way is not in himself; nor is it in a man who walks to direct his steps."

[Jeremiah 10:23]

CONTENTS

Preface and Introduction

Our lives are played out on many stages, and in many roles: at home or at work, at school or at play, in our own country or abroad; and as parent or child, single or married, teacher or student, Jew or Gentile, Protestant or Catholic, Hindu or Buddhist, Moslem or Sikh, atheist or agnostic, black or white or yellow or brown or red. The combinations and permutations of all of these and more are immeasureable. Now introduce the infinite number of differing ideas as a variable, and the possibilities become limitless.

To the enlightened and secular mind, such is the splendor of our civilization, the flower of an educational model largely founded on Greek and Roman thought, and almost universally perceived as the culmination of human achievement.

Yet, despite all of the awesome accomplishments humankind has attained since its beginning, man remains woefully ignorant of the answers to the essential questions of existence:

Why am I here?
Who am I?
Where am I going?
How should I live?
What does all this mean?

Great minds throughout history have attempted to answer these. While psychology, philosophy, social theory, and political science have offered up their conclusions, it is in the world of religion that the most definitive answers may be found. And it is in this domain, which has gathered unto itself billions of faithful adherents throughout the centuries and who embrace a particular existential view, that seemingly right and satisfying answers reside.

But on closer scrutiny, the teachings and doctrines of all of these (religions), simply do not provide the ultimate truth we would seek. Indeed, their ideas and principles, like those who propose them, are fragmented and broken; and it is delusion to believe otherwise.

Today, as the curtain is lifted on the stage of the 21st century, the world is bearing witness to a violent clash of world views, based on religious civilizations founded and perpetuated by sincere and earnest men; a conflict that has the potential to bring utter and complete destruction to all the earth.

How could it be that such exalted ideas, and noble thoughts, articulated by the best and the brightest among us, have brought us to this?

****

There is an answer; and it can overwhelm (us), for it challenges our instinctive, elemental view of our place in the universe.

In order to seriously entertain such an answer, we must divest ourselves of our "selfs", cast off the muddled identities that we claim, shed our stained egos. and take on the role of contrite and humbled servants.

Although the most ascendant members of the human race have given us the best of their gifts, the source of these contributions was found ultimately within themselves. And herein lies the fatal flaw; even the greatest human thoughts are fruits of a poison tree; for mankind is broken physically, emotionally, and spiritually.

Our lives, though often blessed with times of joy, and hope, and fulfillment, are marred by sorrow, frustration, confusion, anger, bitterness, and despair, as we stumble relentlessly toward our earthly destiny and ego's extinction: death and the grave.

So, where then do we go to find the Answer to the essential questions of our existence.

The genuine seeker may take comfort in knowing that there is such a source……. a source not based on human reasoning, experience, or imagination; but on revelation.

This revealed Answer is given to us in a written record known as The Scripture, and in a Living Record, known as the Messiah and Eternal One, the pure and perfect Source of existence itself.

****

This Living Redeemer, sinless and perfect Eternal Teacher, through His Word, is "The Light in the Wilderness" Who will lead us out of the darkness.

****

There are some today who believe that we are living in the last days of human history.

No one can know with certainty whether or not this is true, but even the most jaded among us recognize that there is something disturbingly different about these times.

Indeed, there is a distressing sense that even the best intentions, exercised by our greatest minds, will not be enough to thwart our blind rush to mutual and self annihilation.

We live today on the edge of the wilderness.

Still, it is not inevitable that all will end in destruction.

Indeed, it is a certainty that all history will end starkly, stunningly, and splendidly otherwise.

You are humbly and graciously invited to journey now beyond the edge of this wilderness, to a place where Truth, and Righteousness, and Goodness, and Life will reign eternally; to a civilization founded on, and ruled by the Eternal Creator and Redeemer, as we follow <u>"The Light in the Wilderness"</u>.

Prologue

For more than 2000 years, a seemingly insurmountable wall of partition has separated the two great Abrahamic monotheistic faiths: Judaism and Christianity.

It all began with a humble Jewish rabbi, the son of a carpenter, an itinerant in the land of Israel, who preached a message of repentance, obedient faith, and a redeemed creation and humanity alive for ever in a majestic and hopeful new world tomorrow.

In fulfillment of prophecy, and precisely as "God" had intended, amongst some of His Jewish co-religionists, His Messianic message and mission was met by misunderstanding, disappointment or rejection.

However, there was a significant and zealous number of Jews who truly gave ear, heeding His words and His call. They became the seeds of a seminal Torah-observant Messianic faith community. In Him, they beheld the fulfillment of the Hope of Israel and the nations.

Tragically, but predictably, history was not to be generous or kind to this persecuted remnant; for in a relatively few short years they would be almost completely extinguished by the powerful forces of Roman politics, Gentile military might, pagan doctrines, (Greek) Hellenism, anti-Semitism, sinister compromises, countless concessions, and antinomianism (rejection of the Torah or Law as in the 'Law of God').

Ultimately, the historical truth of Israel's Torah and Israel's Messiah would be sacrificed on the altar of expedience.

****

Historian Will Durant, in his book, "The Story of Civilization", would write:

"Christianity....grew by the absorption of pagan faith and ritual; it became a triumphant Church by inheriting the organizing patterns and genius of Rome....

As Judea had given Christianity ethics, and Greece had given it theology, so now Rome gave it organization; all these with a dozen absorbed and rival faiths, entered into the Christian synthesis."

(Volume 5, Durant pp. 575, 618-619)

****

This early syncretic union of alien, disparate, anti-Jewish and anti-Torah movements and ideas became the foundation of 'orthodox' historical Christian belief and progenitor of Roman and Byzantine, Greek and Coptic, Catholic and Protestant Christianity.

Neither Rome and her Roman Catholicism, nor Germany, Switzerland, Holland, Belgium, France, Scandinavia, England or Scotland, and their Reformation Protestantism, have been fully faithful to the Teaching that is Torah (commonly known as the "Old Testament") and the Redeemer Messiah revealed within its pages.

To those ignorant of Hebrew Scriptures, and the numerous Jewish prophecies pointing over and over again to a suffering and servant Messiah, and to those who would not or could not believe in His atoning death and resurrection, it would appear that this rabbi Who came to reconcile humanity to their Creator and to one another, had missed the mark, and failed [in] His mission.

But appearance is rarely substance. Ultimately, that Messianic mission will wondrously succeed, and be made fully and supernaturally real.

As for His awesome greatness and singular distinction, the Messiah has been variably called deceiver, pretender, liar, lunatic, or legend by some; and "Lord and Savior" by others.

Among the vast multitudes that claim Him as Redeemer and very 'God' Himself, powerful religions have been founded in His Name, with divisions and denominations numbering in the thousands.

It is then both shocking and amazing, that over these last two millenia, not one of these (religions) have taught the full truth of the Messiah, or His revealed Scriptural path to a meaningful and authentic mortal life, and the radical transforming way to attain future immortality.

Only by way of the WHOLE of Scripture, comprised of the Five Books of Moses, the Prophets, and the Writings [known as Torah or Tanach or "Old Testament"], and the Messianic Scriptures [known as"New Testament"] can the full Plan of Redemption be known and lived out.

When one surveys without prejudice or parochialism, but with honest scholarship and intellectual integrity, the origins and development of Christianity and Christendom's hold on the mind and heart of vast multitudes of humanity throughout the ages, that very conclusion becomes inescapable.

In the present day, during these times of extreme turbulence and worldly unrest, this ancient pure and untainted message, proclaimed and embraced by the Messiah, the Torah, and the first faith communities, has never been more urgently relevant or essential.

Bridging that wall of separation between Judaism and Christianity will not come about by glossing over differences, or sentimental slogans about co-existence, tolerance, and common shared beliefs.

Rather, out of this complex web of religious doctrines, born of ignorance, fear, compromise, concession, and human contrivance, concepts and ideas that are radically new and transforming must spring forth so as to shake the very foundations of institutionalized Christianity and Judaism.

****

"The Light in the Wilderness" is a collection of essays of insight, interpretation, and wisdom, inviting the reader to consider life's largest questions, and to re-examine traditional religion's answers.

Along the way, personal creeds, customs, traditions, and beliefs will be met, challenged, and confronted.

At the conclusion of this journey of thought and spirit, it is hoped the reader might be bathed in the light of the Key to Truth.

For all who witness this wilderness light, their vision and world view will be forever changed; but especially for those called and the chosen, the Precious Key will open the door to eternity, inviting the elect to join that great cloud of witnesses, and [to] enter, humbly and repentantly, into His Everlasting Kingdom.

Foreword

The amazing truth about the religions of the world is that all of them share the common belief that MAN IS IMMORTAL; that there is something within man, namely his soul, that already possesses eternal life. Upon that premise, the grand edifices of theology and doctrine have been built over the vast expanses of time. Such a foundational belief is the bedrock on which the great faiths of Judaism, Christianity, Islam, Buddhism, Hinduism, and countless other religions rest.

Yet even more amazing is that this premise, this foundational belief, is utterly and completely false.

The truth is stunningly different; and almost entirely unknown to most of mankind. Shocking to the religious mind, but glaringly obvious to the rational, is the plain and simple truth that MAN IS MORTAL, destined to live for a comparatively few short years, born, as it were, only to die.

Only man's designer and creator, the Almighty YHWH ELOHIM is eternal.* (1Timothy 6:16)

The creature, and present creation itself, has its beginning and its end.

The Eternal Creator, Alone, is without beginning and without end.

Notwithstanding all of this sobering news, the ultimate hope and destiny of mortal man is to escape the prison of his mortality, and ATTAIN ETERNAL LIFE. Indeed, to achieve this transcendent goal is the great purpose of life here on earth.

How to achieve it is the reason for the MOSHIACH* (Messiah) and the Teaching of our Heavenly Father known as TORAH.

As we embark upon this journey that leads to eternal life, you will face scriptural truths that will challenge most, if not all of what you have been taught. Whether you are Jewish, Christian, Moslem, Buddhist, Hindu, Sikh, animist, deist, secularist, rationalist, or any other of the numerous faiths of mankind; even if you have no traditional faith at all, calling yourself atheist or agnostic, this book is for you.

Take comfort in the assurance that the Gates of the Kingdom, the portal to eternal life, are always open to those of humble heart, contrite spirit, and open mind. And although its road is narrow, it can be found!

And once you have found it, there is absolutely nothing that can keep you from reaching that wonderful destination; for it is at this moment that the goal of man is at one with (atoned with) the purposes of Heaven. (Romans 8:33-39).

Transformed from mortality to immortality, from corruptibility to incorruptibility, this NEW LIFE is the crown that AWAITS, through Messiah, the OBEDIENT and FAITHFUL servant sons and daughters of The King of the Universe.(1Corinthians 15:50-58)

This is the life of true "holiness", the life set apart!

It is the life chosen before the foundations of the earth, while yet in its mother's womb, selected for and by YHWH ELOHIM, so that His elect may enter into His Eternal Kingdom, and the 'World to Come'; a world that is truly without end.

Will you travel on this exciting, and life-changing journey?

If and when you do, along the way you may discover the abundantly satisfying nourishment that The Almighty YHWH Elohim has always intended for His children.

This is His Way to eternal life.

This is the **KOSHER** Way!

It is the daily path in the authentic and abundant life of Torah; and nothing less than living the greatest life possible through the atoning, redeeming, and *ETERNAL -LIFE GIVING MOSHIACH[Messiah]!*

****

It can be painfully hard to give up what you have earnestly sought and fiercely conserved all your life; but unless you do, you may never know the heavenly reward that might have been. (Matthew 19:28-30)

Remember, dear reader, whatever you may think you are giving up, (it) is nothing compared to the richest blessings that are promised to you in your faithfulness to Him and to His Word.

And that, friend, is a promise, that is eternal!

****

*Terms and their Meaning

Throughout this book, ("The Light in the Wilderness"), many words and expressions that are either new and/or unfamiliar will appear. While there is a chapter devoted to their explanations, in a "Lexicon", definitions and explanations may also appear in the body of the text or at the end of the chapter in which these words are found.

YHWH: the Proper Hebrew Name of the Almighty, traditionally the unspoken and unpronounced 'tetragrammaton' (name of four Hebrew letters; 'yod, hey, vav, hey')[Exodus 3:13-15] It is variably transcribed as Yahweh, Yahveh, Yahuweh. Since there is no "J" sound in Hebrew, the proper name of the Creator should neither be written nor pronounced as Jehovah.

Elohim:the Hebrew title of the Creator of the Universe, appearing in that role in the opening verse of the Torah (Genesis 1:1) It is the plural form of Elohay, but is most certainly a designation of a singular entity, noting that the singular form of the Hebrew verb on which Elohim acts is always used. It may convey a unity that is not absolute and indivisible, as would be by the Hebrew word 'yachid', but compound, as would be and IS conveyed by the Hebrew word 'echad'as in: "Shema Yisrael YHWH Eloheinu YHWH ECHAD", meaning "Hear O'Israel, YHWH is our Almighty, YHWH is one"(or YHWH alone).

(Unfortunately, such a conceptualization of compound unity has given rise to the false and paganly derived doctrine of the trinity.) When the Unity of the Almighty is properly understood in the light of the Hebrew revelation, the absolute integrity of monotheism is uncompromisingly upheld and the essential nature of Elohim is more clearly illuminated. (Deuteronomy 6:4, 4:35,39)

<u>HaShem</u>: literally translated as "The Name", used as a substitute for YHWH when referring to the Almighty, so as not to take His Proper Name in vain. The title HaShem, while not His Name, is, nevertheless, afforded the honor and respect and awe that is His due. The title "Adonai" is also typically said in Jewish worship and religious discourse, instead of pronouncing YHWH, which is never spoken (in contemporary Jewish conversation).

<u>Torah</u>: Hebrew for Teaching or Instruction, commonly defined as 'Law'.

When used in its narrowest sense, it refers only to the first Five Books of Moses of the Hebrew Scriptures. In its broadest sense, Torah is all teaching given by YHWH Elohim [HaShem], either actually, as in His spoken Word to Moses, or by inspiration, through His proclaimers and messengers, the prophets.

In its most expansive, and most authentic sense, Torah is most perfectly revealed and taught by the Moshiach.

[Orthodox and Traditional Judaism count as "Torah" the written and oral traditions, including the Revelation at Sinai, the Prophets, the Writings, and the full body of 'sacred' manuscripts penned by the rabbis and sages throughout the ages; such as, but not limited to, the Talmud (the Oral Law), Shulchan Aruch (The Set Table-a compendium of Jewish observance), Mishnei Torah of Rabbi Moses ben Maimon (The Rambam or Maimonides), and Pirkei Avot (The Ethics of the Fathers).]

Moshiach: Hebrew for Messiah, Anointed.

The Moshiach is the promised Deliverer and Savior, the Hope of Israel, first declared in the Hebrew Scriptures, perfectly and completely revealed in the Messianic Scriptures (New Testament) in the Person of Yahoshua (Yahshua, Yashua, "Joshua").*

*[The Messiah is named 'Jesus Christ' in Christian doctrine, a paganly derived, non-Hebrew personality, who, as this book will show, has led the whole world astray.

(Matthew 24:23,24; Isaiah 8:20; Matthew 7:15,16; 2Corinthians 11:3,4; Galatians 1:6,7)]

The Valley of
Decision

Are We Lost?

Some Thoughts on Language, Words, and Meaning

We are all familiar with the saying, "It loses something in the translation".

In secular and casual conversation such loss is usually inconsequential. But when we try to communicate the essential elements of eternal significance, like the nature of man, his purpose and his destiny, his responsibility to himself, to others, and to his Creator, any loss in translation is of serious import. Over time, seemingly minor differences in meaning may 'morph' into profoundly different perceptions altogether.

More than two thousand years ago, the ancient Jewish sages lamented that the Greek translation of the Hebrew Scriptures, known as the Septuagint, was a great tragedy for the Jewish nation and the world. Why was this so?

It was because the pure, distinctive, set-apart language, (the 'lashon ha-kadosh'), spoken by The Eternal to Moses and the chosen nation of Israel was Hebrew, and only Hebrew. As the chosen language to His elect, it conveyed perfectly the meaning of the Almighty's message to His messenger Israel, and to mankind.

Greek, (and for that matter Latin, Arabic, or any other language), on the other hand, was a secular tongue, never spoken or used by the Almighty to His chosen messenger(s).

Most significantly, Greek, (and all other languages), carried the weight of pagan custom, belief, and deception in their references to matters of "religious import".

For all these centuries, we have complacently embraced such a dubious inheritance. Virtually all of the words that have become the 'lingua franca' of spiritual matters are glaringly suspect; words like 'holy', 'church', 'cross', 'hallowed', 'sacred', 'sacrifice', 'sanctify', 'glory', 'divine', 'theology', 'bible', 'Christ', "Jesus', 'Lord', 'amen', and even 'GOD'!!

All find their origin in pagan, non-Hebrew, unchosen and alien cultures, strangers to the Truth as it was authentically and originally revealed by the Eternal in Hebrew, the lashon ha-kadosh, "the language (tongue) set-apart".

All can be traced back to ancient astral Babylonian sun worship, revived and restored through Rome, "the second Babylon", as attested to by the early church fathers, rabbinical writers, and reformers.

The Greek and Latin language, as the foundation of this powerful and pervasive religious system, has profoundly altered the meaning and the message of the Hebrew (and Aramaic) Scriptures and their Heavenly Author, leading to false teachings, untenable doctrines, and pagan beliefs.

****

Our own English has given us these familiar sayings:

"Words have power"; and

"The pen is mightier than the sword".

Indeed, few swords have been more powerful than those written in other non-Hebrew words, claiming to be His Word. These (well) intentioned manuscripts, over the centuries, have visited a great and masterful deception upon the nations.

There are literally thousands of sects and denominations extant among 'Christian' and 'non-Christian' religions today. Each have their own customs, traditions, and beliefs; and while they may intesect in some places on principles, practices, and doctrines, each stands firmly in the confident conviction that they alone have the truth.

Sadly, few things could be farther from the Truth!

From the very first, Israel was warned not to learn the ways of the nations, but she did. From its beginning, the writers of the 'New Testament' warned of the intrusion of a different gospel and a different Messiah, which was neither gospel nor Messiah. And this was only a few decades after the Hebrew and Aramaic speaking Jewish Messiah Yahoshua spoke about the Kingdom of His Father Yahuweh and the 'World to Come'.

Nevertheless, this other gospel and its messiah have become the foundation upon which Christianity in all of its forms has been built. In so doing, it has persecuted the Jewish nation as suffering servant and messenger, and the faithful and obedient followers of the Hebrew and Aramaic speaking Redeemer of Israel and the grafted- in believers amongst the Gentiles.

It is a massive and amazing deception, and on its wide road, many sincere seekers have walked and stumbled.

A road built with the vain gravel and mortar of the lies of astral sun worship, pagan religion, human philosophies, and misguided syncretism is a road that leads to a dead end.....literally!!

****

The words and language of this lawless apostasy is the means by which so many have been deceived, ensnared, and held captive. Therefore, after sober reflection, and serious consideration, these religious sounding words will, for the most part, not be found in this book.

In their place, Hebrew and suitable English substitutes will be recruited to convey what it means to live as "The Light in the Wilderness".

****

The original call to Abraham by the Eternal Yahuweh, spoken in Hebrew, is "Lech Lacha"-"Get thee [yourself] out"! (B'reishis 12:7)*

In every age, in every place, the call is the same. To enter into the land of Promise, we must first leave from the land (that is, religions, philosophies, treasured cultural beliefs, and traditions) that we have known. Guided by the Spirit of Truth (John 16:13,18), we will turn away from deception, delusion, lies, and unrighteousness, and turn to the One Who is Truth Himself.

May the carefully chosen words of "The Light in the Wilderness" help you on His Way!

****

*B'reishis is the first book of the Torah or Pentateuch, the Five Books of Moses, also known as the Chumash in the Hebrew. It means 'beginnings' and is the proper Hebrew name for the book commonly called Genesis.

The Torah, the revealed Word of Yahuweh, the Eternal, is a Book of Teaching and Instruction and history and wisdom. It is much, much more than, and different from,the pejorative appelation, the Law, commonly employed by theologians and scholars of the Church.

The Teaching that is Torah, authored and revealed by Yahuweh to His chosen servant nation Israel, and His Messiah Yahoshua, is eternal and will never pass away.

The Hebrew names* for each of the five Books of the Torah are:

1. B'reishis (Genesis)
2. Shemos(Exodus)
3. Vayyikra(Leviticus)
4. Bemidbar(Numbers)
5. Devarim(Deuteronomy)

*The Hebrew names for each of the Five Books of the Torah are drawn from the opening phrase in the Hebrew text and translate as:

1. In the beginning

2. Names
3. (And YHWH) called
4. In the wilderness
5. Words

Lexicon

The terminology used in the book "The Light in the Wilderness" will be new for most of you. The following chapter will illustrate the need for such a 'revised language' in discussing Scriptural Truth(s). Additionally, it will provide concise, sometimes controversial, but historically rich background material.

(The author gratefully acknowledges Dr. C.J. Koster and his extraordinary book, "Come Out of Her, My People" in the preparation of this lexicon.)

*GOD-commonly used as the Name or title of The Deity. It appears in the Book of Isaiah, the Hebrew prophet, as GAD, a pagan Canaanite deity of good fortune (Isaiah 65:11) and as Baal-gad in (Joshua 11:17, 12:7, and 13:5).

GAD has been identified with Jupiter, the Sky or Sun deity. Baal (the god of good fortune).

The word GOD was Teutonic and originally applied to heathen deities, but after "Christianization" became the "Christian deity's" proper name.

Other scholarship traces the origin for this name GOD to the Indo-Germanic 'ghuta', a Sun deity, or 'ghodh', meaning union as in sexual union.

The Hebrew 'Elohim, El, and Eloah' means Mighty One(s). THE PROPER HEBREW NAME FOR THE MIGHTY

ONE is YAHWEH (YHWH)(YAHUWEH), composed of the four Hebrew letters: yod, hey, vav, hey. The Torah (Pentateuch) and the Prophets are clear on this subject. WE ARE COMMANDED NOT TO FORGET, SUBSTITUTE OR DESTROY HIS NAME. Several supportive Scriptural texts include Devarim (Deuteronomy) (12:3-5), Jeremiah (23:27), Isaiah (52:6), Micah (6:9).

In "The Light in the Wilderness", in obedience to Torah, and reinforced by enlightenment through etymology, the word "GOD" will, for the most part, not appear. Instead, the Hebrew YAHUWEH, YHWH, YAHWEH, El, Eloah, Elohim, HaShem (the Name), the Eternal, the Creator, the Almighty, the King of the Universe, the Master of the Universe (Rabbeinu shel Olam), and /or the Set Apart ONE will be used.

*Lord (LORD)-used in translation of the Scriptures almost 7000 times as a substitute for YHWH, Yahuweh or Yah. The title lord has been applied to all heathen deities. It may be traced to Lar (Larth), an Etruscan house deity, invoked in ancient Rome and Greece in the syncretism and polytheism common to those cultures. Other etymological evidence may include Loride or Thor, the Teutonic war deity and Lordo, another deity.

The word Lord will, for the most part, not appear. Instead, the Hebrew 'Adonai' or the English word Master will be used.

*Jesus-the common 'substitution' for the Hebrew Yehoshua, (Yeshua), Yahushua, Yahoshua, (Yahshua), Hellenized in the Greek 'New Testament' as "Ieosus", further Latinized as "Iesus". The Hebrew Name YAH, a shortened form of YAHUWEH, unites with the Hebrew word 'shua' which means 'salvation', to form Yahushua (Yahoshua) or the Salvation of Yah (Yahuweh). In John 5:43, the Messiah declares: "I have come in My Father's Name and you do not receive me......".

Superstition that translated into suppression of the true Torah Name Yahuweh of the post Babylonian captivity, and strong anti-Judaism of Gentile Greece and Rome, led to the distortion and substitution of the true Torah Name of the Messiah Yahushua. The Jews, unduly and wrongly influenced by Babylonish custom, almost completely eliminated the utterance of the Name Yahuweh from their community, notwithstanding (their) 'religious' justification. The Gentiles, on the other hand, abhorred almost all things Jewish, including the Torah, the Torah's Deity YAHUWEH, and the Torah's Messiah YAHUSHUA. The Jewish Savior was replaced by a Hellenized counterfeit, named Ieosus, possibly adapted from the Greek healing goddess, Ieso (Iaso), or the Egyptian son of Isis called Isu or Esu, or sons of Zeus, all traceable back to sun worship. Furthermore, Ieosus abbreviated as IHS, is part of the name of the Greek sun deity Bacchus, also known as Tammuz. This Tammuz, had the Tau (the cross) and the fish as his sign. The ecclesiastical emblem IHS, surrounded by sun rays, betrays his pagan origin.

The verse previously alluded to, John 5:43, concludes:"......if another comes in his own name, him you will receive." And so it happened just as He said it would. Prophetic words, indeed!

Proper names, unlike ordinary words, CANNOT be translated. The given name YAHUSHUA stays YAHUSHUA in Greek, Latin, English, Chinese, German, Spanish, Arabic or any other language on the face of the earth. Simply stated, YAHUSHUA is His Name, a Hebrew name, in any tongue.

The Hebrew prophet Jeremiah rightly declares that the Gentile nations will, in the last days, know that they have inherited lies, repent of their sin(s), and then they shall know the Torah True Name of the Eternal, YAHUWEH. (Jeremiah 16:19-21).

"In that day, YAHUWEH will be King over all the earth, on that day YAHUWEH shall be One and His Name shall be One".

The name Jesus will not appear in this book. Instead, the revealed Hebrew name Yahushua, or Yahoshua (Yahshua) will be used.

*Christ- the traditional name of the Savior, a Greek translation of the Hebrew Moshiach (Messiah), meaning anointed. Both the concept and the identity of the Messiah are irrefutably Jewish. (see Romans 9:4,5)

The name Chrestos referred to Osiris, the sun deity of Egypt. Christ, and Christian are of pagan origin and are part of the syncretism that characterized the early anti-Jewish Christian Church.

The name Christ will not appear in this book. Instead, the Hebrew Moshiach, Messiah, or Anointed will be used.

church-the traditional translation for the Greek word 'ekklesia', meaning called out ones, translated for the Hebrew word 'kahal', meaning assembly or congregation; most likely derived from the Anglo-Saxon 'circe' (Circe) , the daughter-goddess of Helios, the sun-deity, originally a Greek goddess Kirke.

Amen-the traditional rendition of the Hebrew "Amein", which means "so be it" or "surely". This common final word of prayer can be traced back to the chief deity of the Egyptian pantheon, 'Amen-Ra' or Amen as he was known among the Thebans.

Therefore, only the Hebrew 'Amein' is the acceptable word in true worship; the commonly used counterfeit, Amen, violates the First Commandment, and gives honor, albeit unwittingly, to the sun-deity.

Holy-commonly, and wrongly used to describe piety. a translation of the Greek word 'hagios' which in turn was a translation of the Hebrew word 'kadosh'. It is best translated as 'separate', or 'set-apart'. The word holy may be traced back to sun worship, as in HOLI, the Hindu spring sun festival; or heile, the sun's ray, or halo, the sun's disk, or Heil, a Saxon idol.

It should not be used by true worshippers, the followers of Yahuweh, Yahoshua, and Torah.

Hallowed, sacred, sanctified, sacrifice-all traceable back to pagan sun worship (Sakra-the goddess,one of twelve forms of the sun deity). These words, and their derivatives, should not be used.

Glory- translated from the Greek as 'doxa', from the Hebrew 'kavod'. It is better translated as "esteemed" (heavily) or "honored". On the other hand, the concept of glory refers to radiance of light, as in sunrays or sunbeams, and Gloria, a Roman goddess.

As another contaminant of sun worship, it should not be used.

Divine-from the root div, deva, or diu all meaning 'bright' or 'to shine', used to describe the sky sun deity, an abomination according to Torah. see Deuteronomy (12:1-3; 30-32)

These words, including the word deity, should be eliminated.

Bible-from the Greek biblios, meaning books. It did not originally refer to all of Scripture, first gaining acceptance around 400 C.E.

The word bible can be traced back to the Phonecian seaport known as Byblos, home of its sun deity, and the seat of Adonis. It is also an Egyptian city named after the female deity Byblis, the grand-daughter of Apollo, the Greek sun-deity. Byblia was another name for the astral goddess of sensuality, Venus.

****

The lexicon for "The Light in the Wilderness" illustrates the terrible effect compromise has had on the Revealed Faith. The language of traditional religion is born out of syncretism, an attempt to reconcile and unite different, and oftentimes, opposing beliefs, principles, and practice.

Such a language, and such a religion is not of Elohim, the Eternal.

It is not of Yahuweh.
It is not of Yahoshua.
It is not of Israel.

And it should not be of us.

Centuries ago the Hebrew prophet Jeremiah proclaimed:

> "Thus said YAHUWEH: Do not learn the way of the nations, and do not be awed by the signs of the heavens, for the gentiles are awed by them. The customs of these people are worthless....!
>
> (Jeremiah 10:2,3)

These words must speak to us today; cogently, persuasively, radically, and completely. We are a set-apart people, who call upon and worship a set-apart Elohim, the very Creator, Sustainer, and Redeemer of the Universe. Our repentance (teshuvah or turning) toward Him and His Torah (Teaching or instruction, not "Law") is the first essential step to Truth and a life set apart as <u>The Light in the Wilderness</u>.

* "Come Out of Her My People" by C.J. Koster, copyright 1998, Institute for Scripture Research (PTY) LTD, P O Box 1830, 2162 Northriding, Republic of South Africa; 545 Newport Ave. #151, Pawtucket, Rhode Island 02861, USA

PART I:
In His Image: Man

CHAPTER 1

Man and Free Will

WILL:1. the faculty of conscious and especially of deliberate action: the freedom of the will.

2. the power of choosing one's own actions: to have a strong or weak will.

3. the process of willing or volition.

4. wish or desire.

5. purpose or determination

FREE:1. enjoying personal rights or liberty, as one not in slavery.

2, 3, 4. pertaining to or reserved for those who enjoy personal liberty.

5. exempt from external authority, interference, restriction, etc., as a person, the will, thought, choice, action, etc.; independent, unfettered.

(The Random House American Dictionary, 1968 edition, New York, pg. 1396)

"License they mean when they cry liberty."

(John Milton, Sonnet)

"No man is entirely free. He is a slave to riches, to fate, or to the laws; or else the people prevent him from acting as he wishes."

(Euripides, Hecuba)

"No one can be perfectly free till all are free."
(Herbert Spencer, Social Statics)

"There is no free will in the human mind: it is moved to one choice or another by some cause, and that cause has been determined by some other cause, and so on to infinity."
(Baruch Spinoza, Ethics)

"For who among men knows the thoughts of a man except the spirit of the man, which is in him? Even so the thoughts of "God" no one knows except the Spirit of "God"."
(I Corinthians 2:11)

"But a natural man does not accept the things of the Spirit of "God"; for they are foolishness to him, and he cannot understand them because they are spiritually appraised."
(I Corinthians 2:14)

****

It sits at the very core of personal belief. It compels, motivates, chooses, directs, advises, plans, inspires, and ultimately determines the path of a man's life, and in the mind of many, his very destiny. It is fiercely held by atheist and deist, agnostic and gnostic, Hindu and Buddhist, animist and naturalist, Christian and Jew. Its essential verity crosses all national, racial, ethnic, religious, and cultural boundaries.

And whether it exerts its power imminently and immediately, or remotely and finally, most of humanity has held to its certain existence and necessity throughout history.

It is, in truth, a foundational creed that is so global and timeless, that it is practically universal.

"IT" is the "free will" of man.

And it is the greatest deception that has ever been imposed upon humanity.

Rational observation, unfettered by "religious" dogma and decree, must confess that there is no man that truly exercises a 'free will'. Apart from external constraints, the limitations to freedom of the will (free will) are imparted by our very nature. Our genetic composition, environmental influences, anatomical uniqueness, intellectual capabilities....our place in history and space, all conspire together to define and confine the boundaries of our will.

Neurological and behavioural science concede that man uses only a tiny fraction of his brain in cognitive, purposeful, and intellectual pursuits.

What must be plainly evident to the unbiased observer is this:

All options cannot be known at any point in time, and man, at every point of decision, does not have the absolute ability to discern the full dimensions of the choices and the consequences thereof.

But man is not limited to actions determined by instincts alone; and in that regard we may postulate free will, can't we?

No!

Such a concept cannot stand on its own merit. Without comparing man to other creatures, we are forced to confront the folly of the belief that the will of man is (truly) free.

But even apart from the physical realities that unabashedly intrude upon this ego-driven doctrine, there are spiritual ones.

The Scriptures, composed of the so called Old and New Testaments, have been understood by both Judaism and Christianity to support and promote man's free will. Man's dealings with other members of his race and with the Almighty Himself illustrate this obvious fact.

But does it ?

The Scriptures proclaim that man is a created being; but more than that....he is created in the very image of Elohim (God).(Genesis 1:27)

But this is not the finished product. And although man would like to believe he can perfect himself and refine this image, he can never accomplish the crucial transformation from imperfect image of 'God' to perfect image of 'God' without the infusion of another essential element.

This element, represented by the 'Tree of Life', was present at the time and place of man's creation, and was plainly accessible and available to him. (Genesis 1:29, 2:9).

But there was also another tree, the 'Tree of Knowledge of Good and Evil', which was forbidden.(Gen 2:16,17).

Cunningly persuaded, tantalized, encouraged, and deceived by the Adversary and Accuser (Satan) in the form of a serpent, the man Adam and his wife Eve ("freely") chose the forbidden tree, and came to know good and evil, the consequences of disobedience, and death.

This event is known as "the fall of man", and has given us the doctrine of original sin, to which all mankind is heir.(Genesis 3:17-19).

But did man really freely choose the forbidden tree?

And if he did not, what is it that he fell from, other than the opportunity to take from the Tree of Life, and by so doing, truly and authentically, be like Elohim, which is as He (Elohim) ultimately would intend.

Firstly, Adam's choice to follow Eve's bidding, and Eve's choice to obey the Adversary, and disobey Elohim, are the result of deception, and not the product of the exercise of free will in its purest sense. At this point of decision, these two humans were powerfully persuaded to do that which they were commanded not to (do). While both humans must be held accountable, their culpability is not what is so much at issue here.

Rather, this pivotal event in human history illustrates that man without the Spirit of Elohim, represented by the Tree of Life, is ultimately and simply "human".

This is the essential lesson of the Eden story. Two humans, standing before two 'Trees', and two "gods" (Elohim, the true "God" of heaven and earth, and Satan, the false and lying god of this world), are presented two choices.

The wrong choice is chosen; the one that brought death and expulsion from the Garden. This decision, known as "Adam's fall" is believed to be the source of all man's troubles, and is known as original sin.

But the truth of this matter is this:

Original sin did not flow from the "Fall of Adam"; it preceded and led to it.

There was no perfect free will operating at this point of human history, and there was surely no perfect innocent Man before the forbidden fruit was taken and eaten. The decision to disobey Elohim was conceived and nurtured in the heart of Adam and Eve. The Adversary found a most receptive audience in these two (incomplete) images of Elohim. Such was the condition of their heart (that is, their will) before Satan, and such is the condition of man's will now.

The encounter with the Adversary was primarily illustrative, and reveals that apart from the infusion of the Spirit of Life, (the Rauch ha-Kodesh, the Set apart Spirit, the Holy Spirit), man and his will are not free, but in bondage, enslaved by physical, emotional, and spiritual limits, and subject to external and internal forces that lead him farther and farther from the Source of Life Himself.

> "For the flesh sets its desire against the Spirit, and the Spirit against the flesh; for these are in opposition to one another, so that you may not do the things that you please."
>
> (Galatian 5:17)

> "Now the deeds of the flesh are evident, which are: immorality, impurity, sensuality, idolatry,sorcery, enmities, strife, jealousy, outbursts of anger, disputes, dissensions, factions, envying, drunkenness, carrousing, and things like these, of which I have forewarned you that those who practice such things shall not inherit the Kingdom of "God"."
>
> (Galatians 5:19-21)

Furthermore, the tragedy of the human condition is not the consequence of a "fall" from a previous innocent state of grace, but the gritty reality of an unfinished life lived according to the passions and wisdom of the natural man, subject to both internal and external deceptions, exercising his imperfect, 'unfree' will, heeding and gratifying the insatiable appetite of his carnality, without the sovereign, redeeming, gracious, authenticating, and atoning Power of the Spirit of Life.

> "But the fruit of the Spirit is love, joy, peace, patience, kindness, goodness, faithfulness, gentleness, self-control, against such things there is no law."
>
> (Galatians 5:22,23)

At creation, Adam and Eve were driven out of Eden, so they would not take from the Tree of Life, and live forever. (Genesis 3:22-24). But this apparent delay in the Plan of Redemption, and the Authentication of Man, to truly become like Elohim, did not set in motion another alternative 'Plan

B'. On the contrary, this was the intent of Elohim from the very beginning.

For He Who is omniscient, and omnipotent, and Who knows the end from the beginning, had prepared the path of righteousness that leads to the Tree of Life, before the 'foundations of the world'. (Ephesians 1:4)

At the time of restoration, Elohim will give all of his sovereignly chosen people one heart (will) and shall put a new Spirit within them. (Ezekiel 11:19,20; Jeremiah 31:33,34)

It is in that day, at the time of His choosing, that Man will realize his truest potential, be fully authenticated, and for the first time in his history, completely, absolutely, and actually know what it is to think and act and feel and live with a genuine 'free will'.

In that day, man, in the full, true image of Elohim, will be completed and perfected, transformed, as it were, to the very essence of Elohim Himself. All forms of bondage, slavery, deception, and delusion will be removed forever, and he (and we) will finally have tasted the fruit of the Tree of Life.

The Word of Scripture promises such an awesome and wondrous tomorrow:

> 'Beloved, now we are children of The Most High, and it has not appeared yet what we shall be. We know that, when He appears, we shall be like Him, because we shall see Him just as He is.
>
> (1John 3:2)

CHAPTER 2

Mortality, Creationism, and Intelligent Design

The story of creation, as it is told in Scripture, is a familiar one. To some, it is historical fact in every detail; to others it is just a fable. Today, as has been true over the centuries, taking it at its word, literally that is, has been the supreme test that separates the enlightened, rational, 'scientific', intellectual, educated few from the simple, religious, naieve, untutored, believing masses. The Darwinian theory of evolution stands as a beacon to all who would champion and defend human wisdom and reason.

Yet, despite all the weight of academic scholarship, honest scientific investigation has been unable to unequivocally substantiate and prove this 'rational' theory. No missing links have been found to explain the sudden appearance of dramatically different life forms. Evolution's apologists have coined the phrase 'punctuated equilibrium' to explain the conspicuous absence of these transitional life forms that would bridge the gap between sea creature and bird, amphibian and reptile, invertebrate and vertebrate, marsupial, mammal, and man. While changes within a species can be scientifically observed and verified (microevolution), evolution between species (macroevolution) cannot. Notwithstanding great similarities in structure, function, DNA, RNA, cellular organelles and metabolism, the conclusion that all came from a common ancestor will forever be scientifically elusive. And since this is the crux of the evolutionary faith, it can never be ascertained as fact, but will remain forever in the limbo of theory.

The reason for this is simple. The exact environment that existed when reproducible life began is impossible to replicate; hence any experiment that presumes to demonstrate the formation of living from non-living, or change from one species to another, (which are) the essential mechanisms of evolution, are doomed to fail.

The rational, enlightened, and scientific mind should observe what is, and not impose a theory, no matter how elegant, pragmatic, or utilitarian, to fit reality into its construct.

The similarities that exist in all living things need not pre-suppose a common ancestor, as in a single celled origin of life. Rather, all shared characteristics support a common template, or blueprint, as in DNA and RNA, upon which all life forms are founded. Such a conceptualization is observable, repeatable, scientific, and rational.

It is this concept that underlies the Scriptural account of creation: life can only come from life, and each life reproduces according to its own kind.

Life is species-specific.

No primordial soup of "biogenic amines", could, regardless of how many years it took, by chance permutation, and by way of 'spontaneous generation', give rise to life.

The Scriptures are consistent with these reasonable principles, stating from the beginning that a Living One (Elohim or 'God') created the heaven (sky) and the earth; and that living creatures were brought forth, each after their (own) kind. (Genesis 1:1, 1:24,25)

Apart from this, evolution requires mutation and death as operative mechanisms, in order that an ascending complexity of living organisms may occur. The corruption that commonly is wed to mutation is not consistent with ordered ascendancy, and demands extraordinary, nearly impossible combinations of events and elements to support more complicated, viable, and reproducible life.

Furthermore, death itself, the ultimate form of disorganization, disintegration, and chaos, is the 'glue' that links this chain together.

The Scriptures speak of a system quite different, based on design, order, and consistency. According to the original Master Plan, the creature, all ready elegant, and complex, was intended to live forever. Death, external to the original blueprint, intruded upon the arrangement, like a computer virus, and opened the Design to repair and restoration, a plan that was there from the beginning.

Nevertheless, while man may ultimately escape the clutches of death, at his beginning, he was very much subject to it.

The popular ego-driven notion, shared by all of the world's major religions, is that man is immortal.

But the Scriptures teach something quite different.

The Creator-Master-First Cause-Designer "YHWH Elohim" formed man from the dust of the ground and breathed into his nostrils the breath of life (nishmas-breath; chayyim-life, in Hebrew) and man became a living (not immortal!) being or soul (nefesh-soul or being; chayyah-living, in Hebrew). (Genesis 1:26,27; 2:7)

There is absolutely no evidence or Scriptural support that man, drawn from the material earth, whose elements contain the ingredients essential for mortal life, is anything other than material and mortal. The breath of life he received from Elohim is not His Spirit, (Ruach ha-Kadosh in the Hebrew) but a gust of air, as in resuscitation, the kind of air he will breathe as long as he is alive.

The Scripture does not teach or condone the popular and false religious doctine known as 'the immortality of the soul'.

Indeed, it is in the drama of the 'Temptation" that a false promise of immortality is first proclaimed, coming not from Elohim, but from the master of deception and Adversary -Satan:

> "And the serpent said to the woman: "You shall not surely die'."
>
> (Genesis 3:4)

Upon this single verse, and outrageous lie, mankind has found his support for the specious doctrine of the soul's immortality and has constructed the earth's religions.

****

But if man is not immortal, is he simply born to die?

Can he ever attain the immortality that has always been the intention of the Master's Plan?

The Scripture begins to answer that question with the Promise of a "Life Saver" to come.

> "And I will put enmity between you and the woman, and between your seed and her seed; He shall bruise your head, and you shall wound His heel."
> **(Genesis 3:15)**

This verse establishes the historical and prophetic conflict between humanity and the deceiver, assuring the full and complete final destruction of the Adversary by this Seed of woman.

Beginning with Israel, this Redeeming Seed, through Whom all nations would be blessed, is the Promised Life Saver. Through this anointed Being; this Messiah (Hebrew-Moshiach), man will attain immortality; not by usurping eternal life, as if it were possible, as Satan would prescribe, nor by religious contriving, as man would devise, but by receiving Him, as was intended by Yahuweh Elohim from the very beginning.

The Tree of Life, inaccessible, but never prohibited, becomes accessible through the Messiah once again. The death that came with the sin of eating from the Tree of Knowledge of Good and Evil is partially paid for by the death of each mortal, but only One Who all ready possesses eternal life can pay the penalty of sin for all humanity for all time.

In so doing, death and the grave are forever sealed shut, and the gateway to eternal life and the Kingdom is swung wide open to all who would enter in.

****

The Scriptures reveal an account of creation and life that is at once intellectually appealing, and spiritually fulfilling.

By way of a scarlet thread of redemption, deliverance from death unto life is brought about by the imputation of Messiah's sinless, obedient, righteousness, to the redeemed and His priceless gift of overcoming death through the resurrection to eternal life.

Creation began in a material world, subject to corruption, death, and decay; yet the goal of the Creator has always been to redeem this mortal, dying world from its destruction, freeing it from the Adversary and his lies; renewing, restoring, and recreating it, through a transforming event no less radical than a Resurrection from the dead, by the Power and Person of the Creator Yahuweh Elohim's Anointed, the Messiah of Israel and the Nations, Yahoshua ha-Moshiach!

CHAPTER 3

The Challenge of Revelation

The human quest for universal and eternal truth is as old as recorded history. From his very beginnings, man has sought to discern his place in the universe.

Imagination and experience has supplied most of mankind with doctrines that appear to satisfy the yearnings of our hearts. In ancient times, primitive religions, born out of man's own ideas, were the fabric of his community in every corner of the earth. The multiplicity of these doctrines and practices defied and effectively denied the possiblity of One Eternal Being Who created humankind....that is, until the advent of the Revelation that is known as Scripture.

So when we gaze down the tortuous road of human history, it would seem that the Scriptures have been accepted by great numbers of us, only recently to have been replaced by alternative views.

The amazing truth is that almost none of us, at any time in history, have ever really accepted the plain revealed facts of the Scriptural narrative without somehow adding or subtracting our own traditions and beliefs to Scripture's Revelation.

The majesty of man's genesis in a heavenly garden on earth, intimately connected to his Creator and the very real possibility of attaining to eternal life has given way to a chance beginning in a murky swamp without purpose or design. This evolutionary scheme, seemingly scientific and embraced by the modern religious adherent, effectively thrusts humanity from the exalted spiritual plane of Scripture's Revelation and its splendid promises, to the dark and dreary valley of delusion, confusion, and despair, without any authentic hope for release from the burdens of human existence and the certainty of death.

Modern religion, in its desire to be relevant, popular, and politically correct, has largely relinquished any legitimate claim to superior (supernatural) authority and eternal verities by dressing itself in fashionable ideologies.

By so doing, it has returned to the foolish core beliefs of paganism and human doctrines that are both ignorant and incapable of knowing absolute truth.

Now then, if we believe that absolute and eternal Truth does exist, we must conclude that religion cannot and will not lead us to that longed for destination.

A great and broad plain littered with confusing and deluding doctrines and dogmas is the topgraphy of the map that marks the religious route to that eternal goal.

The great religious systems of all civilizations, at all times, throughout the earth are to be found on this crooked and disappointing path.

While this proposition applies to all, the two faiths that have most influenced our culture in North America, and Europe are the primary focus of our study.

Over the last two thousand years, Judaism and Christianity have generously given so much good to us all, both to those inside and outside the faith.

If the goal of religion was only to elevate man's nature, and inspire him to thoughts and acts of selfless devotion and goodness, these (religions) can rightly claim some success; the blight of war, poverty, and injustice notwithstanding.

But religion claims to do more. It purports to invest individual lives with "divine" dignity, and would direct man's steps and his heart onto the path of eternal life.

It is facile to say that having failed this and the many other noble goals set forth, the fault lies not with religion, but with man. In truth, religion has failed to deliver its lofty goals because it is the product of well intentioned but broken and (spiritually) deceived human minds.

****

The remedy for (man's) religion is the authentic Revelation of heaven.

The cure for human despair, and existential loneliness is not to be found in the world's religions but in the (proper)Relationship with the Eternal that is revealed in Scripture.

"The Light in the Wilderness", Who is The Messiah, can and does open the gates that reveal the universal and eternal Truth that we all seek.

But the religious baggage we all carry may keep many true pilgrims from walking through that open gate, and that would be tragic.

Still, the Eternal, Who never changes, proclaims that His yoke is easy, and His burden is light.....and this is the essential doctrine of the Way that leads to His Kingdom of Eternal Life and Truth.

This is the challenge of revelation!

CHAPTER 4

The Reason for Being

(Why on Earth are we Here!?)

"What is man that You remember him?
And the son of man that you visit him?
YET YOU HAVE MADE HIM A LITTLE LESS THAN
ELOHIM,
And have crowned him with esteem and splendor,
You made him rule over the works of Your hands,
You have put all under his feet.

(Psalm 8:4-6)

(translation from THE SCRIPTURES, italics mine)

Most all of us, at one time or another, will ponder the question posed above. The answers we come up with are as many and as varied as we are. If the end of the matter was simply a personal and subjective response, there would be no need for further inquiry. But deep within, we sense that being here (on earth), must signify more than just the pursuit of personal happiness, pleasure, career, love, philosophy, religious belief, or perpetuation of our own self (and species) through our offspring. In short, life has to mean more than simply fulfilling our own ambitions and self-realization.

Over the centuries, great minds have contemplated this elemental question, and have come up with thoughtful and worthy responses. But in the end, despite their intelligence and their wisdom, their answers belong to them, and do not fully satisfy all of us. Truly, isn't it too much to expect of one man, any man, albeit great and wise, to know the heart and mind of all men?

> "For the foolishness of Elohim is wiser than men, and
> the weakness of Elohim is stronger than men.
> `(1Corinthians 1:25)

> **(translation from The Scriptures)**

When one honestly confronts the enormity of this question, the answers of our best and brightest become pale and feeble when placed on the great stage of human history. There is a much greater and grander drama being played out here on earth; and it has largely escaped the vision of the most notable philosophers, scholars, theologians and thinkers of all times.

The answer to this question: "Why on earth are we here?", is found in the Mind of Yahuweh Elohim, the Eternal One, Who created man and put him on this planet. And the Mind of the Creator can be found in His Word, the Scriptures.

In all the vast expanse of the universe, there is only one place that is not under the complete governing Hand of the Almighty. That place is not in some distant galaxy, or remote star, or other dimension.....it is right where we live; it is here.

It is earth!

Our planet is, and has been for countless years, long before the creation of mankind, an outpost for rebels, revolutionaries, and enemies of HaShem. Headed by Satan, the chief accuser of Elohim (and mankind), the earth is ground zero for spiritual warfare between Satan's forces, and Elohim's "army of faithful".

We need only to turn to the inspired words of the Hebrew prophet, Isaiah, to learn of this truth.

"How are thou fallen from heaven, O' morning star*, son of the dawn! how art thou hewn to the ground, crusher of nations! And thou-thou hast said in thy heart: Into heaven will

> I ascend, above the stars of Elohim will I
> exalt my throne, and I will sit also upon the
> mount of assembly, in the farthest end of the
> north; I will ascend above the heights of the
> clouds; I will be equal to the Most High.
> **(Isaiah 14:12-14)**

*(Helel-the sovereign of Babel, ruler of the gentile nations, a manifestation of Satan, the accuser and destroyer.)

The pretender to Heaven's Throne is here on earth.

> "Be sober, watch, because your adversary, the devil, walks about like a roaring lion, seeking someone to devour."
> **(1Peter 5:8)**

> "And the day came to be that the sons of
> Elohim came to present themselves before

> Yahuweh, and Satan also came among them.
> And Yahuweh said to Satan, "From where do
> you come?" And Satan answered Yahuweh
> and said, "From diligently searching in the
> earth, and from walking up and down in it."
>
> **(Job 1:6,7)**

So the evidence is plain. The chief of enemy forces, intent on the overthrow of the Rulership of Elohim in the universe He (Elohim) created, is upon earth. Destruction of this evil-doer should have been the most effective way to rid Hashem of this problem. Enemy angels who followed Satan in rebellion could have been dealt with similarly with summary annihilation, or humiliating surrender. Intuitively, the All Mighty should have done this.....any (human) military strategist would have done so.....but He did not. Not because he could not.....rather He would not, so as to vindicate His character before those misguided messengers (angels) who chose to follow the adversary.

The justice and the righteousness of Hashem was and is the central issue in this war. His absolute right to sit on the Heavenly Throne as King of the Universe had to be validated before His (angelic) creation. One proud angel wanted a regime change, and fomented a spiritual rebellion of unimaginable proportions.

The wisdom of Elohim is illustrated in His Plan for Victory over these agents of deception, delusion, despair, and destruction. The foot soldier in this outpost of rebellion would be a new creation.......he would come from earth, literally.

He would be called Man.

This new creature, distinct from angels, would be in the image of Elohim, but less than Him. Man would be susceptible to the powerful deception of the chief accuser. Indeed, Hashem knew that when he placed His new creature in the same Garden as the enemy, Satan. Before he even tasted the forbidden fruit of the Tree of Knowledge of Good and Evil, evil was in his heart, when man disobeyed His Creator, and followed Satan, just as so many angels had done before. The pretender to the Throne, to the role of Master of the Universe, and Life-giver, sold 'a bill of goods' to Adam and Eve, and seemed to succeed in thwarting Hashem's purposes. But things were not to be as they appeared.

For a little while, it looked as if man had joined with Satan in his rebellion against Hashem, motivated by the false promises of being like the Almighty, and never to die. (Bereishis (Genesis) 3:4,5). But man would realize very soon that he was not like his Creator, and he would die, just as Elohim had said he would. This had to be, not just to confirm that the Word of Hashem is true, but that man by himself, (like angels by themselves), are completely dependent upon Elohim.

Man's inherent weakness is there by design; in effect, it is the potential site of his redemption.

Through this experience, he would recognize the Supremacy of Hashem, and his need for forgiveness and mercy. Indeed, if man simply paid the penalty for his disobedience at creation, in his death, there would be no future for humanity, and the spiritual battle on earth could not move forward to ultimate victory for Hashem, according to His plan.

Instead of taking the lives of Adam and Eve, Yahweh Elohim made garments of skin for Adam and his wife, and clothed them. (Bereishis 3:21).

Life giving blood was poured out by an innocent animal in the Garden to secure this covering. It was obtained by the Hand of Yahuweh Himself. It would prophetically picture the covering of unblemished, obedient, sinless life, in the sacrificial blood that would permit man to escape the punishment due for his disobedience over and over through the rite of animal sacrifice, ultimately pointing to the Anointed One Who perfectly and completely would Personify Yahuweh's Justice and Mercy at the Atonement.

The Destroyer was not to succeed in destroying this potential soldier of Hashem. The deceiver would not send man to the grave. Deliverance from death was made sure in the redeeming Power of Yahuweh through His Messiah, Yahoshua.

> "But thanks to Elohim, Who gives us the overcoming through our Master Yahoshua, Messiah."
> **(1Corinthians 15:57)**

The overcoming is not just escaping the grave, although that itself is beyond measure in its wonder.

It is also the empowerment by the Spirit of Yahuweh, through Messiah, that gives us the strength to fight the

Good Fight, and wage war in every battle the accuser and his forces would have us enter into.

> "For though we walk in the flesh, we do not fight according to the flesh. For the weapons we fight with are not fleshly, but mighty in Elohim for overthrowing strongholds, overthrowing reasonings, and every high matter that exalts itself against the knowledge of Elohim, taking captive every thought to make it obedient to the Messiah."
> **(II Corinthians 2:3-5)**

The psalmist writes:

> "The earth belongs to Yahuweh, and all that fills it, the world, and those who dwell in it."
> **(Psalm 24:1)**

In the Torah, Moses writes:

> "And Yahuweh said, "I shall forgive, according to your word, but truly, as I live, all the earth will be filled with the esteem of Yahuweh"
> **(Bamidbar (Numbers) 14:20-21)**

The prophet Zechariah writes:

> "And Yahuweh will be King over all the earth, in that day Yahuweh will be the only one, and His Name the only one."
> **(Zechariah 14:9)**

In the Messianic Scriptures (New Testament), it is written in the final Book of Revelation:

"And the seventh angel sounded; and there arose loud voices in heaven, saying, "The kingdom of the world has become the Kingdom of our Yahuweh, and of His Messiah; and He will reign forever and ever."

(Revelation 11:15)

Man indeed has a reason for being here. Born on, in, and from the earth, he is the child of Elohim, created in His image. Thrown into battle from his birth, man is assured victory as long as he trusts in, and remains allied with, Hashem [Yahuweh Elohim].

The Torah, the Temple, and the Gospel of the Kingdom of His Father Yahuweh Elohim, proclaimed by Yahoshua Messiah, will win in the end. The accuser and his forces will be defeated; and the Righteousness, Justice, and Mercy of the Almighty will be vindicated before all creation.

****

In the final analysis, *this* is the answer to why, on earth, we are here!

CHAPTER 5

Predestination and Sovereign Election

One of the most widespread beliefs within the Christian faith is the existence of only two classes of humanity: the saved and the lost. According to this position, if one does not make a decision for "Christ" in this lifetime, and is not "born again", he will go to a Christless grave, having lost all hope, and will endure conscious torment, separated from 'God', in hell, for all eternity.

This doctrine rests on several false assumptions:

> 1. everyone, at all times, everywhere, has had the opportunity to choose 'Christ'.
> 2. everyone has had an equal ability to make the decision for 'Christ'.
> 3. everyone already has eternal life because we possess an "immortal soul".
> 4. death is a state of conscious eternal existence, either in heaven with 'God' and 'Christ'; or in hell, separated from 'God' and 'Christ'.
> 5. every person, each in his own unperfected human-ness, apart from regeneration by the Spirit of 'God', can choose 'Christ'.

All of these assumptions, according to Scripture, are FALSE!

This dogma of religious tradition has caused untold anguish and sorrow for countless generations throughout the ages, promoting the greatest deception the world has ever known.

Can it really be that this is the only day of salvation?

Consider the consequences if the answer is yes.

The multitudes who lived before the Resurrection are lost.

The multitudes who have not heard or understood the Gospel since the Resurrection are lost.

The unborn millions who did not come to birth because of abortion are lost.

The mentally defective, incapable of understanding the message are lost.

The members of religions or traditions that deny or alter the Gospel and its power to save are lost.

****

The righteousness and justice of The Eternal demands that each and every person who has ever lived, who was ever conceived, have their eyes opened and their hearts prepared by His Spirit, so that they all have a fair chance to decide for or against Him.

Mortal man, in his own carnal nature, apart from the Spirit (Mind) of the Almighty, does not acknowledge his need for salvation or a Saviour, neither does he desire the Almighty and His Kingdom; rather, he seeks only his own gratification.

Before any one can truly decide, he must be called, he must be invited, he must be chosen!

Messiah Himself testifies to that fact!

> "No one can come to Me, unless the Father Who sent Me draws him, and I will raise him up on the last day."
>
> **(John 6:44)**

> "You did not choose Me, but I chose you and appointed you, that you should go and bear fruit, and that your fruit should remain, that whatever you ask of the Father in My Name, He may give it to you."
>
> **(John 15:16)**

The apostle Paul, in his letter to the Romans underscores this principle of 'divine' election.

> "So then, it does not depend on the man who will or the man who runs, but on 'God' Who has mercy."
>
> **(Romans 9:16)**

This regeneration of the natural mind must precede the opportunity to know the Gospel and all it represents; for without this infusion of the Spirit or Mind of 'God', no meaningful decision is possible.

There are numerous verses in Scripture that point to predestination as a central part of the plan of redemption, but the message is no plainer than (it is) stated here:

"And we know that 'God' causes all things to work together for good to those who love 'God', to those who are called according to His purpose.

> For whom he foreknew, He also predestined to become conformed to the image of His Son, that He might be the first-born among many brethren; and whom He predestined, these He also called; and whom He called, these He also justified; and whom He justified, these He also glorified."
>
> **(Romans 8:28-30)**

The predestination that the Scripture teaches is not to salvation or damnation, but to election. It does not eliminate the will of man; rather, through The Eternal's prevenient, antecedent, and anticipatory grace, the will is properly prepared and suited to meet the challenge of truly hearing the message of the Messiah and the Gospel of the Kingdom.

It is only then that the reprobate will of man is truly made free! Only through this regeneration of the human spirit can man be enabled to enter into salvation and eternal life.

There is no injustice with Elohim ('God'). He denies no one an opportunity for salvation.

Most of humanity has simply not been called at this time; but there will be a time when everyone will have their chance. The billions who have lived and died, in bondage to their human will and nature, without illumination or regeneration, shall, at the resurrection, be given their full opportunity to really "see" the Messiah, and hear the Good News, without the deceptive power of the carnal, unregenerated, natural mind (the flesh) or the accuser (the devil).

As the children of Abraham, Israel was chosen by Elohim ('God') for a witness to the nations before the Messiah's first appearing. Now, there are people of all nations, spiritually grafted in to Israel through Messiah, who are also chosen by Elohim for a witness.

> "I will call those who were not My people, My people,
> and her who was not beloved, beloved."
> **(Romans 9:26, Hosea 2:23)**

The issue at hand for the community of faith is not whether one is "saved" or "lost", but whether one is called.

The overwhelming majority of all humanity today, and in ages past, is neither saved nor lost; they just haven't been called. Their fair chance has not yet come.

Today is not the only day of salvation.

Today is not yet their time.

But as sure as the Scriptures are true, and The Eternal and His Messiah are just and fair; their day will come!

PART II:
The Redemption of Man

CHAPTER 6

Israel and the Messiah

He was, like his father Isaac, the product of a miraculous birth. (Genesis 17:19; 21:2,5,7; 25:21) His life was certainly not unblemished; and by any standard, was not of faultless and most noble character. Like his grandfather Abraham, he would, when he thought necessary, speak in half truths. (Genesis 12:11-13; 20:2) Indeed, his penchant for deception was evident even before his birth, while still in his mother's womb, even at the moment of (his) delivery. (Genesis 25:23-26) For the blessing of the first born, he supplanted his elder brother Esau. In adult life, with his father's vision dimmed by age, he deceived his dying father Isaac, so as to definitively secure that blessing. (Genesis 27:18-29) And for the love of Rachel after twenty long years of servitude, he dissembled his uncle and father-in-law Laban. (Genesis 30:41-42; 31:20).

Yet, for all of this, Jacob is the chosen heir to an eternal covenant, initiated and forever honored by Yahuweh; the same Yahuweh Elohim of his father Isaac, and his grandfather Abraham. (Genesis 17:1-16).

To Abraham, The Eternal had once appeared as one of three men, hungry and journeying wayfarers, at the terebinths of Mamre, bearing important news. This vital message would serve both to forge the character of Abraham, and to confirm a covenant that seemed impossible to keep, since

Abraham and Sarah were already well beyond the age of childbearing. (Genesis 18:1, 10-19, 23-33).

To Isaac, The Eternal appeared in Gerar to confirm the covenant once more. Like his father Abraham, when speaking of Sarah, Isaac would echo the same half truths about Rebekah, calling her only his sister, and not his wife, before the Philistines and Abimelech. (Genesis 26:2,7).

Now to Jacob (Ya'akov in Hebrew), The Eternal appears first in a dream.(Genesis 28:12-16). But later He comes as a 'Man', in a night-time wrestling contest, where Jacob is transformed from a supplanter*, who prevails by deceit*, into Israel* (Yisra-El), the champion of "El" (God or Mighty One), a contender for Heaven, who will conquer by the spirit and power of Yahuweh Elohim. This transformation comes through heavenly blessing, change of name, and ultimately, change of nature.

Unlike the previous vision of a stairway linking heaven and earth with ascending and descending angels, this physical and spiritual encounter with The Eternal is not a dream, for it leaves the man Jacob with an injury to his thigh, and a limp. (Genesis 32: 25-30)

The anthropomorphisms of these three appearances compel us to consider a seeming impossibility, that the Infinite Being the Torah calls Elohim, and Yahuweh, at least for a time, took on human form. Indeed, such a revelation occurred first in Eden, when Yahuweh Elohim was heard walking in the Garden toward the cool (breeze) of the day. (Genesis 3:8).

Each of these encounters are critical in establishing the personal and intimate relationship that secures and sustains the covenant between servant Israel and Yahuweh Elohim.

Neither a disembodied other-worldly voice, nor a dream-like vision, could be adequate for this covenant of witness and redemption. Only a face to face, "mano-a-mano" connection between Creator and creature would do.

Jacob becomes Israel; not because of his physical prowess, or strength of character. He is chosen to serve, witness for, and represent Elohim, because the King of the Universe has sovereignly elected him for that purpose.

[The Eternal confirms the covenant of Abraham and Isaac with Jacob in yet another appearance, where he is reminded that he is no longer Jacob, but Israel. (Genesis 35:9-12).]

In all of these appearances, The Eternal intimates his immediacy, and His desire for a close personal relationship with man.

Centuries later, in His ultimate Appearance, the Eternal would reveal Himself in the Person of the Messiah, the same Messiah Who is (likely) the One who first appeared in the Garden of Eden and then later to Abraham, Isaac, and Jacob. These 'pre-incarnate' revelations form the thread of redemption that began in Eden, weaving through the whole history of Israel, and leading to the end of the age and all the way to the Eternal Kingdom.

The story of Israel and the Messiah is a rich saga of history, destiny, election, epistemology, sovereignty, prophecy, eschatology, and theophany. It is a tale rooted in reality that carries Israel and all peoples from their beginning through atonement, justification, and redemption, to the end of history, and onward to a new heaven and a new earth.

In a very real sense, the story of Israel and the Messiah, is the story of us all.

*Jacob: The English equivalent of the Hebrew Ya'akov, which itself is derived from the Hebrew word 'ekev', means 'heel'. Since Ya'akov held onto his brother Esau's (Esav) heel at birth,(Genesis 25:26, Hosea 12:4) so as to be delivered together with his "older" twin, he has come to be known as 'supplanter'. His behaviour in later life caused him to acquire the unflattering reputation of 'deceiver'.

*Israel: The English equivalent of the Hebrew Yisra'el, which means "he who strives with El" (from the Hebrew Elohim, commonly translated as 'God').The name change originates with Elohim during the night-time wrestling match between Jacob (now Israel) and a mysterious heavenly being, a "God-Man", (Genesis 32:25-33, especially v.31; Hosea 12:4 identifies Him as "Et-Elohim") Who blesses Jacob as Israel, and wills Israel to prevail.

CHAPTER 7

The Redeemer of Israel

A Portrait of Joseph

He was the first born son of Jacob's first love, Rachel. His name was Joseph, conceived in the barren womb of his mother, whom Elohim remembered, hearkened to, and "hath taken away her reproach", and "added to her another son". (Genesis 29:31; 30:22-24)

His name was Joseph. In all, he had eleven brothers: six born of Leah: (Reuben, Simeon, Levi, Judah, Issachar, and Zebulun); two born of Rachel's handmaid Bilhah: (Dan and Naphtali); two born of Leah's handmaid Zilpah: (Gad and Asher); and one full brother, born of his mother Rachel: (Benjamin).

Jacob's father, Isaac, lived 180 years. After his passing, Jacob settled in Canaan, the land of his father; and it is here that the story of Joseph is told.

A child of Jacob's later years, Joseph is loved more than Israel's (Jacob's) other children, and they know it. His coat of many colors, marking him for chieftainship of the tribes at his father's death, left no room for doubt about his unique inheritance. And if this alone was not enough to arouse the bitter envy and hatred of his brothers, Joseph's two dreams of dominion assured his fate in this sibling world of jealousy and disdain. Yet his father Israel (Jacob) quietly approves the future lordship of his dear son, seeing signs of Elohim's hand in the matter, even as his other sons conspire to slay him. (Genesis 37:11,18)

Seeking his brethren and his father's flock, on Israel's bidding, Joseph, like his great grandfather Abraham, answers "Hineni" ("Here I am") when called. Like his grandfather Isaac at the 'akedah' (the binding "sacrifice"), Joseph is cast into a pit with his treasured coat dipped in goat's blood, and becomes symbolically dead. But for his aged father Jacob, this is no mere symbolism; for distraught Jacob, his beloved son Joseph is dead.

But Joseph, of course, is not dead. The intercession of his brothers Reuben and Judah constrain the others from their hateful and murderous intent, and Joseph's life is spared. Midianites lift Joseph up out of the pit, sell him to Ishmaelites for 20 shekels of silver, and he is brought into Egypt. Here, he is sold to Potiphar, the captain of Pharaoh's guard; "And Yahuweh was with Joseph" ("YHWH Et Yosef"). Joseph prospers, so that even the pagan Potiphar recognizes that YHWH was with him. For the sake of Joseph, YAHUWEH (YHWH) blesses the house of the Egyptian, according to the promise of the covenant with Abraham. (Genesis 12:3; 39:5)

The contingencies that befall the Hebrew Joseph in this Egyptian household will prophetically portray the future experience of the children of Israel in this nation. Falsely accused by Potiphar's wife of romantic advances, and unfairly condemned by his garment left behind in his flight from her devious scheme of entrapment, Joseph ends up in prison. Steadfast in his righteousness, his virtue shines forth when he asks: "How then can I do this great wickedness, and sin against Elohim?" (Genesis 39:9)

As it was in the house of Potiphar, so it was in prison; Yahuweh was with Joseph, and caused him to prosper.

Here, Joseph the dreamer, proclaiming that interpretations belong to Elohim. is called upon by Pharaoh's imprisoned chief butler and baker to interpret their dreams. (Genesis 40:8)

For both men, their dreams will be fulfilled in three days. The butler will be lifted up by Pharaoh and restored to his office; the baker will hang from a tree.

One hangs, and one is restored and exalted, all in three days.

Later, on the recommendation of the chief butler, Joseph is called upon by Pharaoh himself to interpret his dream. For those who have read this story, it is the familiar dream of seven years of plenty, followed by seven years of famine. None of the wise men or magicians of the Egyptian court can interpret this dream; only the Hebrew Joseph can.

And Pharaoh said, "Can we find one such as this, a man in whom the spirit of Elohim is?" (Genesis 41:38)

And so, Joseph is freed from prison, and is made Grand Vizier of Egypt. Through the wisdom and understanding given to him by Elohim, Joseph was appointed over all the land of Egypt; and because of the famine over all the face of the earth, he is also the designated executive for the sale of corn (food) for all the nations, even the brethren of Joseph, the sons of Israel.

Through the masterful hand of Elohim, the poignant encounter between Joseph and his brothers is finally brought about. Joseph's dream of his brother's sheaves of wheat bowing before his (sheaf) is now fulfilled, as the brothers all bow before him. Joseph is not recognized in either name or appearance; "but (Joseph) made himself strange unto them." (Genesis 42:7) He is known in Egypt as 'Zaphenathpaneah', 'food man of the life'. (Genesis 41:45)

Still, for all his challenges and rough speech, Joseph never seizes the opportunity for revenge. Once again, his righteous character shines forth. By helping his brothers confess their sin toward him, and sincerely repenting of it, he forgives them, lavishly, abundantly, and completely.

> "And Joseph said to them on the third day: 'This do in order that ye may live, for I fear Elohim.'"
> **(Genesis 42:18)**

Moved by the pathetic and anguished pleas of Judah, and the remembrances of his aged father Israel, the 'Egyptian Grand Vizier' finally reveals his true identity to his eleven brothers, as their Hebrew brother, Joseph.

> "I am Joseph your brother, whom ye sold into Egypt. And now, be not grieved, nor angry with yourselves, that you sold me here, for Elohim sent me before you to preserve life."
> **(Genesis 45:4,5)**

In this sweeping prophetic declaration, Joseph reveals his unique and singular purpose in the life of his family, his people, and in all the nations of the world.

> "And Elohim sent me before you to give you a remnant on the earth, and to save you alive for a great deliverance."
>
> **(Genesis 45:7)**

The son of the 'barren' Rachel, who, except for the will and providence of Elohim, would have never been born, had become a most powerful instrument in Yahuweh's redemptive plan for the ages. His dreams and interpretations were not ordinary, but inspired.

A pattern of three days, a pattern that will reappear in the death and resurrection of the Messiah, repeats itself throughout these stories:

for the baker, the third day seals his death;

but for the chief butler, the third day brings pardon and 'new life'.

The life of Joseph is more than just the heartwarming tale of a righteous man. His entire being is bound up not only with his father and his brothers, but also with all the nations of the whole earth.

Joseph had been pre-destined and fore-ordained by Elohim to be where he was, when he was there. As the chosen servant of The Eternal, 'bloodied' Joseph, thrown into a pit, symbolically dies, and yet lives. Taken from his own household, he is exalted to a post of great power and authority over all the world. His mission was to save a remnant alive for a great deliverance, and he fulfills his call perfectly.

Joseph, the miraculous son of Rachel and Israel, rejected and hated by his own brothers, and written off as dead by his own father, is received by the Gentile nations as a wise and beneficent ruler. At the conclusion of all, Joseph returns to his father and brothers, giving (them) assurance of Yahuweh's redemption, providence, and blessing.

Joseph, Elohim's chosen agent of deliverance, is a wondrous portrait of the Suffering Servant of Yahuweh, exquisitely described in the fifty third chapter of the Jewish prophet, Isaiah.

Yahoshua ha-Moshiach, the Messiah Yahoshua, fulfills the promise of the first coming of Yahuweh Elohim's Redeemer as a Suffering Servant, portrayed centuries before in the life of Joseph.

Rejected by his own brothers, and mourned by his father Jacob (Israel), he is received by the Egyptians and the Gentiles. After his service is completed amongst these nations, he returns to bind up the wounds of his own, the family of Israel.

The life and story of Joseph is one of wonder and great comfort; revealing the Master's Plan of Salvation by first showing us a Messiah that must endure suffering and rejection, as "Moshiach ben Yosef" (Messiah, son of Joseph), before He will return triumphantly as "Moshiach ben Dovid" (Messiah, son of David). Then He ascends to His throne in Jerusalem, and will finally and fully be King of Israel and all the earth.

> "And I will pour out over the house of David, and over the inhabitants of Jerusalem, the spirit of grace and supplications; and they will look upon Me, the One they have pierced, and they will mourn for Him, as one laments for an only son, and weep bitterly for Him, as one weeps bitterly for the first-born."
>
> **(Zechariah 12:10)**

> "On that day shall there be a fountain opened to the house of David and to the inhabitants of Jerusalem, for cleansing from sin and for purification."
>
> **(Zechariah 13:1)**

> "For I do not want you, brethren, to be uninformed of this mystery, lest you be wise in your own estimation, that a partial hardening has happened to Israel until the fulness of the Gentiles has come in;

and thus ALL ISRAEL WILL BE SAVED;
just as it is written,

The Deliverer will come to Zion,
He will remove ungodliness from Jacob,
And this is my covenant with them,
When I take away their sins.

(Isaiah 59:20,21)
(Romans 11;26, 27)

CHAPTER 8

Come unto Me

From the cloud covered 'tent of meeting' ('ohel' in Hebrew) and the 'esteem' ('kavod' in Hebrew) filled 'tabernacle' ('mishkan' in Hebrew), Yahuweh calls to Moses. The first verse of Leviticus, seamlessly connects the narrative with the last verses of Exodus, where it is proclaimed that the Tabernacle is complete, and the "Kavod Yahuweh" (esteem of Yahuweh) filled the Tabernacle. (Exodus 40:34)

And it was for this very reason that Moses could not enter in. (Exodus 40:35)

For Moses, and for Israel, this would make Yahuweh distant and unapproachable, creating an insoluble predicament. But the solution was all ready in the 'hand' of Elohim, for He would remind Israel that the key to this locked gate was the KORBAN, a Hebrew word which means 'that which brings (or is brought) near'. (Leviticus 1:1-2)

The KORBAN is really neither a sacrifice nor an offering as it is traditionally translated and understood. Yahuweh Elohim does not benefit from depriving His children, nor does He require gifts of tribute or appeasement. Nevertheless, the TORAH of KORBAN, as written in the first seven chapters of Leviticus, teaches timeless lessons of Yahuweh's righteousness, man's sinfulness, and the crucial issues of punishment, death, reconciliation, fellowship, and atonement.

The purpose of KORBAN can be first seen in Eden, when Yahuweh made for Adam and his wife garments of skins, and clothed them, to cover their shame as fig leaves could not. (Genesis 3:21)

In the lives of Adam and Eve's children, Cain and Abel, the lesson is taught yet again, when Yahuweh accepts Abel's firstlings and fat of the flock, but rejects Cain's fruit of the ground. In both cases, blood is shed; first by the 'hand" of Yahuweh Himself, then by the hand of Abel, but for entirely different reasons.

Juxtaposing these two pivotal events in Torah offers a profound lesson.

Drawing near to Yahuweh exacts an immeasureable cost; the death of an innocent, unblemished life: a life that is in stark contrast with the profane, rebellious, unrighteous life of the men who slaughter and bring forth the KORBAN (offering).

Through pressing or leaning one's hands between the horns of the KORBAN, identity is transferred, the innocent animal becomes substitute, and the process of expiation is begun. The life of the KORBAN is now legally and spiritually, by Heaven's authority, the life of the offering sinner. Its blood, the seat of its life (soul) (Leviticus 17:11), now reckoned as the life of the sinner, is dashed about the altar by the priests (kohanim) (Leviticus 1:5), and its pieces are wholly burned (holocaust) as an "olah"- a burnt offering which ascends to Elohim in a perpetual fire. Never to be consumed, this fire is constantly refreshed with wood by the sons of Aaron, who are charged with this special task.

The altar was, in effect, the gateway to Heaven, where Yahuweh is seated on His Throne of Mercy. Through the KORBAN, the means to draw near to Yahuweh was achieved, and an apparently insoluble predicament was solved.

The goal of the KORBAN was not death, but life!

Still, it was only through the KORBAN's death that the life in its blood could be procured. In this mystical transaction of double imputation, the innocent and unblemished KORBAN, and the worldly and sin-stained offerer, effectively exchange places. By imputation, an innocent [Korban] life "becomes" sinful and must be given up, so that a repentant sinner may "become" righteous, and live.

From his position of impurity, unrighteousness, sinfulness, and mortality, man is brought near to Yahuweh Who is Pure, Righteous, Sinless, and Immortal.

Through the blood of the KORBAN, sinful man passes through the Gateway to Heaven at the altar, and 'stands' in the Presence of The Eternal. This innocent life-blood 'covers' ('kaper' in Hebrew) and makes atonement for sinful man, while man's unrighteousness is (legally) transferred to the KORBAN, which must give up its life as payment for the penalty of sin. Through this imputed righteousness, man is delivered from the punishment of death to life, again and again; each time the KORBAN is brought to the altar, providing justification, reconciliation, atonement, and "new life".

From the very beginning, in the Garden of Eden, Yahuweh Elohim showed man how to come near to Him. In the life of Cain and Abel, in the life of Abraham and Isaac, in the Passover Story of Redemption, in the Tent and Tabernacle in the Wilderness, and in the Temples in Jerusalem, the means to draw near and full atonement has always required the giving up of innocent life.

Indeed, the currency of reconciliation could be no less, for all of us have disobeyed and dishonored the Life-Giver and Law-Giver, Yahuweh Elohim, and all of us are deserving of death. (Ezekiel 18:4; Genesis 3:3; Romans 6:23).

Yahuweh's mercy and justice are conferred and adjudicated over and over again in the Torah of Korban ("laws of sacrifice").

But alas, the innumerable deaths of so many innocent animals was not the ultimate purpose or goal of Torah's means of drawing near to Elohim. The animal skins in Eden, the fat and firstlings of the flock of Abel, the ram of Isaac and Abraham, the lamb of Passover, and every living creature brought to the altar in the wilderness' mishkan and Jerusalem's Temple, all pointed to a better way; a way that would testify Itself to be the end, goal, and fulfillment of the Laws of Sacrifice: the Ultimate and Supreme KORBAN.

****

The altar of the Second Temple in Jerusalem is no longer standing, having disappeared from human history in 70

C.E. The followers of a Pharisee named Rabbi Jochanan ben Zakkai, who feigned his own death to escape from the Roman's siege of Jerusalem, diverted Judaism in a new direction, and had formulated a Judaism in exile, a diaspora faith without a center of worship, without an altar, without a KORBAN- without a means for man to draw near to Yahuweh. This post-Temple Judaism faced an even greater predicament than did Moses and Israel in the wilderness: coming near to Yahuweh without an altar, and without a KORBAN.

The new guardians of the faith were now the rabbis, since there was no longer a Temple priesthood. In their wisdom, they sought a solution, and they came up with this. Selecting supporting texts in the Scriptures, the rabbis declared that animal 'sacrifice' would be replaced with the 'bullocks of our lips' (Hosea 14:1,2). The currency of reconciliation was now tefillah (prayer in Hebrew), teshuvah (repentance), and tzedakah (acts of righteousness, or charity). Authority for such a dramatic change was now assumed and appropriated by these well-intentioned teachers, who hold such influence to this very day. Historical necessity, and rabbinic triumphalism, would suggest that this was the only solution.

Nevertheless, notwithstanding religious affirmations to the contrary, there was another solution. Like the former, it came from a Rabbi, and was proclaimed and perpetuated by His disciples.

The followers of a Nazarene rabbi, Rabbi Yahoshua ben Yosef, who actually died at the hand of others, TO LIVE

AGAIN IN RESURRECTION FROM DEATH, were called out to realize the better way. The Judaism of this Teacher did not require a physical place of worship, or an altar, where countless innocent animals as korbanot (offerings) would be required. The Supreme Korban had come, just as the Torah and the Prophets had said He would, in the Person of the Rabbi-Messiah, the Rabbi Yahoshua ben Yahuweh, Son of Man and Son of Elohim.

The earthly Jerusalem Temple and its altar were now in the hearts of the obedient faithful followers of the Servant-Messiah. As Advocate for His elect, His Spirit would transform the lives of His chosen believers.

The Key to the Gates of the Kingdom of Heaven, and Eternal Life, as promised in the Torah and the Prophets, had now come.

In this day, and for all time, Yahoshua, Messiah and Korban, continues to call to all who would hear, saying "Come unto Me."

*The Hebrew word 'KAVOD' is usually translated as 'glory'. However, 'KAVOD' actually means honor, esteem, and repute, literally meaning to be "heavy" or "weighty". In popular American English, one might speak of a "heavy subject", or "weighty topic".

The word glory refers to radiance or emanations of light, historically connected to the sun and sun-worship. "Gloria" was herself, a Roman goddess, associated with sun-worship.

The Hebrew Yahuweh Elohim and Messiah Yahoshua command that we are to neither have nor mention other 'gods' besides Him. (Exodus 20:3; 23:13).

Therefore, the Hebrew "KAVOD YAHUWEH" should not be rendered as the 'glory of the LORD', but more accurately as, "the Esteemed Honor of YAHUWEH".

CHAPTER 9

The Name Above All Names

Since the beginning of time, He has been called by many names and by many nations. Yet, it is by the name 'God' or 'Lord' that most of us know Him. Indeed, the people who consider themselves Jewish, or Christian, or Moslem, the three great monotheistic faiths, all call Him by the same name; 'God'.

Yet, can it be that the Adonai or Elohim of Judaism, and the Jesus Christ of Christianity, and the Allah of Islam (Moslem), are all the same 'God'? Today, in a world of political correctness and tolerance, this is the commonly held belief; but do the accounts of this 'God' in the Hebrew Scriptures (the Jewish Torah), and the Christian New Testament, and the Moslem Koran support such a claim?

I do not believe they do!

While all describe a deity who is similar in some ways, He is sufficiently different in so many, as to challenge and refute the possiblity that these three faiths reveal, revere, and worship the same 'God'.

How could this be? After all, these three great religions derive their essential doctrines of faith from the same source, the first Book of Scriptures known as Genesis or

"B'rayshis" in Hebrew. It is here, in this Book of Beginnings, where the answer to this "mystery" begins to be revealed.

The Torah, in its most narrow and traditional definition, is the first Five Books of Moses, known as the Pentateuch or 'Chumash', meaning '5' in the Hebrew. In the 'Christian Bible' it is called the 'Old Testament'. And in the Islamic Koran, with modifications, this 'sacred' text also appears. All three agree that the Torah either is or contains the Word of 'God'.

But the name "God" never appears anywhere in the Torah! In fact, that name (God) derives from the pantheon of Canaanite deities; gods whom we are expressly forbidden to acknowledge, let alone worship! (Exodus 20:3)

So what name does appear in the very first verse of Genesis; the well known "In the beginning"? It is the Hebrew word ELOHIM. This then, must be the name of the true Creator.

Astonishingly, it is not!

You see, Elohim, like Adonai, are names given to Canaanite deities, like El and Ba-al. They are not Hebrew but Canaanite titles for the pagan gods of Canaan and Babylon. Furthermore, Elohim is a plural form of Eloha, suggesting more than one god. And it is in this plural form, Elohim, that the Creator is first spoken of in Torah. However, take note, that the Hebrew word for 'created' is 'bara', the singular form; emphatically affirming that this 'ELOHIM' is not many gods, but ONE, Who has a plenitude of characteristics but simultaneously, an inscrutable and essential oneness, ('echad' in the Hebrew).

Why then does the Torah, the Word of the Eternal, in its very first verse, use the name of a Canaanite deity to reveal the Creator of heaven and earth?

The short answer is this: it does not!

While there is an apparent similarity between Torah's 'God' and the Canaanite god, it is no more than that; for in the Torah's first verse, the name Elohim does not appear alone, but with the unique Hebrew word "ET", as "ELOHIM ET". Composed of the first and last letters of the Hebrew alphabet, 'aleph' and 'tav', 'ET' is the first intimation in Scripture of the nature of the Hebrew ELOHIM. He is the 'first and the last', the 'rishon and acharon' in the Hebrew, elucidating the nature and essence of Elohim. It is later in Scripture that this Being, Who existed at the Creation, and was active in Creation, is revealed as the Anointed, the Messiah, the Saviour and Redeemer.

But if "ET" is the only characteristic of the Hebrew Elohim, why did the Eternal One reveal Himself in the plural in Genesis 1:1 rather than the singular. Here again, the answer to this question is revealed later in Scripture; specifically in Genesis 2:4, when the name Yahuweh Elohim first appears.

The rabbis have prohibited the true articulation of the Name Yahuweh, prescribing instead 'Adonai' wherever YHWH appears. The tetragrammaton YHWH is never pronounced as written, based on the belief that such use would be considered taking His Name in vain. But by not calling upon the Name Yahuweh (YHWH), and substituting Adonai, we (albeit) unintentionally call upon the Canaanite deity, elohim adonai (Lord God), and not the Hebrew One and Only, Yahuweh. This was surely not their goal, yet the practical effect is as if it were.

Even the rabbis acknowledge that while Elohim denotes 'God' as the Creator and moral Governor of the universe, YHWH (Yahuweh) stresses His loving kindness, His mercy, and His condescension and revelation to mankind. And it is precisely in that fulness of His Person that He wants us to know Him. For that very reason, He declares this unique Name to His chosen people.

In the Torah's second Book, in Exodus' third chapter, at the farthest end of the wilderness, at the mountain of Elohim, named Horeb, Moses, the deliverer, mediator, prophet, and teacher, meets the Eternal in the bush that burned with fire, but yet was not consumed. It is in the seventh verse that Elohim further declares Himself "Yahuweh", Who has seen the affliction of His people that are in Egypt, and Who will deliver them and bring them up out of that land to a land flowing with milk and honey. Moses is to be that man chosen to propel forward this redeeming mission of Yahuweh for His elect.

But Moses must know the Name of this 'God' Who redeems, anticipating the question from all Israel.

And so Elohim answers. saying:

"Ehyeh asher ehyeh",which translates "I am that I
am....('I AM' has sent me unto you).

(Exodus 3:14)

This NAME and its declaration reveals the self-existence
and eternality of the Hebrew Elohim, the Torah's 'God'.
And in the very next verse He proclaims Himself to be:

"Yahuweh Elohay avosaychem", which translates
"Yahuweh, the Mighty One of your fathers. "This is
My Name forever,and this is My Memorial Name
unto all generations."

(Exodus 3:15)

Amazingly, the very Name by which the One and Only
Eternal Elohim is to be remembered, the Name YAHUWEH,
is never spoken, and as a result, forgotten or ignored.

The Almighty, the Creator, the Deliverer and Redeemer, the
Saviour, and King of Kings has proclaimed to His creation
His One and Only Personal Name; it is not Elohim, it is not
Adonai, it is not Jesus Christ, it is not Allah!

IT IS YAHUWEH!

In simple and straightforward language, the Eternal tells
us that it is in this Name YAHUWEH, and in this Name
only, that Elohim, the Mighty One of Israel and the fathers
Abraham, Isaac, and Jacob, is to be known and remembered
forever and for all generations.

And in a later day, in the prophesied fulness of time,
His Anointed, the Messiah YAHOSHUA, whose Name
translated means Yahuweh saves, or the salvation of Yah,

Who first appeared as the Word "ET", symbolizing the First and the Last, with Elohim at Creation, will take on His image in humanity, as a carpenter and Jewish rabbi from Nazareth, and make Himself to be known to Israel and to all the nations of the earth.

In this wondrous saving incarnation, the Name of the Father Yahuweh is in the Name of the Son, Yahoshua, and all Creation, for all eternity, shall know Him.

The prophet Zechariah foresees that splendid day when he proclaims:

> "V'neh'ehmar: v'hauyauh YAHUWEH l'melech al kol ha-aretz; ba-yom ha-hu yih-yeh YAHUWEH echad u'sh'mo echad."

which translates:

> "As it is written: And YAHUWEH shall be King over all the earth; in that day will YAHUWEH be One, and His NAME ONE!"
>
> (Zechariah 14:9)

May that Day come soon.

CHAPTER 10

A Name Like None Other

In Hebrew, the language of Torah, a name is more than just a title. It reveals the character and essence of the person being named. As it is for mortal humans, so it is for the immortal Elohim ('God').

The Hebrew Torah proclaims in its opening statement that "Elohim 'ET' " created the heaven and the earth.

("ET", composed of the first and last letters of the Hebrew alphabet, is the Word spoken of in the Gospel of John 1:1; the Word that was with 'God' (Elohim), and the Word that was 'God'.)

> "B'rayshis bara Elohim ET ha-shamayim v'ET ha-aretz."
>
> (Genesis 1:1)

Through Genesis 1:1 to Genesis 2:3, the Almighty is called by the title-name Elohim, meaning 'Mighty Ones'. But beginning in Genesis 2:4 that name is refined to the proper and personal Name, Yahuweh Elohim.

Traditionally unspoken, and read as Adonai, the Name of Four Letters, YHWH or YHVH (yod-hay-vav-hay), known as the tetragrammaton, is derived from the Hebrew letters hay-yod-hay, and may be understood to mean the 'eternally self-existent One".

It is here that YHVH speaks of His personal and intimate involvement with Adam and Eve, the man and woman created in His image. And here too is the story of Eden, the Tree of Knowledge of Good and Evil, and the Tree of Life.

The personal Name YHVH appears twelve times from Genesis 2:4 and Genesis 3:1.

Then, suddenly, Satan, the subtle and deceiving angelic spirit adversary and opponent of YHVH, incarnated as a serpent, ignores the personal Name YHVH, and substitutes the impersonal title Elohim alone.

But YHVH Elohim reappears in Genesis 3:8, in the familiar encounter between Yahuweh and disobedient Adam and Eve, where man attempts to deceive YHVH, as Satan had deceived man. The consequence of human disobedience and false witness brings about YHVH's judgement against His adversary, Satan, (Genesis 3:14-15), and against his partner, man. (Genesis 3:16-19)

Responding with compassion to the shame of Adam and Eve, Yahuweh covers their nakedness with 'garments of skins'. Mercifully, and justly, the mortal and imperfect Adam and Eve are expelled from the Garden of Eden so as not to eat from the Tree of Life, and live forever in their shame and sinfulness.

Securing the garments of skin by Yahuweh required the death of an innocent life, and the consequent shedding of innocent blood, which brought about judgement, expiation, atonement, and reconciliation, while Adam and Eve were yet in Eden. Although temporary, this becomes the prototype and foundation of the Sovereign's economy of redemption when dealing with the problem of disobedience and sin.

Even without their confession or repentance, Yahuweh, in His infinite mercy and unbounded grace, gave Adam and Eve pardon; effectively restoring the lives they had forfeited, by eating from the very tree that would guarantee their death in that day. (Genesis 2:17)

The fig tree girdles, crafted by the man and his wife, were wholly inadequate to cover their shame; only Yahuweh, the Law-Giver and Life-Giver, could restore life to the first parents of the human race, who otherwise would have died.

Later, the Torah would identify blood as the currency of reconciliation. This has been called 'the scarlet thread of redemption'.

> "For the life of the flesh is in the blood, and I have given it to you on the altar to make atonement for your souls; for it is the blood by reason of the life that makes atonement."
>
> (Leviticus 17:11)

The Torah declares, and Judaism has rightly understood, that as YHVH (Yahuweh), the Eternal is revealed in close relationship with men and with nations. As YHVH, His compassion, mercy, lovingkindness, and nearness to His children is manifest.

That same faithfulness and care is illustrated dramatically and powerfully in the encounter between Moses and the Almighty just prior to Israel's redemption from bondage in Egypt, when Moses meets with Elohim and learns again that His Name is YHVH.

The Hebrew words, spoken by Elohim Himself are:

"EhYH asher ehYH" ("I am that I am")

The Personal Name of YHVH is written in the Hebrew language with the letters 'yod-hay-vav-hay' and as 'yod-yod'. These are derived from the Hebrew verb 'hay-yod-hay' (HYH) meaning 'to be', as an ongoing state, as in: was, is, and shall be, an action in progress, an eternal being.

In Scripture, the Hebrew letter 'vav' (v) is used as a device that reverses the tense in a sequence of verbs. It may also be the Hebrew conjunction, 'and', which is added to the beginning of a word, but not written as a separate word.

So then; as 'YY' (yod-yod) is a contraction of Eh'Y'H asher Eh'Y'H, so YHVH is a contraction of YHvYH.

Here, the Scriptural device of the reversing 'vav' changes the first "YH" in the verb sequence from the perfect tense "was", to the imperfect tense "shall be"; so that "I AM THAT I AM' becomes in YHvYH, "I WAS AND I SHALL BE".

The reversing 'vav' is usually translated as 'and'; but since it serves to link sequences of events, it may also be translated as 'then', or 'so', or 'when'.

Torah narratives often begin with the Hebrew word 'vyhy' (vav-yod-hay-yod), pronounced as va-yi-hee, a shortened form of YHYH, with a reversing 'vav', and translated as: "and it came to pass".

Similarly, the Hebrew word 'hyh' (hay-yod-hay), with the reversing 'vav' appears as 'vhyh' (vav-hay-yod-hay), pronounced as vihawyawh, and translated as: "and it shall come to pass".

By joining these two words together, we get: "vyhyvhyh", pronounced as va-yi-hee-vi-haw-yawh, and translated as: "and it came to pass and it shall come to pass".

In its shortened and contracted form, these two words may become one, as in YHVH (Yod-Hay-Vav-Hay), the Personal Name of Elohim.

In conclusion, both 'YY' (Yod-Yod) and 'YHVH' (Yod-Hay-Vav-Hay) may be traced to the Hebrew word 'HYH' (hay-yod-hay), meaning "to be", appearing in Scripture as 'EhYh asher EhYh', "I AM THAT (I) AM".

YHVH, the Personal Name of Elohim, reveals the essence and character of "The Mighty One(s)", proclaiming His Eternal Being twice!

Yahuveh Elohim is not just "I AM", but "I AM that (and) I AM".

Within the richness and fulness of His Name YHVH, (Yahuweh) is:

1. The Creator of the Universe and Sovereign Elector of Israel;
2. The Redeemer of Israel and the Nations, and Redeemer of all Creation;

3. The Author of a first Covenant and Author of a New Covenant. (Jeremiah 31:31-33);
4. "ET" (as in Elohim ET in Genesis 1:1): the aleph and the tav, the alpha and omega, the first and the last;
5. The Suffering Servant and The Triumphant Savior;
6. The Eternal Father and His Eternal Son.

Finally, in the words of the Son, Yahoshua, speaking of His Father, as Yahuweh, there is an assurance and affirmation that bears witness to all who would hear:

"I AND MY FATHER ARE ONE."
(John 10:30)

CHAPTER 11

One Little Word

Some years ago, well within the lifetime of many of us, there was a popular American song entitled "Little Things Mean Alot". More often than not, those "little things" are not things but ideas, communicated and carried in symbolic thought we call "words".

The story of the beginning of all history is contained in one of the world's most treasured books, 'The Scriptures', composed of tens of thousands of words.

And among this vast ocean of ideas, and the words that represent them, is one upon which rests all of Torah's Truth.

That one little word, pronounced 'ET', is created with just two Hebrew letters, 'aleph' and 'tav'; the first letter and last letter of the Hebrew alphabet. In effect, within 'ET', is everything from "A" to "Z" in the English, or from "Alpha" to "Omega" in the Greek.

And while 'ET' appears many times throughout the Hebrew Scriptures, it is no small matter that 'et' makes its Appearance at the very first, in the familiar opening verse of Hebrew Scripture:

[The English translation of the phonetic Hebrew appears in brackets.]

The Light in the Wilderness

> "B'reishis (In the beginning) bara (created)Elohim
> (" Mighty Ones [God]") 'ET' (untranslated) ha-
> shamayim (the heaven) v' 'ET' (untranslated) ha-
> aretz (the earth)."

(Genesis 1:1)

The untranslated word 'ET', known as the direct definite object marker, is an instrument of Hebrew syntactical construction, preceding the definite object on which the verb's action is directed.

According to traditional linguistic scholarship, this Hebrew Word has no meaning. However, there is nothing in the Scripture that is superfluous and without purpose. Indeed, in order for man to live by EVERY WORD that proceeds out of the mouth of Yahuweh, each and every word must have meaning. (Deuteronomy 8:3; Matthew 4:4)

As it is written:

> "So shall My Word be which goes forth from My mouth;
> It shall not return to Me empty,
> Without accomplishing what I desire,
> And without succeeding in the matter for which I sent
> it."

(Isaiah 55:11)

And so it is that this one little word simultaneously conceals and reveals the essential Truth of Torah and all of Scripture.

Appearing twice in this revelation of Creation, 'ET' is, at once, closely connected to Elohim, and to His creation, positioned significantly and remarkably, between Him

86

(Elohim), and the heaven (ha-shamayim) and the earth (ha-aretz) which He created.

In these first seven words of Scripture, the Word 'ET' sits, in Its first appearance, notably, historically, prophetically, and even eschatologically, in the midst of the seven.

'ET' shares with Elohim existence before creation, and prophetically, will appear twice in creation, in a first and second coming or appearance.

Of all the attributes given to the nature of Elohim, the 'first and last', being without beginning and without end, are solely and uniquely His. And so it is that 'ET', the little word made of the first letter 'aleph' (alpha or "A"), and the last letter 'tav' (omega or "Z"), reveals an element of the nature of Elohim that is intimately part of His identity. (Revelation 1:17-18)

In the third Book of Torah, Leviticus, which teaches the concepts of 'holiness', sacrifice, and atonement, 'ET' is revealed even further.

In Leviticus 8:2, 'ET' appears seven (7) times in a verse that includes the Hebrew word 'ha-moshichah', from which the title "Moshiach", meaning Anointed or Messiah, is derived, and elaborates on the priestly work of atonement.

In Leviticus 16:14, the blood of the atoning sacrifice is sprinkled seven (7) times on the ark-cover.

The Hebrew mind, established within the revelation of Torah, conceived in the number '7' , fulness and completeness in the order of creation.

In these verses, the anointing oil (shemen ha-moshichah), the high priest, the atoning sacrifice, and the unleavened bread (the Passover symbol of affliction, freedom, and sinlessness) all appear together where the atoning blood, sprinkled seven times, is inextricably linked to the Word 'ET', which appears seven times in Lev. 8:2.

So then, in the Hebrew Scriptures alone, it may be deduced that 'ET' is part of Elohim, eternally self-existent, active in Creation, and the central Figure in the Plan of Redemption and Atonement.

****

The Messianic Scriptures (New Testament) reveal with even greater clarity the identity of this one little Word.

The Gospel of John proclaims:

> In the beginning was the WORD, and the WORD was with "God", and the WORD was "God". He was in the beginning with "God". All things came into being by Him, and apart from Him nothing has come into being that has come into being. In Him was life, and the life was the light of men. And the light shines in the darkness, and the darkness did not comprehend it.
>
> (John 1:1-5)

> And the WORD became flesh, and dwelt among us, and we beheld His glory, glory as of the only begotten from the Father, full of grace and truth.
>
> (John 1:14)

> What was from the beginning, what we have heard, what we have seen with our eyes, what we beheld and our hands handled, concerning the WORD of Life-and the Life was manifested, and we have seen and bear witness and proclaim to you the eternal life, which was with the Father and was manifested to us-what we have seen and heard we proclaim to you also, that you may also have fellowship with us; and indeed our fellowship is with the Father and with His Son, Yahoshua Ha-Moshiach. And these things we write, so that our joy may be made complete.
>
> (1John:1-4)

The WORD of the Gospel of John, and the WORD of the Epistle of 1John is NOT the Greek "LOGOS", which permeates all of Christianity's theology and scholarship.

The identity of the Messiah is not to be found in Greek words (LOGOS) which symbolize Greek thought, Greek philosophy, and Greek religion. To believe this would lead to spiritual darkness; eating, as it were, the fruit of a barren, poisonous, pagan tree. (Jeremiah10: 1-3)

The WORD proclaimed by the Gospel of John and the Letter of 1John is not Greek, but Hebrew!

It is not LOGOS.

It is "ET"!

Comprised of the first and last letters of the Hebrew alphabet, appearing in Genesis 1:1 and John 1:1, 'ET' is intimately and inextricably bound to the work of the High Priest, the Blood of Sacrifice, sinlessness, and atonement, to Creation, to the Father, and part of Elohim.

As "ET" appears twice in the first verse of Scripture, He will appear a second time in a 'New Creation', restoring and redeeming the world from its brokeness, through the Atoning Work of His First Appearing, and His triumphant Kingdom Reign in His Second.

This one little "WORD" is not little after all; for He who has seen "ET", [The WORD], has seen the Father.

The only Saviour there is must be Elohim Himself....and "ET" is the Person of Elohim Who is the One Anointed to Redeem and to Reign eternally as the Messiah, Yahoshua ha-Moshiach.

Some Additional Reflections on "The WORD"

*In the Hebrew language, the word for "word" and "speak" is *'DiBaR',* composed of the three Hebrew letters 'dahlid', 'bet', (also called 'vet'), and 'resh'[DBR].

The Fifth Book of Moses, [the Pentateuch or Torah], called Deuteronomy (meaning Second Law from the Greek), is known in Hebrew as 'Devarim', meaning "Words".

The Fourth Book of Torah, called Numbers, is known as 'BemiDBaR' in Hebrew, meaning "In the Wilderness". It is intriguing that the root of this word is composed of the same three letters that make up the Hebrew word for "Word", DBR, as dahlid, bet, and resh.

In a very real sense, the Word [DBR] is [The Light] in the Wilderness [bmDBR].

****

Indeed, "DiBaR" [or "DiVaR"] appears over and over again throughout Hebrew Scriptures:

To Abram [Abraham], regarding the promise of a son, and a covenant:

> "Achar ha-d'varim ha-ayleh hayah DiVaR-YHWH el Avram bamachazeh laymohr:....."
> [After these things the WORD of YHWH (the LORD) came to Abram in a vision, saying:]
> **(Genesis 15:1)**

> "V'henay DiVaR-YHWH aylav laymohr...."
> [And behold, the WORD of YHWH (the LORD) came to him, saying:....]
> **(Genesis 15:4)**

To Moses, being instructed on the ordinance of the Passover:

> "VayiDaBayR YHWH el Mosheh laymohr:"
> [And YHWH spoke to Moses saying:]
> **(Exodus 13:1; 14:1)**

To Moses, from within the wilderness tabernacle, at the Mercy seat, above the Ark of the Covenant:

> "....v'yishma ET-ha-kol me-DaBayR aylav may-al ha-kaporet"
> [and he heard the Voice making itself as speaking from above the ark cover (or)
> and he heard the Voice from the WORD from above the ark cover]
> **(Numbers 7:89)**

To Ezekiel, regarding the vindication of the Name of Yahuweh through Israel:

> "Vayihee DiVaR-YHWH aylee laymohr:"
> [Now the WORD of Yahuweh came to me saying:]
> **(Ezekiel 36:16)**

and to Elijah, before an epiphany of YHWH, upon the mountain, when:

> "the WORD of the Lord[YHWH] came to him, and He said to him, 'What are you doing here, Elijah'?"
> **(1Kings 19:9)**

****

The WORD is described as both a noun and a verb. Indeed, in the Hebrew, it is both, as DBR means both 'WORD' and 'to speak'.

In Psalm 119:160: "Thy WORD is Truth".

In Psalm 107:20. the WORD "heals".

In Jeremiah 23:29, the WORD is "like a hammer which shatters a rock."

In Isaiah 40:8, the WORD "stands forever".

To Abram, the WORD came to him.

To Moses, the WORD spoke.

To Ezekiel and Elijah, (and to others), the WORD came [to them].

In the Messianic Scriptures (New Testament), the writer of Hebrews 11:3 proclaims: the WORD created the worlds.

In Hebrews 4:12, he declares: the WORD is living and active, piercing the soul and spirit, able to judge the thoughts and intentions of the heart.

The WORD, then, is not just a major feature of Torah; the WORD is The Living Torah.

Ultimately, the conclusion of the Revelation of all Scripture is revealed in the Gospel of John 1:1-4:

The WORD was with Elohim in the beginning.

The WORD was Elohim from the beginning.

The WORD is a Person with Elohim.

Through this Person-WORD, all things came into being.

In this Person-WORD was [and is] LIFE, and the LIFE was [and is] the LIGHT of men.

The WORD is the revelation of the Source of life and light.

The WORD is the Messiah, and the Messiah is ELOHIM!

CHAPTER 12

It Takes Two: The Template of Torah

It has long been the best selling book of all time. Translated into countless tongues, and found in every nation on earth, you would think it would be the most powerful unifying force that humanity has ever known. But it is not!

Unique in its Authorship, and its exclusive claim for Truth, it has spawned, some would say surprisingly, a multiplicity of religions and creeds. These diverse systems of belief have planted the seeds of fear and distrust between and among the nations. Across the millenia, as these disparate systems of belief have germinated, (except for a notable few), almost all have sprouted, bore, and brought forth the bitter fruit of wars, inquisitions, bigotry, genocide, and terrorism. Rather than inspire the best in the heart of man, it gave way to the worst. Still, it would be grossly unjust to hold it culpable for the abysmal confusion that remains in its wake as it sails through the centuries.

It has always had the potential for great and lasting 'good'; but such a 'good' has been tragically thwarted by massive deception and the innate tendency toward rebellion, delusion, and evil in the heart of man.

"It", of course, is that Book the world knows as the "Bible"; a name that itself has its roots in heathen religion, and pagan deception*. Known by the ancients who inherited the True

Faith as "The Scriptures", we would also do well to reclaim this appelation.

In majesty and elegant simplicity, The Scriptures give sweeping account of the universe's creation, the origin of man, the call of a nation, a constitution of laws, statutes, and ordinances, ordinary people made extraordinary by faithful obedience to a sublime vision, sin and sorrow, repentance and restoration, and the ultimate hope of a Kingdom governed by the righteous rule of the Eternal Creator and King.

All along the way, this supreme Book of Books tells its tale, following a template patterned in 'twos'. It reveals a Plan whose primary purpose is to secure a consanguinous familial relationship between the Eternal Father Yahuwheh and His son Israel, (and by extension all who are grafted in) that reflects the essential unity within the eternal relationship that has always existed between the Father, Yahuweh Elohim, and His Son, Yahoshua.

This grand design is achieved by way of two covenants: a first and former one, that relies on man's imperfect will, and a new and latter one, that is secured with Yahuweh's Spirit. From Elohim's Laws written on tables of stone, and symbolically sealed with the blood of mortal creatures as illustrated in the animal offerings at the altar and the rite of circumcision, to His laws written on the human heart, eternally sealed with the blood of the Messiah of Israel, these two covenants perfectly picture the Eternal's Plan of Redemption.

It begins in Eden, the Garden at the focal point of the creation story. In it are two people; a man and a woman. In it, also, are two trees; the forbidden 'tree of knowledge of good and evil', and the (now largely inaccessible) "Tree of Life". And in it, too, are two supernatural beings, one created, the other Creator; each calling for the faith and obedience of the man and the woman. The created one is Satan, meaning Adversary or Accuser in Hebrew, the Other is the Creator Elohim, meaning "Mighty Ones" in Hebrew. Satan appears in the form of a serpent; Elohim in the form of a Man, in Whose likeness and image the man and woman were created. Suffering the immediate consequence of sinful disobedience, by rejecting Elohim and believing the lie of the Adversary, Adam and his wife Eve, the first two humans, are expelled from Eden.

Soon after, Eve gives birth to two sons; first Cain, and then, Abel. The story of these two brothers, will, like their parents, be marked by sinful disobedience, and tragic consequences. It is a bitter tale that will repeat again and again throughout Scripture.

Cain murders Abel, Ishmael hates Isaac, Jacob deceives Esau, eleven brothers conspire against Joseph, who himself has two sons, Ephraim and Manasseh, each with very different destinies. Their Hebrew names serve to foretell their future.

Manasseh, Joseph's first born, means, "making to forget".

Ephraim, his second born, means, "fruitfulness". And so it came to pass, that their grandfather Israel (Jacob), who himself was the younger of two brothers, and according to the will of Elohim, conferred the blessing of the first born, which was 'rightfully' Manasseh's, onto the second born and younger, Ephraim.

The birth order of Israel (Jacob), and his adopted grandson Ephraim, does not predict or secure the blessing of the first born, since both are second-born, but both are counted by Elohim as if they were first.

> "Thus says Yahuweh, "Israel is my son, My first-born'."
>
> (Exodus 4:22)

> "With weeping they shall come, and by supplication I will lead them; I will make them walk by streams of waters, on a straight path in which they will not stumble; For I am a Father to Israel, and Ephraim is My first-born."
>
> (Jeremiah 31:9)

According to the prophetic blessing of their father Jacob (Israel), two sons and brothers, Judah and Joseph, are destined to be at the center of redemptive history. (see Genesis 49: 8-12; 22-26).

But of all of Jacob's blessings, the very best are given to his beloved son Joseph, and to Joseph's son, Ephraim. (see Genesis 49:22-26; 48:14-22).

Joseph, the man of vision and dreams, is also the man of great character, morality, compassion, and forgiveness. The Torah's rich and honorable recognition of Joseph is meant to convey much more than just a detailed account of a noble man in the history of Israel.

And like a prince, eminent and distinguished among his brothers, Joseph is a perfect picture of the 'Suffering Servant' portrayed in the 53rd Chapter of the Prophet Isaiah. Such a figure is as much a representation of the promised Messiah of Israel, as is the Triumphant and Conquering Redeemer, long awaited by the Jewish people.

The destiny of this (Jewish) people is bound up in Joseph's two sons; the naturally first born, Manasseh, and his brother, the prophetically ordained "first-born", Ephraim. As in the meaning of his name (Manasseh), the Jewish people (Israel) is "made to forget" the 'Suffering Servant'; but only for a time! In the days to come, they, like Ephraim, shall be "doubly fruitful".

The Messianic Scriptures powerfully proclaim this with certainty.

> "I say then, they did not stumble so as to fall, did they? May it never be! But by their transgression, salvation has come to the Gentiles to make them jealous. Now if their transgression be riches for the world and their failure be riches for the Gentiles, how much more will their fulfillment be!"
>
> (Romans 11:11-12)

> "For I do not want you, brethren, to be uninformed of this mystery, lest you be wise in your own estimation; that a partial hardening has happened to Israel until the fulness of the Gentiles has come in; and thus all Israel will be saved; just as it is written, 'The Deliverer will come from Zion, He will remove 'ungodliness' from Jacob, and this is my covenant with them when I take away their sins.' From the standpoint of the gospel, they are enemies for your sake, but from the

standpoint of Elohim's choice, they are beloved for
the sake of the fathers; for the gifts and calling of
Elohim are irrevocable."

(Romans 11:25-29)

The historical suffering and persecution of Israel, (the Jewish people), might persuade some, that the greater blessing has been taken from her. Replacement or Covenant theology in religion, and all forms of anti-Semitism, are too often the basis of this fallacy. Such grave injustice is rooted in (the Adversary's) hatred of Yahuweh Elohim and His Kingdom, expressing itself as the physical and spiritual oppression of Elohim's chosen people, the Jews.

But according to Scripture, this is not to be the future destiny of Zion.

"But Zion said, 'Yahuweh has forsaken me, Yahuweh
has forgotten me'.
` Can a woman forget her nursing child, and have no
compassion on the son of her womb?
Even these may forget, but I will not forget you."

(Isaiah 49:14-15)

Ultimately, Zion, the first-born natural son of Elohim, will receive not the blessing of Manasseh, but the greater blessing of the "fruitful" Ephraim. The identity of Israel is bound up in the life of two brothers and two sons: Joseph and Judah, and Ephraim and Manasseh.

And just as Israel is one people with two blessings, Israel's Messiah is one Redeemer with two natures.

He is the 'Suffering Servant' of Isaiah 53, and the son of David, the King.

He is the 'Star' that shall come forth from Jacob, and the 'Scepter' that shall rise from Israel. (Numbers 24:17).

He is the 'Stone' which the builders rejected (and the One) that has become the 'Chief Cornerstone'. (Psalm 118:22).

He is the Son of Man and the Son of Elohim.

Do you recall those two trees in Eden? The one known as the Tree of Life was neither touched nor eaten. The history of mankind gives painful witness to the consequence of partaking of the other tree. Although not without blessing, its fruits have given Israel and the nations untold sorrow and suffering.

But the Plan of Redemption, as told in Scripture is not finished!

The Scripture and its tale of 'twos' reveals that His Story (history) will end in restoration and victory. Israel, and the redeemed of all nations, at the Messiah's Second Coming, will be welcomed into a renewed earth, and a Kingdom ruled from a new Jerusalem, by the King of Kings Himself.

Here, the gates shall be flung open to a Garden where the Tree of Life, previously inaccessible except to an elect few, will finally bless all of humanity.

> "And on either side of the river was the Tree of Life, bearing twelve kinds of fruit, yielding its fruit every

> month; and the leaves of the Tree were for the healing
> of the nations."
>
> (Revelation 22:2)

The Scriptures tells its Great Story following a template of 'twos': beginning in the Garden of Eden in Genesis, and concluding in the New Jerusalem in Revelation, all the while pointing to the Messiah, Who as Priest and Korban (sacrifice), Suffering Servant and Victorious King, destined to appear twice in history, is a Man of two natures, Son of Man and Son of Elohim. His mission was to save two peoples, Israel and the Gentile nations, as the Mediator of the New Covenant*, and the Faithful Son of His Eternal Father.

At long last, at the end of the age, with Sceptre and Crown, Yahoshua, the Messiah of Israel and the Nations, will bring the Kingdom of Heaven to the new Earth, where He will rule and reign from the New Jerusalem, for ever!

*Bible: the word derives from the Greek 'biblos' or 'biblion', meaning 'books'. This Hellenized term was first applied to all of Scripture around 400 C.E. While the use of the term "Bible" appears reasonable enough, closer scrutiny reveals that it is not innocent.

"Byblos" was the Greek name of the Phonecian seaport where Adonis, Isis, and Osiris were all worshipped. The female deity "Byblis" (aka "Byble", "Biblis") was the grand-daughter of Apollo, the sun deity of the Greeks. "Byblia" was also a name for "Venus", an astral goddess, and goddess of sensuality. As a part of this greatest deception of all nations, even the name of the Scriptures, through syncretism, have been covered in the counterfeit clothes of paganism. (referenced from "Come Out of Her My People", C.J. Koster, p.75-78)

> "And in all things I have said unto you take heed; and make NO mention of 'the name of other mighty ones (gods)' (v'shemelohim achayrim), neither let it be heard out of your mouth."
>
> (Exodus 23:13)

*The New Covenant is first promised in Eden (Genesis 3:15), fulfilled by the Messiah Yahoshua (John 14:6), and defined by the prophet Jeremiah (Jeremiah 31:31-34).

> "Behold, days are coming, declares Yahuweh, when I will make a New Covenant with the house of Israel and the house of Judah.(v.31)
>
> But this is the Covenant which I will make with the house of Israel after those days, declares Yahuweh. I will put My Torah (Teaching, Instruction, or Law) within them,and on their hearts I will write it; and I will be their Elohim, and they shall be My people. (v.33)

The New Covenant, in its complete fulfillment, will be the radical transformation of the nature (heart) of humankind. The sinful inclination of man will finally be conquered and vanquished, and he will be ruled by the righteousness that is Torah, now inscribed upon his heart, in the Power of the Spirit of Elohim and the Messiah living in and through Him. In this transcendent newness, man will at last realize the reason for his creation, and through translation or resurrection to eternal life, change from the image and likeness of Elohim to the very nature and substance of Yahuweh Elohim Himself. (1Corinthian 13:12; 1John 3:2).

The New Covenant is most emphatically, NOT a "New Testament", superceding and replacing an "Old Testament". A testament is a legal instrument, formally declaring, usually in writing, a person's wishes as to the disposition of his property after death. In neither the Hebrew Torah, nor the Messianic Scriptures, is the initiating Party to this agreement dead, for that would be impossible.

Yahuweh Elohim and Messiah Yahoshua are Immortal and Eternal, without beginning and without end, and not subject to the natural consequences of corruption and decay.(1Timothy 6:16). The word testament is inappropriate and deceptive, and has led to false doctrine and teaching. leading the whole world astray!

Covenant, (B'rit in Hebrew, Diatheke in Greek), on the other hand is a contract between two living parties, written and confirmed throughout Torah, and sealed by the Messiah in the symbol and source of life itself: blood. As the Author of all the covenants of Scripture is eternal, so too, The New Covenant will endure for all time and forever.

CHAPTER 13

A Sure Foundation:

The Stone of Jacob and The King of the Universe

(A Father's son meets the Father and Son)

There is a connection that exists between humans that transcends race, religion, ethnicity, and national boundaries. It is contained in space and time, and simultaneously is beyond them. This connection is a life giving relationship; it is the bond between a parent and a child, a father and his son.

Appearing at the very beginning of history, in the creation story (Genesis 1:26,27 and 2:7), one can persuasively conclude that the first man, Adam, is the son of his Creator, Yahuweh Elohim (the"LORD God").

This unique and special relationship reappears again and again early on, first with Abraham and his 'chosen son', Isaac (Genesis 22:2); then with Isaac, and his 'chosen son', Jacob.

Indeed, the whole nation of Israel is reckoned by Elohim as Yahuweh's son, even His 'first-born'.

> "And you shall say to Pharaoh: Thus says Yahuweh: Israel is My son, My first-born."
>
> **(Exodus 4:22)**

Upon this human landscape of a father and his son, is reflected the Personal nature, character, identity, and historical redeeming role of Yahuweh Elohim (the "LORD 'God'").

At the behest of his father Isaac and his mother Rebekah, Jacob (Yaakov), their younger son, and brother of Esau, is charged to leave Canaan (the Promised Land) and Beersheba (Hebrew for "the well of good fortune") for his uncle Laban who resides in Paddan-aram (Mesopotamia) to find a suitable wife and escape the vengeful wrath of his brother, Esau.

Before he takes leave, his father Isaac calls upon the Almighty to give to Jacob the blessing of Jacob's grandfather, Abraham.(Genesis 28:3,4)

Along the way, at the end of the day, travelling toward Haran, Jacob comes upon "the place".

> "And he lighted upon the place, and tarried there all night, because the sun was set; and he took one of the stones of the place, and put it under his head, and lay down in that place to sleep."
>
> **(Genesis 28:11)**

The Hebrew word for the place is "ha-Makom", and often signifies throughout Scripture, where the Almighty is, whether on earth or in heaven. As the sun was set, Jacob will stay in the place for the entire night. At the hour of sleep, Jacob takes one of the stones* to rest his head.

*[The Hebrew word for stone is 'ehben' (or 'ehven'), composed of three Hebrew letters: aleph-bet-nun. The first and second letters, aleph-bet, spell "ab" or "av" meaning "father" as in "abba". The second and third letters, bet-nun, spell "ben" meaning "son". "The second letter of the Hebrew word, 'ehben' is bet, shared by both "ab" (father) and "ben" (son),

linking the two together into the one word, 'ehben', meaning stone. The letter bet itself is a word in the Hebrew, and means "house".]

When one carefully and rightly divides the 'word' "ehben", and diligently seeks its deeper significance, it now becomes clearer why Jacob called the stone (ehben), Bet Elohim, The House of Elohim, The House of the Mighty Ones, that is, the House of the Father (Ab) and the Son (Ben).

For Jacob, who had just experienced a powerful life changing dream and vision, this stone portrays the house where the Father(Ab) and Son(Ben) co-exist. In that dream, Jacob saw "Malachay Elohim"* ascending and descending on a ladder that connected heaven and earth.

[*"Malachay", the constructive possessive form of the Hebrew plural word "malachim", are the messengers, angels, representatives, or manifestations of Elohim. Elohim is commonly translated as 'God', but literally means"The Mighty Ones".]

Immediately after this description of "Malachay Elohim" descending on the ladder, Yahuweh is standing beside Jacob. In the context of this vision, the "Malachay Elohim" may best be perceived not as angels, which has been the historic and common perception, but as a theophany or manifestation of Elohim as Yahuweh. This interpretation is supported by Jacob's own understanding of this vision, when he calls the place "Bet Elohim and Sha'ar Ha-Shamayim" (The House of God and The Gate of Heaven)[Genesis 28:12-17].

This conclusion will be affirmed by Jacob some twenty years later, after his service to Laban, his marriage to Leah and Rachel, and the birth of all of his children except for Benjamin. Upon concluding a treaty between himself and his father-in-law (and uncle) Laban, before "stones of witness", Laban departs, and this time Jacob actually encounters the "Malachay Elohim".

> "And Jacob said when he saw them: This is 'machanay Elohim' (the camp or company of Elohim). And he called the name of that place 'machanyim' (a pair of camps)."
>
> **(Genesis 32:2,3)**

At a later time, possibly taking this as a sign from Providence, and in desperation and prayerful supplication to Yahuweh, Jacob will divide his own camp into two camps (sh'nay machanot), in preparation for the fateful encounter he is destined to have with his estranged brother, Esau. (Genesis 32:8,11)

In a word that is favored by theologians and scholars, the Bet Elohim that is "ehben", the stone, is (alphabetically) comprised of Father (Ab) and Son (Ben) and illustrates the essential nature,character, person, and identity of the "Godhead".

Now, let us return again to the Scriptural narrative.

Jacob has dreamt of a ladder connecting earth and heaven, with Malachay Elohim travelling up and down between the two, and YAHUWEH, the Eternal Himself, standing beside him. The promise and covenant given to his grandfather Abraham, and to his father Isaac, is now given to him.

Jacob, chosen by Yahuweh before his birth to receive his father Isaac's blessing, intended for the first born, had held his "older" twin brother Esau's heel ('ekev'=heel in Hebrew and hence the name 'Yaakov' meaning one that takes by the heel or supplants) at birth, so that THE TWO WOULD COME OUT AS ONE. (Genesis 25:26)

As a grown son, at his mother Rebekah's insistence, Jacob finally receives his father's blessing, ultimately fulfilling the Plan of Yahuweh. (Genesis 25:23 and 27:6-29).

Having taken Esau's birthright and blessing, Jacob must flee from his brother's rage, and the only home he had ever known.

The memories of his life must have flooded his thoughts as he escaped to save himself from Esau's fury. Most of all, the complex and tortured relationship he had with his father, who favored Esau, and yet gave to him the blessing, would have been uppermost in his mind.

In the space of this powerful human drama, Jacob realizes that this was no ordinary dream, no ordinary place, and no ordinary stone.

> "And Jacob awaked out of his sleep, and he said: 'Surely Yahuweh is in this place (makom), and I did not know it.' And he was afraid, and said:'How full of awe is this place (makom)! This is none other than the house of Elohim, and this is the gate of heaven.'"
>
> **(Genesis 28:16.17)**

Jacob takes the stone (ehben) upon which he rested his head, applies oil to the top of it, sets it up as a pillar, declaring that this stone shall be Bet Elohim, the house of the Almighty. (In effect, Jacob anoints the stone.) (Genesis 28:18, 22)

At first glance, that a particular stone (or place), no matter what it may signify, could be the House of the Infinite Yahuweh Elohim appears primitive and naieve.

Yet the great patriarch Jacob, the father of the twelve sons of Israel, and heir to the promise and blessing of Abraham, may be called many things, but primitive and naieve are none of them.

Jacob knew that Elohim, the Creator, Sustainer, and Upholder of the universe was separate from (His) creation. Jacob was no pantheist.

Still, this dream-vision revealed very personally that Elohim was not remote nor removed from the world or from Jacob. Indeed, although Elohim was surely transcendent and eminent, He was also concurrently, intimate and imminent. Indeed, Jacob would call this very 'place' Beth-El, (meaning House of God), and make the first vow in Scripture, dedicating his life to Yahuweh.(Genesis 28:19,20)

The Sovereign of the Universe, revealed by individual personal disclosure, that He is, and will forever be there, permeating natural and supernatural history, ruling purposefully and providentially.

Jacob knew that his own personal destiny, and the greater destiny of his people called by his new name, Israel, were established and confirmed at The Place (ha-Makom) where he rested his head on The Stone (Ha-Ehben).

The promised land , the increase of his people, their spread over all the earth, and the blessing of all the families of the earth, in Jacob and in his seed, is proclaimed by the Eternal. Such an awesome occurence compels us to diligently seek to understand why Jacob would call this stone Bet Elohim, the House of the Eternal Mighty Ones. (Genesis 28:22)

Jacob recognized that in this stone, this 'ehben', the full and true identity of Elohim YAHUWEH was to be found.

[Recall again: the Hebrew word for stone is the combination of two Hebrew words, 'av' or 'ab' which means father; and 'ben' which means son. In 'ehben', in the 'stone', is the deepest revealed identity of Elohim (the Mighty Ones), as the Father and Son in One Eternal Being.]

Indeed, on the very next day after the supernatural dream-vision, he comes upon a well in the field, covered by a great stone (ha-ehven gedolah), and three flocks of sheep.

Now, in his waking hours, firmly grounded in real life, in a real place, the identity of the stone is confirmed. Here, in its place (makom), the stone (ehven), opens and closes the well from which the flocks of sheep are watered. (Genesis 29:2,3)

The appearance of the well is not gratuitous or incidental, but is, like all of Scripture, intended to convey an essential truth message.

Jacob departed from his father, his mother, and his home in Beersheba, (the well of good fortune). Like those sovereignly called and chosen by Elohim who came before him, he embarks upon a journey toward a new and better place.

So another well appears. In this encounter, and because of an awesome dream, he meets the covenant keeping Eternal Yahuweh, Who promised that "I will never leave you until I have done that which I have spoken to you of." (Genesis 28:15)

The imagery of water as the Spirit of Elohim, the faithful as His sheep, and Yahuweh as Shepherd, are well known and appear throughout Scripture.

At this moment, Jacob saw confirmation of his dream.

In the centuries that would follow, the children of Jacob (Israel) would encounter 'this STONE' again and again.

In the wilderness, and in his anger, Moses, who had all ready seen the messenger of Yahuweh as Yahuweh (malach YHWH or angel) in the burning bush at Horeb, the mountain of Elohim, and heard the Eternal's voice, would fail to recognize the Identity of the Rock when he (Moses) twice strikes It and does not speak to It as Yahuweh had commanded, to obtain water for his flock, the children of Israel.

Like the Stone of Jacob, which he called Bet Elohim, this was no ordinary Rock (in the Hebrew, the word for rock here is 'sela'), for it would bring forth water. By striking the rock, Moses in his anger and disbelief, dishonored the Eternal. (Exodus 3:1-16, Numbers 20:1-13)

> "(It is noteworthy that in another place in the wilderness, to quiet the murmuring of the congregation and to quench their thirst, Moses is instructed to strike the

rock for water. This time, in the sight of the elders, Yahuweh would stand upon the rock in Horeb. The Hebrew word for rock here is 'tzoor'.)

(Exodus 17:6)

The prophet Isaiah declares:

"Then He shall become a sanctuary;
But to both houses of Israel, a STONE to strike and a ROCK to stumble over,
And a snare and a trap for the inhabitants of Jerusalem."

(Isaiah 8:14)

The psalmist declares:

"The STONE which the builders rejected
Has become the CHIEF CORNERSTONE,
This is Yahuweh's doing;
It is marvelous in our eyes."

(Psalm 118:22-23)

The prophet Isaiah again declares:

"Behold, I am laying in Zion a STONE, a tested STONE,
A costly CORNERSTONE for the foundation, firmly placed.
He who believes in it will not be disturbed."

(Isaiah 28:16)

Finally, and ultimately, the prophet Daniel, in his interpretation of the dream of Nebuchadnezzar, the king of Babylon, proclaims:

"You, O King were looking, and behold, there
was a single great statue;...........................
You continued looking until a STONE was cut out
without hands, and it struck the statue on its feet of
iron and partly of clay,   and crushed them.................
....
'But the STONE that struck the statue became a great
mountain and filled the whole earth".

(Daniel 2:31-35)

And in the days of those kings, The Elohim of Heaven
will set up a Kingdom which will never be destroyed,
and that Kingdom will not be left for another people;
it will crush and put an end to all these kingdoms, but
it will itself endure forever. Inasmuch as you saw that
a STONE was cut out of the mountains without hands
and that it crushed the iron, the bronze, the clay, the
silver, and the gold, the great Elohim has made known
to the king what will take place in the future; so the
dream is true, and its interpretation is trustworthy.

(Daniel 2:44,45)

What then, is this thread that weaves through Scripture
and history, proclaiming one profound and powerful
message?

The STONE of Jacob, the STONE of Isaiah, the STONE
of the Psalmist, the "ROCK-STONE" of Moses in the
wilderness, and the STONE of Daniel's grand prophecy,
are all Yahuweh Elohim, the Almighty and Eternal, the Bet
Elohim, the 'Ehven' ('Ehben'), the Father and the Son, the
Place of Two Camps or Companies (as a pair of similars,
as machanayim, and not sh'nay machanot, that is any two,
according to the Hebrew), Yahuweh as Father and Yahuweh-
Yahoshua as Son, the Anointed Messiah, the Source of

Living Water, the Shepherd of His sheep, the Great King of His Everlasting Kingdom.

He is our sure and eternal Foundation,

the Rock of Israel and the Ages, the Sustainer and Governor of this world, and the Ruler and Hope of the World to Come.

PART III:
Father and Son

CHAPTER 14

The Almighty Appears

Among the many controversies that exist within religious debate, one of the most critically divisive is the one known as the theophany, that is, the appearance of "God" in Scripture.

Although the language of such occurences may appear straightforward enough in the original Hebrew, (and even in translation), preconceived notions embraced by influential and powerful "religious experts", would have us believe otherwise. In effect, these self and societally appointed "keepers of the faith", have tilted the debate away from the plain word of revelation to the tradition of their particular religion. Having muddied the waters of honest inquiry with their prejudices, the Revelation of the Almighty becomes nothing more than symbolic, or metaphorical, even mythical, rendering the truly awesome appearance of the Almighty as a weak and anemic shadow of the Presence of Elohim in history, in His personal encounter with His chosen servants.

Whether it is called a visitation, dream, or vision, these theologians and scholars would insist that the anthropomorphic language of Scripture must not be understood to mean what it says.

Their arguments can be cogent and persuasive. First, they declare that the Almighty is infinite, and that man is finite, a generally accepted foundational truth. But then they proceed to build their house of doctrine and dogma, reasonably proclaiming that the Infinite "God" must communicate to finite men in language that they could understand; and herein lies the problem, for they insist that the Infinite Creator and Sovereign of the Universe could not possibly appear as a Man.

Yet the Torah, the Prophets, and the Writings would have us believe otherwise.

When Scripture plainly declares:

"And Yahuweh appeared to Abram...." as it does in Genesis12:7,
 and again in Genesis 18:1 where we read,
"And Yahuweh appeared to him by the terebinths of Mamre...."
 and to Isaac in Genesis 26:2,24
 and to Jacob in Genesis 35:1,9
 and to Moses in Exodus 3:2, 16
 and to Moses, Aaron, Nadab, Abihu and the seventy elders of Israel in Exodus 24:9-12
 and to Israel in Exodus 16:10
 and in the 'mercy seat' in Leviticus 16:2
 and in the 'meeting tent' in Numbers 14:10
 and to Gideon in Judges 6:11,12 as an angel (messenger)
 and to Manoah in Judges 13:3,10,21 as an angel (messenger)

****

The revelation to Manoa(c)h and his wife is unique and merits a closer look. It describes the annunciation and foretelling of the birth of Samson [Shimshon in Hebrew], a Nazirite, who was (to begin) to save Israel from the Philistines. A mysterious Being performs this sacred mission. He is called by a variety of titles in Hebrew. Among them are:

"malach-YHWH" meaning angel or messenger of Yahuweh.

"eeysh Elohim" meaning man of Elohim ('God').

"malach-Elohim" meaning angel or messenger of Elohim.

When Manoah asks the Name of this Being [Judges 13:17], the answer given is identical to the one given to Jacob, when he wrestled with a mysterious 'Man' in [Genesis 32:29,30].

It is, "Lamah zeh teeshal leesh'me....?"

which translates:

"Why do you ask my Name....?"

At this moment, Jacob is blessed by the 'Man'.

But for Manoah and his wife, something even more wondrous takes place; for upon the rock-altar where Manoah was instructed to offer meal and kid, this "Malach-Yahuweh" ascended in the flame to heaven, and appeared no more.

And just like Jacob, Manoah realized that he and his wife had seen Elohim ('God'), and yet lived.

Such appearances as these are not gratuitous, but essential and purposeful, bringing Elohim near to his elect.

In the annunciation of the birth of Samson, foretelling a type of saviour, *the Messenger becomes the Message,* picturing the future substitutionary atonement and redemption of His people Israel in the Person of the Messiah.

Appearing to Manoah and his wife as "malach-YHWH", "eeysh Elohim", "malach-Elohim", this mysterious Being is the 'pre-incarnate

Yahoshua ha-Moshiach, the Messiah, Who offers Himself as an offering to Yahuweh [the Father].

****

and to Samuel in 1Samuel 3:21
and to David in Chronicles 3:1
and to Solomon in 1Kings 3:5 in a dream
and in many other appearances, (believing that the Scriptures are trustworthy and true), we are then compelled to give these accounts serious consideration.

Whether He chose to appear in dreams, or visions, or in a burning bush, or in clouds of "glory", as an Angel (messenger). or even as a Man, the Appearances of the Eternal, according to the Torah, Prophets, and Writings, are palpable, immediate, visible, verifiable, authentic and real.

How remote and "spiritual' this 'god' of religious doctrine appears when compared to the vibrant and robust Reality that our patriarchs, prophets and the people of Israel surely must have witnessed!

The Revelation of the Almighty's appearances in Tanakh* as Man, critically challenges our preconceived notions of the Deity and His possibility of "taking on the face of common humanity"; yet the conclusion is inescapable, for according to the plain word of Scripture, that is exactly what Elohim has done.

In the final analysis, when we let the Word that is Torah, speak for Itself; plainly, and without prejudice or precondition, the possiblity of the Eternal manifesting Himself as Man is not just credible, but compelling.

And it is from this foundational Truth, grounded in the reality of human history and a redeeming Creator, Lawgiver and King, that Yahoshua, Son of Man and Son of Yahuweh, the Moshiach (the anointed Messiah) of Israel, and Redeemer of all mankind, springs forth.

> He is the image of the invisible Elohim (Almighty), the first born of all Creation; by Him all things were created, both in the heavens and on earth, visible and invisible, whether thrones or dominions or rulers or authorities-all things have been created by Him and for Him; and He is before all things, and in Him all things hold together; He is also the head of the body, the called out ones; and He is the beginning, the first born from the dead; so that He Himself might come to have first place in everything; for it was the Father's good pleasure to have all the fulness to dwell in Him. (Colossians 1:15-19)

That the Almighty has really appeared to humanity in history means more than just doctrinal differences, nuanced language, or religious interpretation. It is at the heart of His story (history), and in the plan of redemption, it is the essence.

The hope of humanity for a redeemed world, the good news (gospel) of the Kingdom, and the promise of the world to come (olam habah in the Hebrew) all join together in the certainty of the actual appearance of the Almighty in His Torah, to His Prophets, and in His Messiah.

*Tanakh [Tanach] is an acronym for the 3 divisions of Hebrew Scripture:

1. 'T'orah (the 5 Books of Moses, the Pentateuch)

2. 'N'evi'im (The Prophets)

3. 'K'etuvim (The Writings)

CHAPTER 15

The Young Man and the River

His name was Jacob, [Yaakov in the Hebrew], derived from the Hebrew word 'ekev', because he held his twin 'elder' brother Esau's heel (ekev=heel or supplanter) while yet in his mother's womb, so he should come forth simultaneously from his mother Rebekah's painful and difficult pregnancy as the twins were born. Barren Rebekah, the wife of Isaac, the gentle promised son of his aged parents Abraham and Sarah, was like her mother-in-law Sarah, favored by the Eternal, and in His mercy, despite her natural infertility, was saved from her barrenness, and graciously given a son.

Yaakov [Jacob], like his father Isaac before him, was conceived not in the ordinary way, but through the supernatural intervention of Elohim, the Almighty. And like his father Isaac before him, who supplanted his older (half) brother Ishmael, so that Elohim's purpose in election could be fulfilled, Jacob would replace his "older" brother Esau, so that the "older shall serve the younger".(Genesis 25:23)

Jacob, the grandson of Abraham, the patriarch called out from his people and his culture; Jacob, the son of Isaac, the patriarch who came close to death in the "Akedah" or binding for sacrifice to Elohim; Jacob, whose tiny hand was guided by YHWH even before he was born, to take hold of his heavenly ordained destiny by grabbing the heel of his naturally first-to-be born twin brother Esau is, through Sovereign election, the son of promise. And in a very real sense, not just the son of Isaac, but like his father, the son of the Eternal Elohim, Whose entry into these marriages brought forth these blessed young men through whom all the nations on earth would receive blessing.

Jacob knew that his brother Esau was born before him, even though he held his heel so they would be born as one. Jacob, the quiet shepherd who lived in tents, his mother Rebekah's favored son, would secure the birth-right and the blessing of the first born, a priestly and spiritual inheritance, for a pot of red bean stew and some bread for his brother Esau, and a bowl of savoury venison and some wine for his father Isaac.

Secure in the blessing of the first born, Jacob would find a wife among Rebekah's brother's, (his uncle Laban's) daughters. In such a union, the blessings first given to his grandfather Abraham would surely be bestowed upon him. And so Jacob marries, first Leah, and then, his beloved Rachel.

Contrarily, Esau married the daughters of Canaan. Later, in a misguided effort to please his father Isaac, he marries his cousin, the daughter of his father's half brother, Ishmael.

Jacob's dream of the ladder connecting heaven and earth, with its great throng of angels (heavenly messengers), and most importantly, Yahweh Himself, would further assure Jacob of the special relationship he would enjoy with the Eternal.

Indeed, the salvation Jacob sought would be forthcoming upon his confrontation with his avenging brother Esau. Out of his fear and distress, Jacob in humility, kindness, and generosity, would find reconciliation with Esau, but not until he would experience a strange encounter with a Man in the night.

That same night he could not sleep, knowing that Esau and four hundred men were approaching. He sends his two wives, Leah and Rachel, and his two handmaids, Zilpah and Bilhah, and his eleven children, and all his possessions over the stream to the other side, across the ford of the Jabbok, a tributary of the River Jordan.

Seemingly alone, in the stillness of the night, by the water's edge, Jacob soon discovers that he is not alone after all. The dream of the ladder and its angels and the Eternal Who stood above and beside him must have come to Jacob's mind. The struggles with Laban, his father-in-law, and his brother Esau, must also have come to mind.

But the encounter this night is no dream, and the One with Whom Jacob strives and wrestles is no ordinary man. The Man Who would (choose) not (to) prevail in a natural wrestling match, would bless Jacob, giving him victory, blessing, and a new name. This new name, Yisra-El (Israel), means "he who strives (wrestles) with 'El' or Elohim", "for you have striven with Elohim and with men, and have prevailed. (Genesis 23:29). And although the Man does not reveal His Name; Jacob, now to be known forevermore as Israel, knows that this Man with Whom he wrestled, and by Whom his new name was given, and by Whom he was blessed, was not just a man, nor even an angel, but Elohim, the Eternal, Himself. Indeed, Jacob (Israel), recorded and sealed this transforming encounter by receiving his new name, and calling the name of the place Peniel, which translates as "the face of El (Elohim)", "for I have seen Elohim face to face and my life is preserved" (Genesis 32:29-31).

Now limping from his struggle with Elohim, he is readied to meet Esau and his company of 400 men, a meeting that will go well, "for I have seen your face as one sees the face of Elohim, and you have received me favorably." (Genesis 33:10)

The meeting of Jacob with his Redeemer at the water's edge pre-figures in many ways the future of Israel. In their exodus from Egypt, this broken enslaved people would limp to the edge of the Sea of Reeds (Red Sea), seek deliverance, and would find it in Elohim, just as Jacob did at the edge of a river stream. Only by entering that water, and coming out on the other side, would a new and redeemed people be born.

The Man Who wrestled and blessed this man Jacob, and this people Israel, would appear again, in the latter days, as Redeemer and Messiah. But this time it would not be by night, but by day, and He would not come to wrestle, but to teach, to save, to reconcile, and to forgive.

As His identity was not made known to Jacob in that lonely, transforming night-time encounter, His identity would still be unknown to many from the House that is known by the name Israel.

Still, Elohim would use Israel to bless the nations through this Man-Messiah-Elohim.

And as the Man of the night promised Jacob (Israel), who had wrestled and striven with Elohim and with men and prevailed, so too shall every generation of Israel wrestle and strive with Elohim and men.....and prevail.

One day, in the not too distant future, Israel will meet her Messiah-Redeemer when He will make Himself known to her.

And so, limping, struggling, persecuted, misunderstood, confounded, sorely afflicted, suffering, and ultimately saved---- Israel, will, at long last, finally 'cross the river' to the Promised Land, to fully realize, and vividly comprehend her destined call, as the other son and suffering servant of Yahuweh Elohim.

[Exodus 4:22; Jeremiah 31:9; Hosea 11:1; Romans 9:4, 11:25-27]

CHAPTER 16

The Word, the Sign, and the Stone

The Torah (Teaching or Law), the Prophets (Nevi'im), and the Writings (Ketuvim), together known by the Hebrew acronym "Tanakh", is the written record of the revealed Truth and Wisdom of Almighty YHWH.

Among the many recurrent themes that appear in these remarkable documents of eternal worth are three that are particularly significant.

They are the "sign", the "word', and the "stone".

The word "sign" in the Scriptures, is composed of three Hebrew letters: 'aleph', 'vav', and 'tav', and is pronounced "oat".

[You may recall that in Hebrew, each letter composes not only words, but has numerical significance.]*

'Aleph' and 'Tav' are the first and last letters of the Hebrew alphabet. The Hebrew word "ET" (aleph and tav), read from right to left, the reverse of most languages, and pronounced "et", appears repeatedly throughout the Scriptures.

In the very first verse of Torah, in "B'reishis" (Beginnings or Genesis), the word "et" appears twice.

In English, it is the well known and familiar:

"In the beginning 'God' created the heavens and the earth".

But in the Hebrew, it actually reads like this:

"B'reishis bara Elohim et ha-shamayim v'et ha-aretz".

This may be translated linguistically as:

"(In the) Beginning created Elohim 'et' the heavens and 'et' the earth".

The untranslated word 'et', composed of the first and last letters of the Hebrew alphabet, is itself a sign. It signifies the One Who claims to be "the First and the Last", the "Alpha and Omega", the "Aleph and the Tav".

As it is written:

> "Thus says YHWH, the King of Israel, and His
> Redeemer, the YHWH of hosts:
> 'I am the First and I am the Last,
> And there is no Elohim besides Me.'"
>
> **(Isaiah 44:6)**

(see also Isaiah 41:4 in the Prophets, and Revelation 1:17 in the Messianic Scriptures.)

So then, YHWH and His Redeemer, the "First and the Last", aleph-tav, or 'ET', makes His appearance at the very beginning of (B'reishis) Beginnings. He (as 'et') appears before the heavens, (ha-shamayim) and the earth, (ha-aretz); He is the Creator of the Heavens and the Earth, and He appears (as 'et') twice.

"And He is the image of the invisible Elohim.
the First born of all creation.
For by Him all things were created, both in the heavens
and on the earth, visible and invisible, whether thrones
or dominions or
rulers or authorities-----all things have been created
by Him and for Him.
And He is before all things, and in Him all things
hold together.

(Colossians 1:1-17)

The Word "ET", AND NOT "LOGOS", (the Greek translation for 'Word'), is the 'Word' that John speaks of in his Gospel.

John is a Jew, and a son of Israel, taught by the rabbis and raised up in the Hebrew Scriptures (Tanakh). He would no more borrow from the Greek language to communicate essential Jewish theological truths than he would assimilate Hellenistic philosophy and religion into his Jewish Gospel of the Promised Messiah of Israel.

And John, in his testimony of the Messiah would write:

"In the beginning was the WORD, and the WORD
WAS WITH ELOHIM , and the WORD WAS
ELOHIM'.

(John 1:1)

As "ET", the Word, appears twice in the very first words of Torah, so too will "ET" (Elohim) appear twice in History; first as Suffering Servant, and at the last, as Victorious Ruler-King and Redeemer.

In traditional Hebrew thought, which has declared a Messiah Redeemer with two natures, the Servant is portrayed in the figure Joseph, (Moshaich ben Yosef which means 'Messiah, Son of Joseph') and the Ruler-King, portrayed in the figure of David (Moshiach ben Dovid which means 'Messiah, Son of David').

The Torah and the Gospels boldly proclaim the identity of the One Who fulfills both natures and intimates how and when He will appear in history.

There is not to be two Messiahs with one appearing, but one Messiah with two appearings. Having come once to suffer, serve and atone, He is prophesied to return; to rule, reign and redeem.

****

'Vav', is the sixth letter of the Hebrew alphabet.

In the story of Creation, [in Genesis- B'reishis], man is created on the sixth day.

In Hebrew thought, and according to numerical equivalency of the Hebrew alphabet, the sixth letter 'vav' may signify 'man'.

Now recall that the Hebrew word for sign, is comprised of aleph-vav-tav, [pronounced "oat"].

Symbolically then, 'man' (vav), appears within the Hebrew word for sign, between the letters 'Aleph and Tav', the Word we have come to know as "ET".

Man, symbolized by the letter 'vav', appears then, within the very Name "ET" (Aleph-Tav), the Word Who is Elohim, Creator, Messiah, and Redeemer.

The prophet Isaiah declares in the well known Messianic prophecy:

> "Therefore, Adonai Himself will give you a sign "
> ["Aleph-Vav-Tav"]: Behold, a maiden (almah, virgin)
> will be with child and bear a son, and she will call His
> Name Immanuel."
>
> **(Isaiah 7:14)**

This sign (signal) is that man (vav) will be enveloped in the Deity (ET).

The Son of Man and the Son of Elohim, is the divine incarnation proclaimed by the Hebrew prophet Isaiah, and His Name Immanuel means 'El' or Elohim is with us.

****

This very sign is also the stone.

The 118th Psalm declares:

> "The stone which the builders rejected has become the
> chief cornerstone.
> This is YHWH's doing; it is marvelous in our eyes."
>
> **(Psalm 118:22,23)**

The Hebrew word for stone is composed of the letters aleph, bet and nun, pronounced as "ehven" or "ehben".

This three lettered word has two very important words within it, they are: "av" and "ben".

In the Hebrew, "av" means father and "ben' means son.

The Hebrew word for stone, then, is comprised of the Hebrew words for Father and Son.

The Messiah proclaimed that He and His Father are One.

(see John 17:11, 21,22, 23).

The stone appears in Exodus 34:1 and Deuteronomy 9:9, 10 as the TWO tablets of stone written by the finger of Elohim, the tablets of the Covenant made with Israel at the mountain from the midst of the fire on the day of the assembly.

The stone appears in the Book of Daniel, when the prophet interprets the dream of the Gentile king of Babylon, and proclaims that a stone cut out 'without human hands' will shatter a great statue, and will itself become a great mountain that will fill the whole earth.

(see Daniel 2:34,35)

****

With sublime Hebrew symbolism, the great and awesome Plan of Yahuweh is pictured in a word, a sign, and a stone.

The Messiah is, and shall be, the Redeemer and King.

On this, there is little debate.

That the Messiah is not just a Man but also Deity has been a major theological point of separation for rabbinic Judaism and the Messianic faith.

The heavenly language of Hebrew, the tongue by which YHWH spoke and wrote His Truth, profoundly expresses the fullness of the nature of Elohim and His Redeemer.

The Word (ET), the Sign (OAT), and the Stone (EHVEN), together, sublimely proclaim the Eternal Father and the Eternal Son as One; the Son of the Father and the Son of Man as One; fully disclosed in the Person of the Messiah Yahoshua Who is One in Elohim.

****

These three Hebrew words, which for centuries have been ignored, misunderstood, or unappreciated by those who would claim the authority to teach the great truths of Scriptural faith, and (who), although well intentioned, misguided the many sincere seekers who sought their instruction, reveal the essential elements of the Torah's revelation of Elohim and His salvation.

In these last days, as the Great Day of Redemption draws near, Yahoshua HaMoshiach, Who is the way, the truth, and the life, will reveal His judgement and salvation; and every eye shall surely see Him, and every heart shall surely know, that the Word, the Sign, and the Stone we have waited and hoped for, is here for us all, and will be with us, forever .

*In the Scriptures the Hebrew word for 'sign' can also be found composed of the two letters, 'aleph and tav', written alphabetically exactly like the WORD "ET", but pronounced as 'oat' with its "O" sounding vowel, appearing as a dot above the aleph. In this rendering, the letter'vav' is absent.

Here, the unity between the sign and the word, sharing the same alphabetic construction, is plain, and profound in its significance in Scriptural revelation.

CHAPTER 17

The 'Man' in the Middle

Mortal man was made by the Creator YHVH Elohim, according to His Own Word, "in Our image, after Our likeness" (Genesis 1:26) on that penultimate sixth day of creation week. As His image and likeness, man was conceived so he may reflect and mirror the character of his Creator, and bear witness to his supernatural heavenly origins and his supreme transcendent potential.

Now it may be recalled, that in the language and world view of the Hebrew, a name is more than just a title; it is a graphic symbolic representation of the nature and essence of its bearer. And no where is this truer than in the Name of the Creator, YHVH, and his creation, man.

Hebrew letters may be used to represent cardinal (as in 1,2,3) or ordinal numbers (as in first, second, third). In the Hebrew alphabet, the first letter is 'aleph', the last letter is 'tav', and the sixth letter is 'vav'. Man, created on the sixth day (or day 6), has historically been represented Hebraically, by the Hebrew letter 'vav'. In appearance, 'vav' looks most like the small letter "l" without the horizontal base seen here.

The great "I AM THAT I AM", also known as "I AM" (aleph-hay-yod-hay in Hebrew and pronounced "ehyeh") describes the eternal nature of Elohim, but "I AM" is not His

Name! (Exodus 3:13-14). His Name, translated as "LORD" in English, is YHVH (Yahveh, or Yahweh, or Yahuweh), composed of the Hebrew letters "YOD-HAY-VAV-HAY", and is His Memorial Name for ever. (Exodus 3:15).

Since this tetragrammaton (four letter Name) appears immediately after the descriptive **"I AM" (aleph-hay-yod-hay) that "I AM" (aleph-hay-yod-hay)** , pronounced as **EHYEH asher EHYEH**, the final composition of His Memorial Name shares the 'yod-hay' from the two "I AM"'s; but instead of the second 'yod', there is the 'vav'.

(If Y=YOD and H=HAY and V=VAV, you might expect His Name to be written as YHYH as YOD-HAY-YOD-HAY, but instead it is YHVH as YOD-HAY-VAV-HAY.)

> (An amazing and wondrous revelation comes from rightly dividing and analyzing the etymology of the Name Itself. The Hebrew Elohim YHVH is therefore "I AM-I AM", simultaneously illustrating the plurality and the unity of The essential nature of Elohim, which literally translates as 'The Mighty "ONES" '.

> Hence, the central confession of Judaism upon which the Greatest Commandment according to the Messiah is this:

> "Hear O' Israel, YHVH (I AM-I AM) is our Elohim, YHVH (I AM-I AM) is ONE".
> > (Deuteronomy 6:4; Matthew 22:37)

Within Elohim's Memorial Name is the Two "I AM"s, revealing that the ONE Elohim is not just a plurality, but   as YHVH, He is really Two Eternal Persons, Being as ONE!)

In the previous chapter, we explored one possible explanation for the 'vav' in the Name YHVH. But there may be another that is even more compelling!

It has already been stated that 'vav' is the letter symbol that denotes 'man'. Could it be more than incidental that the same letter 'vav' appears in the "middle" of the Memorial Name YHVH (Yod-Hay-VAV-Hay). This temporal, ephemeral, mortal created being, intended to reflect and mirror the great "I AM", is represented symbolically as the Hebrew letter 'vav', within the very Name of his Creator YHVH.

But there is also an Eternal Being Who is pictured within the Name YHVH, the second "I-AM" of Elohim, (as it were), where the first "I-AM" (YH) is The Father. This 'Son of Man', Who is at One with His Father, fulfills the potential of mortal man by perfectly reflecting and mirroring the character of Elohim, since He is also "Son of Elohim (God)".

Bearing witness to YHVH, this Son of Man and Son of 'God' is the sign (aleph-vav-tav in the Hebrew) given to the House of David.

> "Therefore, YH'V'H Himself will give you a sign: (aleph-'vav'-tav): Behold a maiden will be with child and bear a son, and she will call His name Emmanuel (meaning Elohim with us)."
>
> (Isaiah 7:14)

141

The letter 'vav', representing the Son of Man and Son of Elohim, that appears in the "middle" of the Memorial Name YHVH (I AM-I AM), is the same 'vav' that appears in the "middle" of the Word ET (composed of Aleph and Tav) that was with Elohim (God) and was Elohim (God) (John 1:1)(Genesis 1:1). As the First and the Last Letters of the Hebrew alphabet, Aleph is the Alpha and Tav is the Omega in the Greek equivalent in Scriptural translation, and Hebraically represent the Eternal YHVH, Who is The First and the Last. (Isaiah 41:4; Revelation 1:8)

The 'VAV' in the middle of ET, (aleph-'vav'-tav, pronounced "oat"), boldly proclaims that a Son, as seed of woman, will represent Elohim (dwelling) with us.

****

"Vav", the Hebrew letter, graphically written as a stroke of the pen in Torah, is symbolically the 'Man in the Middle' of the Name YHVH (Yahuweh), in Whose Name He appears throughout Scripture. He is the 'Man in the Middle' (vav) in the Sign of the Son of Man and God (Elohim) when He appears as Israel's Saviour and Messiah in the fulness of time.

The incarnation, whereby YHVH Elohim, takes on human form and appearance, is woven into the very fabric of His nature, as revealed by His Hebrew Name and the sign He promised through His prophet Isaiah. Such a picture of Israel's Redeemer is neither imported from alien cultures, nor a legacy of heathen heritage. Rather, it is, from the very beginning, within the essential Person of Torah's God (Elohim).

Theophanies, or appearances of YHVH (the LORD) as a Messenger-Angel-Man, APART from dreams and visions, occur throughout the Torah. Beginning in the Garden of Eden, YHVH makes Himself known to Abraham by the oaks of Mamre (Genesis 18:1-33), and as Melchizedek (Genesis 14:18); to Isaac as Guide and Benefactor (Genesis 26:2-5); to Jacob as a wrestling Man (Genesis 32:24-30); to Moses at Horeb in the burning bush (Exodus 3:1-22), to Moses, Aaron, Nadab, Abihu, and seventy elders before the giving of the Ten Commandments at Sinai (Exodus 24:9-12); to Joshua as the Captain of the host of YHVH (Joshua 5:13-15), and to Israel, Gideon, and Manoah, in the Book of Judges (Judges 2:1-5; 6:11-24; 13:2-25).

In the Messianic Scriptures (New Testament), the Apostle Paul proclaims that YHVH has appeared in the Person of the Messiah Yahoshua,

> "in Whom we have redemption, the forgiveness of sins. And He is the image of the invisible Elohim (God), the first born of all creation. For by Him all things were created, both in the heavens and on earth, visible and invisible, whether thrones or dominions or rulers or authorities-all things have been created by Him and for Him. And He is before all things, and in Him all things hold together."
>
> (Colossians 1:14-17)

The proper Hebrew name of the Messiah is Yahoshua and not the Greek name Jesus! Indeed, as servant and successor of Moses, the man Yahoshua (Joshua) was a type of the Messiah Yahoshua. As Moses declares; YHVH will go over the Jordan before Israel, so too shall Yahoshua. (Deuteronomy 31:3). After the death of Moses, the servant of YHVH, Yahoshua is commanded to "Rise", cross the Jordan and receive the Promised Land. (Joshua 1:1-2)

So too does Yahoshua the Messiah, in His Resurrection and Entry into the Kingdom.

His Name is composed of five Hebrew letters "Yod-hay-'vav'-shin-ayin" and means 'YAH saves' or 'the salvation of YAH'. Here too, the 'vav', Hebraically representing man appears, as the third and middle letter of this five letter Name. Thus, in the very Name of the Savior Yahoshua (Joshua) the Messiah, the Immortal 'Man in the Middle' is there!

This Man in the Middle links the two immortal Great "I AM"s, the Eternal Father and the Eternal Son, to each other, and bridges the gap between mortal man on earth and his Father in Heaven. As YHVH He created us, led us out of Egypt into the Promised Land, gave us His Torah (Law), and came as Yahoshua, the Son of Man, as one of us, to be our Messiah and Redeemer.

In a day that will soon be here, YHVH will come again, as Yahoshua, the Son of God (Elohim), to be creation's Messiah and King!

CHAPTER 18

The "Other" Man in the Middle

In the previous chapter, we presented evidence that the MAN in the middle is the Son of Man and Son of Elohim, the Messiah Yahoshua Himself. Based on the symbolism and significance of the sixth letter of the Hebrew alphabet, (the letter 'vav'), we discovered three critical places where this representation of the MAN was revealed. They are:

1.within the Hebrew Memorial Name of Elohim: "YHVH"

[spelled 'Yod-Hay-VAV-Hay'; written in various English forms as Yahveh, Yahweh, Yahuveh, Yahuweh, Yahovah, Jehovah].

2. within the Hebrew word for sign: spelled
"Aleph-VAV-Tav"
and pronounced 'oat'.

3.within the Hebrew Name of the Messiah:
"YAHOSHUA"
[spelled 'Yod-Hay-VAV-Shin-Ayin'].

In these three domains, the identity of the True Deliverer and Redeemer, Who came in the Name of His Father (John 5:43), was made known.

But the Scripture gives sober warning that another man, another spirit, or other men would come and deceive many.

These counterfeits have been called the Anti-Messiah or the Anti-'Christ' .

There are many references to him (or them) throughout Scripture; appearing in (1John 2:18, 22; 4:3; 2John 7; Isaiah 14:12-14; Daniel 7-11; Matthew 24:4-5,11,12,15; John 5:43; 2Corinthians 11:4; 2Thessalonians 2:2, 3, 7,9-12; Revelation 13:16-18). Here, it is declared that this man of lawlessness, this son of destruction, who opposes and exalts himself above all that is called Elohim, sets himself within the Temple or Dwelling Place of Elohim, and shows himself as Elohim. Today, since there is no Jerusalem Temple, the Dwelling Place of Elohim is in the hearts of [His] people. (2Corinthians 6:16; John 14:23; John 2:19-21)

There has been much speculation about the identity of this individual over the centuries; with theories pointing to Satan, politicians, Popes, kings, emperors, The Roman Catholic Church, ancient Rome, the European Union, the Jews, Christian and non-Christian religions, and any myth or mortal whose misfortune it is to be caught within the wide net of man's theories of conspiracy and delusion.

But the Scripture gives us more than just useful clues as to his identity. It provides an accurate road map that leads us right to him, if we have the courage to follow the trail to its end.

This much we do know:

> 1.The Anti-Messiah (Anti-'Christ'), both opposes the True Messiah, and puts himself in His Place.

2.He is contrasted with Truth, which is the Word of Elohim ('God'), as revealed in the TORAH.

3.As one who opposes Truth and Torah, he is a man of sin, deceit, unrighteousness, delusion, falsehood and lawlessness, all of which is "Torah-lessness".

4. He is a religious power, capable of signs and wonders.

5. He is or possesses a lying and deceiving spirit.

6. He masquerades as a messenger of light, but he is a beast.

7. He is used by Satan, the Adversary, because Satan, the father of lies, is behind them all.

So, in truth, there is quite a bit of useful information about the Anti-Messiah.

Still, there is one last piece of the puzzle we need that will lead us to the identity of this fake.

That final clue is found in the last book of the Scriptures, where we read:

> "Here is wisdom. Let him who has understanding calculate the number of the beast, for the number is that of a man: and his number is 666!"
> **(Revelation 13:18)**

This verse declares that the beast is a man, but not just any man. If that were the case, the number of man, being "6", as in the day of his creation, and as in the 6th letter of the Hebrew alphabet, would have appeared just once. But it appears THREE times!

This powerful deceiver is the agent of Satan, the master of deception, whose use of great delusion, has led the whole world astray.

The True Messiah has been identified as The Man in the Middle.

As Son of Man, and the Incarnation of YHVH, apart from the fulfillment of all prophecy about Him, and even apart from His resurrection, His credentials are supported by:

> 1. His relationship to His Father by heritage and genealogy in YHVH.
> 2. His Sign.
> 3. Name as Yahoshua.

All three of these were demonstrated by the central place of the "number of man","[6]", as 'VAV' in the Hebrew Memorial Name [YHVH], the Hebrew word for Sign [aleph-VAV-tav pronounced 'oat'], and the Hebrew Name of the Messiah and Son [Yahoshua].

As the true identity of the Messiah and King is founded on these three, the deceiver cleverly uses each domain to oppose and deny Him, so another messiah ("christ") can be put in YHVH's and Yahoshua's place.

Let's look at each one of these to see where Satan and his counterfeit have done their dastardly deed.

1. The Memorial Name: YHVH

The Eternal Elohim, The Two Great "I AM"s, reveals the Nature of the Almighty, composed of Two Persons, Father and Son, eternally co-existing, forever as ONE! In language used by the world's theologians, this "Godhead", then, is made up of Two Persons, and is plainly revealed in Scripture. The real "Man in the Middle", the True Messiah, Yahoshua and YHVH, comes from this Eternal Elohim.

The Other Man, the Counterfeit, claims this heritage and legacy; but he comes as a member of a godhead made up of three 'persons', a so-called "trinity", "Father-Son-Holy Ghost", which is declared a mystery by the church and the religion that proclaims this dogma. Indeed, in this paganly derived scheme of 'three-in-one", one of its members is not even a person but a spirit, (as in the holy ghost-spirit). Generated from the lying mind of a created, fallen, angelic being himself, Satan has deceived the whole world with his counterfeit Messiah and 'Lord'.

2. The Sign

There are many signs in the Scriptures. The sign of the Messiah's incarnation was the birth of a son to a young maiden who, though betrothed, was yet a virgin. But there are other signs YHVH gives for His Identity and His Covenant between Elohim and his people. Blessed at Creation on the 7th Day, the sign of the Sabbath was given as an everlasting perpetual covenant between YHVH and His people, and confirmed by the true Messiah, when He says, "For the Son of Man is Lord of the Sabbath". (Matthew 12:8; Exodus 31:13-17; Ezekiel 20:12-20).

The reality and time of the resurrection is the cornerstone of the identity of the True Messiah, the Real Man in the Middle. The sign of Jonah is given as such proof, declaring that the Son of Man would be in the heart of the earth for three days and three nights.(Matthew 12:39-40)

The counterfeit messiah takes the sign of the incarnation and joins it to the birthday of the sun deity, Sol Invictus, establishing near the darkest day of the year in the Northern Hemisphere, on December 25th, one of the most beloved holidays of the Christian Church and the world, Christmas, declaring (falsely) that this is the day of the savior's birth. No such command or record of this is evident in Scripture or in the early apostolic community.

Furthermore, the eternal sign of the 7th Day Sabbath, instituted at Creation by YHVH, and given at Sinai as His fourth Commandment of the Ten, by Him Who does not change, has been first opposed, then denied, then nullified and cancelled, and finally changed by the counterfeit "Lord". For most of Christianity, the Sabbath is part of the "Old Testament", nailed to the cross at Calvary, of no effect; and like all of the 'Law', has been done away with, replaced with the better 'law of Christ'.

Finally, he takes the resurrection, removes it from its relationship to the Passover and First Fruits, and transfers it to the pagan Easter Sunday with its Lenten-Good Friday tradition, thereby denying the identity of the Passover Lamb, its role in the Deliverance of Israel, and the necessity of Blood as covering. As the only sign Yahoshua would give to support His claim as Messiah, the Sign of Jonah; the liar nullifies it. (Matthew 12:38-40)

Of the legacy of lies foisted over the centuries upon so many sincere seeking people, few are more egregious than Christianity's abolition of the 7th Day Sabbath, and the doctinal institution of the Sunday resurrection, which they call "The Lord's Day".

Historians have long recognized that this transmogrification from the Scriptural 7th Day Sabbath to the first day of the week, Sunday, the day of veneration for the 'Sun-deity' of pre-Messianic paganism, came about through cunning, deceit, compromise, concession, and theological sleight-of-hand, all played out on a backdrop of passionate and virulent anti-Jewish, anti-Torah sentiment.

The final nail that "crucified the Sabbath" was hammered into Christian history and destiny by the anti-Semitic Church fathers, when they proclaimed Sunday as the day of the 'Lord's Resurrection'. In arrogant self aggrandizement, this momentous change deepened and widened the rift that had formed between Judaism's Messiah believing remnant and Gentile Christianity, an almost unbridgeable chasm that persists to this day.

Jesus Christ, the messiah of Christendom, is claimed to have been slain during 'Passion Week', on 'Good Friday', and rose from the dead on 'Easter Sunday'. Beginning with Palm Sunday, and preceded by the 40 day Lenten season, this is the most sacred week of the Christian Church calendar.

Amazingly, there is absolutely no basis for this account in Scripture. It is, like so much of Christianity, the result of syncretism.

Indeed, the Scriptures do not leave us clueless as to when these things would happen. When carefully studied, the death and resurrection of the Messiah of Torah and Israel, Yahoshua, can be discerned and made known.

Let's take a close look at the Word in Scripture to see what it really says, "proving all things and holding fast to that which is good" [1Thessalonians 5:21], and "handling accurately the Word of Truth." [2Timothy 2:15]

1. According to Daniel 9:24-27, Messiah would put a stop [an end] to sacrifice and grain offering in the middle of the one week he makes a firm covenant, when He would be cut off [slain].

That firm covenant is the institution of the "LORD'S Supper", the Passover meal, when He takes the commanded symbols of the Exodus deliverance, the matzo (unleavened bread) and the wine, and now makes them emblems of His atoning Body and Blood.

With His death, the sacrificial system does come to an end, as He declares, "It is finished!" [John 19:30], and the curtain in the Temple was torn in two from top to bottom. [Mark 15:38; Exodus 26:33,34]

Since it is universally recognized that Sunday is the first day of the week, and there are 7 days in a week, the "middle of the week" must be on Wednesday, positioned halfway between Sunday, Monday, Tuesday, and Thursday, Friday, Saturday.

Scripture shows that Messiah, therefore, was killed in the middle of the week, on Wednesday, and NOT on Friday.

Therefore, there is no Scriptural basis for a Friday crucifixion, and the 'Good Friday' tradition.

2. The Messiah would die on Passover, since He is called, our Passover, and the Lamb that takes away the sins of the world. [1Corinthians 5:7, John 19:14, John 1:29]

3. Messiah's Death would be on the Passover, the Preparation day before a Sabbath, but not just any weekly 7th day Sabbath; it would be the Sabbath of Unleavened Bread, the sabbath that follows Nisan 14, the Passover. This "Preparation" was the removal of all leaven from the homes of Israel, in "proper anticipation" of the Feast of Unleavened Bread, the first day of which is a Sabbath. [John 19:31, Leviticus 23:5-8] Hence, the Sabbath after the death of Messiah, was not Saturday. In point of fact, in the week of His Death, it was Thursday.

4. Messiah said the only sign that would be given to that generation, to support His claim as Messiah was 'the sign of Jonah', when He said:

> "for just as Jonah was 3 days and 3 nights in the belly of the sea monster, so shall the Son of Man be 3 days and 3 nights in the heart of the earth."
>
> **(Matthew 12:40)**

Further references to the necessity of this sign are confirmed by Scripture where it says Messiah would rise from the dead on the third day [Matthew 16:21], would rise again after 3 days [Matthew 27:63,64], and as the Temple, would raise up in 3 days [John 2:19].

Since there is no conceivable way to count 3 days and 3 nights from Friday to Sunday, (without resorting to devious explanations for this obvious defect in Christian doctrine], the Friday crucifixion-Sunday resurrection doctrine could not possibly be true!

What is true, is that the real Messiah of the Torah and Israel was slain on Passover, Nisan 14, in the middle of the week, on Wednesday. He was taken down from the tree on which he was hung that day, before sunset, and laid in the tomb before Nisan 15, the Sabbath of Unleavened Bread, where He remained 3 days and 3 nights.

He rose from the dead exactly when He said He would, 3 days and 3 nights after that Wednesday Passover, on the 7th Day Sabbath!

5. Early, before dawn on Sunday,the first day of the week, the day after the weekly Sabbath when He had all ready risen from the dead, the evidence of the Resurrection was the empty tomb, as it was witnessed by Mary Magdalene, and the other Mary. [Matthew 28:1,6]

Sunday was not Resurrection Day; it was simply the day that the Great Sabbath Resurrection became known to His chosen disciples.

Hence, just like 'Good Friday', there is no Scriptural basis for the "Easter Sunday" tradition.

6. Turning back to Daniel 9:26, he prophesied that "the people of the prince who is to come will destroy the city and the sanctuary." He goes on to say, in Daniel 9:27, "on the

wing of abominations will come one who makes desolate, even until a complete destruction, one that is decreed, is poured out on the one who makes desolate."

Such a destruction and desolation is prophesied and revealed in [Revelation 17; 18:2, 31].

History tells us that 'the people of the prince' are the Roman legions.

But who is this 'one who makes desolate'?

By now, it should be clear that he is none other than a counterfeit messiah, a false syncretic 'Christ', who is no saviour at all!

Indeed, this pretender, this "other man in the middle", at least regarding the day of his death, was not even in the middle [of the week].

Despite all of this, He remains the central object of worship of Christianity! [Matthew 24:24, John 5:43]

In fact, the very name of this religion is named after him.

This 'other man', the pretender to the Throne of Torah's Messiah Yahoshua, has taken the Signs of YHVH, and brought them to destruction.

3. The Name YAHOSHUA

Finally, it is the NAME itself that reveals the identity of the True Messiah, and of the other man, the counterfeit.

Born of a Jewish mother named Miriam (Mary), in a Jewish village named Bethlehem, and raised by a Jewish father named Joseph, the miracle Child of this Hebrew maiden would be given a Jewish Hebrew name. That name was YAHOSHUA, (Joshua), which means Yah shall save, Yah saves, or the salvation of Yah. Yah is the Name of His Father, as in Hallelulyah, meaning Praise Yah!

After all, Yahoshua did say He came in the Name of His Father, YHVH.

> "I have come in my Father's Name, and you do not receive Me; if another shall come in his own name, you will receive him."
>
> (John 5:43)

Indeed, another 'man' did come in his own name. He was received by the whole world; and in his name a religion has been founded, and a church has been established.

The counterfeit "messiah and lord" comes in the name of another.

He is an agent of the master of deception and delusion.

He has joined forces with all the powerful religious, spiritual, political, and military forces that have ever emanated from Babylon and the evil one himself.

He is the antichrist, and the antimessiah.

He holds the whole world in his sway.

His name is "JESUS CHRIST"!

PART IV:
The Torah's Atonement

CHAPTER 19

The Messiah and the Torah

The tenth day of the seventh month of the year, according to Scripture, is the most sacred of the annual cycle of " Seven Sabbaths" proclaimed in the 23rd chapter of Leviticus; and it is known as 'Yom Kippur', (Hebrew for the "Day of Covering"). This day of the soul's affliction, expressed by personal fasting, is dedicated to the Atonement of Israel before the King of the Universe, the Eternal YaHuWeH.

Since the destruction of the Second Temple in Jerusalem by Titus and his Roman legions in 70 C.E., the ordained form of service, as commanded by YHWH in His Torah (Leviticus 16:1-18:30) could not be fulfilled.

Originally, the first High Priest, Aaron, the brother of Moses would perform the annual ceremony of purification and atonement at this extraordinary intersection of sacred time and sacred space. Dressed in a holy linen tunic, breeches, girdle, and mitre, and bathed in pure fresh water, Aaron enters the 'Holy Place' with a young bullock for a sin offering for Aaron and his own house, a ram for a burnt offering, and two male goats for a sin offering. Through the casting of lots, one goat is assigned to YHWH, the other to "azazel".

YHWH's goat is slaughtered and serves as a sacrificial sin offering.

The goat assigned to 'azazel' is best understood from the Hebrew, as the goat of dismissal, set apart as the "scapegoat", to be sent away from Israel alive into the wilderness.

Here, on Yom Kippur, the Day dedicated to atonement and forgiveness, is the confluence of a unique crucial event that will bring reconciliation for the whole congregation of Israel. The death of one goat, and the concurrent sending forth of another, onto whom the sins of Israel have been symbolically transferred by the High Priest, is not just remarkable, but prophetic.

Substitutionary sacrifice, vicarious atonement, and the shedding of innocent blood is the method of reconciliation taught in the Torah, and commanded over and over again by YaHuWeH.

> "For the life of the flesh is in the blood; and I have given it to you upon the altar to make atonement for your souls; for it is the blood that makes atonement by reason of the life."
>
> (Leviticus 17:11)

In the fleshly denial of the soul's affliction, the fasting penitent symbolically gives up his life, seeking atonement before the Heavenly Judge.

Dr. J.H. Hertz, the late Chief Rabbi of the British Empire, in his commentary on Deuteronomy 21:22-23) from the "Laws of Kindness" (The Pentateuch and Haftorahs, 2nd ed., Soncino Press, 1988, p.842) declares:

"Death, Judaism teaches, atones his sin; therefore his body shall, at the earliest moment, receive the same reverent treatment that is due to any other deceased. The hanging was delayed till near sunset. so that the body might without delay be taken down for burial."

Rabbi Hertz's observation on death and atonement are faithful to Torah's principles, and represent, in the main, the teachings of modern rabbinic Judaism.

In the High Holy Day Prayer Book known as the 'Machzor', the Akedah (binding) of Isaac for sacrifice by his father Abraham is recalled in supplication, as we ask that YHWH remember the merit of this event, and apply it to our own individual and collective sin-ridden lives, fully aware that there is nothing we can offer up to Him that would make us deserving of His grace and forgiveness.

While the Eternal is longsuffering and abundant in mercy, willing that none perish and that all come to repentance, He is also perfectly just.

Consequently, Torah declares:

> "....everyman shall be put to death for his own sin."
> (Deuteronomy 24:16)

That is why the Torah soberly warns that no human being is regarded as morally spotless, or perfectly righteous.

> "The LORD looketh down from heaven upon the children of men, to see if there be one intelligent, one who seeketh for GOD. They are all gone aside, they

are altogether become corrupt; there is none that
doeth good, no, NOT EVEN ONE!"

(Psalm 14:2,3)

"If Thou LORD shouldst treasure up iniquities, who
would be able to stand?"

(Psalm 130:3)

"For there is no man that does not sin."

(1Kings 8:46)

"For no man is so righteous upon earth, that he should
always do good, and never sin."

(Ecclesiastes 7:20)

As payment for sin, the rabbis have taught that 'Tefillah
(prayer, "the bullocks of our lips"), Teshuvah (repentance),
and Tzedakah' (acts of righteousness, beneficence and
charity) will turn away the evil decree, the "curse of the
Law", that is , the penalty of death.

But if the fabric of perfect justice and righteousness is the
thread by which the Torah is woven, can this be the basis
upon which we can be sure of our forgiveness?

While the rabbinic formula for atonement was an ingenious
necessity after the destruction of the Temple in Jerusalem,
it fails to meet the Torah's basic principle of offering an
innocent life for a guilty one.

Indeed, even in the Garden of Eden, an innocent animal
was slaughtered after Adam and Eve sinned, so as to cover
their shame before YaHuWeH and one another. On Mount
Moriah, at the 'Akedah', in the place of Abraham's only

son Isaac, YHWH provides a ram caught in the thicket as a substitute sacrifice.

The following words of anguish and faith echo painfully but hopefully throughout the ages, as a distraught father answers his son:

> "My father.....behold the fire and the wood, but where is the lamb for the burnt offering? And Abraham said: Elohim(GOD) will provide Himself the lamb for the burnt offering, my son."
>
> (Genesis 22:8)

The innocent blood of the sinless substitute provides life given up in sacrificial atonement, providing the essential element in the Master's plan. To be sure, apart from genuine repentance, it is an empty ritual, and of no worth before the Throne of Judgement. (Isaiah 57:14-58:14). But when an innocent and good life is combined with sincere 'teshuvah' (turning again to-ward YHWH or 'repentance'), absolute and total forgiveness can be assured, for it is the Torah's formula for atonement, given by the Source of Forgiveness Himself.

The two goats of Leviticus 16-18, like the Red Heifer (Parah Adumah in the Hebrew) of Numbers 19, represent an awesome and inspiring law of purification. In both of these rituals, the drama of defilement and cleansing, the imputation of sinfulness and righteousness, and death and life are all played out. While at first difficult to fully understand, their deepest significance may be revealed in the prophet Isaiah 53: 10-12. In these words, we may discern the abiding truths of sin and death, offering and offerer, priest and sacrifice, vicarious atonement and imputed righteousness, and ultimately Heaven's forgiveness leading the forgiven mortal to eternal Life.

The Torah prophetically speaks of One Who will be both sinless and yet bear the iniquity of many. Like the anointed Aaron, such a person will provide Atonement.

But far more than any High Priest (Kohen Gadol in the Hebrew), this Anointed Messiah and Mediator will be both Priest and Sacrifice (Korban in the Hebrew), Suffering Servant and Triumphant Redeemer, whose Atoning Work is boundless and timeless, transcending the confines of an earthly Temple, to be an eternal Advocate for a repentant humanity in the Heavenly Temple (Beit HaMikdosh or HaMakom in the Hebrew).

There is One Who, in the course of Jewish history, has fulfilled this role. The Eternal One, Who abides with the contrite and humble in spirit, forever exalted, condescended to be with us. High and lofty, far above all human eminence, He came to us as the Anointed, the Moshiach (Messiah), with a just, compassionate, righteous, and merciful nature, manifested fully and completely within YaHuWeH's inscrutable Oneness. (Philippians 2:5-11)

His atoning, vicarious death and saving resurrection, was at once supernatural and preternatural (fore-ordained by Elohim).

Drawing from the accumulated wisdom of centuries of Jewish scholarship, where two Messianic figures have been proposed, we may identify Him, in His first Appearing, as

Moshiach ben Yosef, Messiah, the Son of Joseph. and in His Second Appearing, Moshiach ben Dovid, Messiah, the Son of David, all the time being Messiah, Son of YaHuWeH.

The prophet Isaiah, in these inspired words proclaims:

> "And He will destroy on this mountain the face of the covering which covers all the people, and the veil that is spread over all the nations.
> He will destroy death forever, and YHWH Elohim will wipe away the tear from off all faces, and the shame of His people will He remove from off all the earth; for YHWH has spoken it. And men will say on that day: Lo, this is our Elohim (GOD), for Whom we have waited that He would help us, this is YHWH for Whom we have waited, we will be glad and we will rejoice in His salvation."
>
> (Isaiah 25:7-9)

For the Jewish people, who have longed for this glorious Day of Redemption, one could almost hear the hopeful, sweet songs of national hope and personal faith in 'HaTikvah' ('The Hope'), and 'Ani Ma'amin' ('I Believe').

This is the Day of Moshiach; when Suffering Servant and Triumphant Redeemer King "become" ONE.

The ancient Hebrew hymn, "Ein Keihoheinu", ("None like our GOD"), teaches an essential truth in Jewish faith. In its final verses, the lyrics triumphantly proclaim:

> "You are our GOD,
> You are our LORD,
> You are our KING,
> You are our SAVIOUR."

Indeed, there is NONE else!

There is much more in the Torah that tells of Messiah, redemption, and the wonderful world to come.

The Redeemer far exceeds the character and nature of any mortal man, and yet He partakes of it while He is ever Elohim.

In Him, the paradox of the red heifer, the two goats, the history of national Israel, the suffering and dying Servant, and the victorious and everlasting Redeemer, Saviour, and Messiah is resolved and revealed.

His Name in Hebrew is YAHOSHUA, which translates (from the Hebrew) as the 'salvation of YAH or YaHuWeH. Moses speaks of Him prophetically in Deuteronomy 18:18. The NAME (Ha-Shem in the Hebrew) of His Father Yahuweh (Yah) is in His Name as Messiah and Son.

The Torah leads in every ordinance, statute, judgement, and commandment to Yahoshua Ha-Moshiach, Yahoshua the Messiah, the Hope of Israel, the Assurance of the Resurrection, and Life in the World to Come.

CHAPTER 20

The Mystery of the Red Heifer

In the nineteenth chapter of the the fourth Book of the Torah, known as Numbers or Bamidbar (meaning 'in the Wilderness' in Hebrew) we discover one of the most mysterious statutes of Torah, the sacrifice of the Red Heifer, or as it is known in Hebrew, the Parah Adumah.

It is a mysterious law of purification, assigned to the priesthood of Israel, and is devoted to ritual cleansing from the ultimate defilement, contact with the dead.

The Parah Adumah (red cow or heifer), which must be faultless, unblemished, and upon which never came a yoke of burden, is the sole creature for atonement in this statute.

Slaughtered by the priest, its blood is sprinkled toward the front of the tent of meeting seven times. Then, the skin, flesh, remaining blood, and dung is burnt; co-mingled with cedar wood, hyssop, and scarlet. Finally, its ashes mixed with water forms the 'water of sprinkling' for the congregation of the children of Israel, as a purification from sin.

The deep significance of this statute has not been fully understood by the rabbis over the centuries, perceived as a statute which human wisdom cannot penetrate. Seemingly, a mystery of supernatural proportions, the paradox of the

Parah Adumah is that it simultaneously defiles and sanctifies, contaminating the priest and cleansing the sinner.

But there may indeed be a solution to this mystery. It begins with the word 'adumah' itself. Derived from the same Hebrew word from which the first man Adam was created, 'adamah' means the soil of the earth or ground. The redness of good rich soil explains why adumah takes on such a descriptive role. Furthermore, the Hebrew word for blood is 'dam', the root for adamah (earth), adumah (red), and adam (man)!

So then, the redness of the heifer is more than just a rare and peculiar color (for a cow). It imparts to this unique animal of sacrifice, through a remarkable ritual of purification, the identity of man, blood, and the earth itself.

The central focus of this majestic ritual is the final chord of life's symphony, death itself.

Since man's expulsion from the Garden of Eden, mortality and death has been his fate. Without access to the Tree of Life, the days of man are numbered and finite, and must, at some point, come to an end.

Immortality, the exclusive and essential nature of the Eternal Creator, has, for now, been witheld. Through his sin of disobedience, by eating of the forbidden fruit of the Tree of Knowledge of Good and Evil, Adam had confirmed the fate of mankind and all creation, apart from the Spirit of Yahuweh, suffering the consequence of his failure to honor the only prohibition that was imposed upon him in Eden. Acquiring the Knowledge of Evil, Adam had invited the final enemy, Death, into history. Previously unknown, a formerly innocent creation would become all too familiar with all of death's associates: sorrow, loss, pain, corruption, decay, disease, manslaughter, war, terrorism, torture, and murder.

Any contact with the dead resulted in uncleaness for seven days for the native born Israelite, and the stranger that dwelt with them. The ritual formula demanded that he be sprinkled with the water of purification on not just one day; and not just any day, but on the Third Day, and on the Seventh Day.

Why did Yahuweh choose the seventh day as a day of sprinkling?

To answer this, we may look to the special days of Yahuweh identified in Leviticus 23. The weekly Sabbath, the final day of Tabernacles, and the final day of Unleavened Bread, are all " the seventh day", and point to some future time of perfect rest, atonement and sinlessness: a time when death itself shall be no more.

But what are we to make of the Third Day of sprinkling?

Here, in order to solve the mystery of the Parah Adumah, we must turn our eyes beyond the vision of the rabbis, to the perfect fulfillment of Torah and Prophecy, realized in the Messiah Himself!

As Son of Man, Messiah became, as it were, a second Adam. Through His perfect obedience to His Father Yahuweh, and His Father's Torah (Instruction or Teaching), He was unblemished by sin (that is, transgressing any of the laws of Torah. [1John 3:4]). Yet, by the design and purpose of the Almighty Himself, the Anointed Son of Man would bear the burden and yoke of the penalty for sin, (the 'curse of the law'), death itself. The shedding of the Messiah's blood, in which resided eternal life, would be that 'water' of sprinkling to cleanse and purify all creation, contaminated by death. And as the first earthly Adam secured death by disobedience unto life, the second heavenly Adam, Yahoshua the Messiah, would secure life by obedience unto death.

The Resurrection on The Third Day sealed the Heavenly Design for atonement and restoration.

The Suffering Servant Son of Israel, as Son of Man and Son of Elohim, is the Messiah; anointed to remove death, the final enemy from creation, and succeeded in reversing the downward spiral begun by the first (deceived) Adam. He had 'finished' the Work of Salvation (from sin and death), restoring access to the Tree of Life and reclaiming the original purpose of the creation of man, (which is) eternal life shared in perfect obedience with Yahuweh Elohim, his Creator, and His Son, Yahoshua, man's Messiah.

Death is repugnant and alien to Yahuweh Elohim, the source of Life itself. Therefore, this statute of purification was given in His mercy and grace, providing access to the Eternal by every being contaminated by death, and prophetically picturing a better sacrifice to come.

The Messiah, like the Parah Adumah, simultaneously purified and defiled, bearing both life and death. He is at once priest and sacrifice, sinless and sinner, blessed and cursed. The paradox and mystery of the Red Heifer is answered in Him. The wisdom of the statute of purification can now be understood. The water of sprinkling that purifies is both the Messiah's blood and the Spirit of Elohim, cleansing us from all unrighteousness, beginning on the third day, the Day of His Resurrection, and completed on a seventh day still to come; imputing unto us, a righteousness apart from ourselves, a Righteousness perfect and pure, given to mankind by Yahuweh Elohim through His Son, Yahoshua, the Messiah.

CHAPTER 21

Seasons In Reflection

When you look into a mirror, you see a likeness of yourself. A face that appears to be real, actually is only a representation, an image in reverse.

But, when you look into the Scriptures, you see not just an image, but you as you are, and most importantly, you as you were meant to be, for you were made in the image, and after the likeness of Elohim, the Eternal Almighty Creator of the universe. And in the absolutely clearest picture of reality that can ever be revealed, there is, above it all, YAHUWEH (YHWH), the Creator of heaven and earth; Giver, Revealer and Author of the Scriptures we know as the Torah. YHWH is the Name for Being (or what it means to exist) itself!

In various books of the Torah, but most particularly in the twenty-third chapter of Leviticus, and the twenty - eighth and twenty-ninth chapter of Numbers, there is a proclamation of appointed times, (mo'edim in the Hebrew), set apart as distinct convocations for the people of Israel. These seven unique times of remembrance are distinguished from the daily, new moon, and the weekly seventh-day Sabbath offerings.

Of the seven, three mo'edim appear in the spring.

They are:

(1)Passover (Pesach) [Leviticus 23:5; Numbers 28:16]
(2)The Feast of Unleavened Bread, (Chag Ha-Matzos)
[Leviticus 23:6-8; Numbers 28:17-25]
(3)The Feast of Weeks, or Chag Ha-Shavuos [Exodus 34:22, Deuteronomy 16:10]; also reckoned as Seven Sabbaths or Sheva Shabbatot [Leviticus 23:15,16], also named as First Fruits or Yom HaBikurim [Numbers 28:26], additionally known as Feast of the Harvest or Chag Ha-Katzeer [Exodus 23:16], and most recognized in the non-Jewish community as Pentecost meaning '50' in the Greek and Chamesheeym Yom (50 Days) in the Hebrew [Leviticus 23:16].

The four mo'edim that appear in the autumn are:

(4)Trumpets, (Yom Teruah), also known as Rosh Hashanah, meaning head of the year or new year
[Leviticus 23:24,25; Numbers 29:1-6]
(5)Atonement, (Yom Kippur), meaning day of covering,
[Leviticus 23:27-32; Numbers 29:7-11]
(6)Tabernacles or Booths, (Sukkot)
[Leviticus 23:34-36; Numbers 29:12-34]
and finally,
(7)The Eighth Day of Assembly, (Shemini Atzeres).
[Leviticus 34:36,39; Numbers 29:35-38]

These set apart appointments, repeated each year, according to their times and seasons, reveal to us the vast eternal plan of Yahuweh Elohim. They illustrate, in painstaking detail and precision, a progressive revelation of redemption for the people of Israel, and individual persons from the nations (who are) called by the Almighty.

(1) The springtime mo'edim, the appointed times to meet with YHWH, begins with Passover (Pesach), at dusk, between sunset and the full darkness of nightfall, on the

14th day of Aviv (also known as Nisan), in the first month of the year. (Leviticus 23:5; Numbers 28:16)

It is a memorial day, to be kept throughout all generations, for all time. Today, the Passover is remembered in the 'Seder', a meal of symbolic foods, (lamb shank, bitter herbs, and unleavened bread [matzo]), during which the miracles of YHWH's mighty Redemption of Israel from Egypt is retold.

On the very first Passover (Pesach), a year old unblemished kid ("seh" in Hebrew), was taken from either the sheep or the goats on the 10th day of this first month (Nisan), kept until the 14th day, and was killed at dusk (twilight) on that day (Nisan 14). The blood of this 'pesach', this Passover lamb, was placed on the doorposts and lintels of the Hebrew homes, and was a sign to Israel, and to YHWH, that Israel would be saved from death on that fateful night. (Exodus 12: 1-14)

But for those Israelites who could not participate in the Passover of the first month, it is worthy and timely to note the institution of "The Second Passover" of the second month ("Pesach Sheni" in the Hebrew).[Numbers 9:1-14].

Here, the Torah leaves no doubt that the Passover was to be celebrated and memorialized on the 14th day of the month [Numbers 9:11], and not the 15th day, as it is observed in rabbinic Judaism.

Furthermore, prophetically, the Second Passover reveals the graciousness and mercy of Yahuweh-Yahoshua, the Saviour and Redeemer King, Who provides for 'another chance for redemption'.

(2) The Feast of Unleavened Bread, is on the fifteenth day of the same month. This is a seven day festival, the first and seventh day of which are set apart gatherings, on which no servile labor is to be done. (Leviticus 23:6-8; Numbers 28:17-25).

The prescribed offering for this First Day of Unleavened Bread was two bulls, one ram, seven male year old unblemished lambs, and one male goat.

> *(On the day after the first weekly (7th day) Sabbath of Passover-Unleavened Bread, that is, on Sunday, is the wave offering of the sheaf (Omer in the Hebrew) of the firstfruits (barley) of the harvest [Leviticus 23:10-14]. On this day, a year old unblemished male lamb, as in the first Passover, is also offered. Here, in this first-omer celebration, a lamb, joined with the first -fruits of the harvest, is a stunningly dramatic reflection of the lamb that had to die to redeem Israel. It intimates to the people the profound truth of the essential nature of the Redeemer of Israel, the Savior from Egyptian bondage (symbolic of despair and death), and the Giver of new life (symbolic of hope and resurrection), as "the living Bread of Life".*
> **(Leviticus 23: 9-14, 1Corinthians 15:20)**

(3) The third spring mo'ed is Shavuos (the Feast of Weeks, Pentecost, or Yom HaBikurim). It is observed 50 days later, that is, seven Sabbaths plus one day (49+1) after the first Sabbath of Passover and Unleavened Bread, (the day) when the first sheaf (omer) of the barley harvest, and the year old unblemished lamb is offered. (Leviticus 23:15-16)

On this day, two loaves of 'leavened' bread are offered, along with seven male year old unblemished lambs, one bull, and two rams, as burnt offerings, one male goat, as sin offering, and two male year old lambs as peace offerings. These two leavened loaves, and two additional lambs, not specifically prescribed to be without blemish, are waved before YHWH, but not placed upon the altar, and may symbolize Israel and the nations, in their present condition, leavened and blemished, not yet completely set apart for YHWH, for a mixed multitude (wheat and tares) also went out with them (Exodus 12:38). Standing before the Almighty, as His firstfruits of redemption, Israel in her miraculous deliverance from servanthood in Egypt, realizes her new role as the Servant of Yahuweh, a kingdom of priests for Israel and the nations . This is also a day of no laborious work. (Leviticus 23:17-21)

(4) The autumn times of meeting with YHWH begins with the fourth mo'ed, The Day of Trumpets, (Yom Teruah), (modern Rosh Hashanah), a memorial day, as is Passover, the first springtime mo'ed. It is to be observed on the first day of the seventh month, and is a day of no laborious work. (Leviticus 23: 24-25) On this Day of Trumpets, the prescribed offerings were one bull, one ram. seven male year old unblemished lambs, and one male goat, for a sin offering to make atonement for you. This is beside the offerings of the new moon, which were two bulls, one ram, seven male year old unblemished lambs, and one male goat. (Numbers 28:11-15) (Numbers 29:1-6)

(5) The fifth mo'ed is The Day of Atonement, (Yom Kippur), observed on the tenth day of the seventh month. (Leviticus

23:27-32) It is the "Sabbath of Sabbaths", a day of humbling, and repentance. On this Day of Atonement, the prescribed offerings were one bull, one ram, seven male year old unblemished lambs, and one male goat for a sin offering. (Numbers 29:7-11).

This is besides the ordinances for atonement commanded in Leviticus 16, where two goats are taken for a sin offering, and by lots one is chosen to die upon the altar, and the other, upon whose head all the sins of Israel are placed, is sent away, alive, to a land which is cut off, into the wilderness.

(6) The sixth mo'ed is The Feast of Booths, or Tabernacles (Sukkot), observed on the fifteenth day of the seventh month for seven days (Leviticus 23:34-36; Numbers 29:12-34). On its first day, the fruit (the esrog or citron) of good trees, and the branches of palm trees, twigs of leafy trees, and willows of the stream, (the lulav), are taken, and there is rejoicing for seven days. On this occasion, two rams, fourteen male year old unblemished lambs, and one male goat for a sin offering are offered each of the seven days of Sukkot. This is TWICE the prescribed number of lambs proclaimed for the Days of Unleavened Bread, Pentecost, Trumpets, and Atonement, and like the two loaves of Pentecost, may represent Israel and the nations.

Even more remarkable is that the number of bulls offered begins with thirteen on the first day of Sukkot, decreases by one each day of the Festival, and ends with seven (bulls), on the seventh and last day of Tabernacles. The sum of bulls offered over the seven days of Sukkot is 70, (13+12+11+10+9+8+7) considered to represent the gentile nations of the earth, to serve as an atonement for all mankind. This seventh final day of Tabernacles is known as Hoshanah Rabbah, the day of Great Salvation and Praise.

(7) The seventh and final mo'ed is The Eighth Day of Assembly, also known as Shemini Atzeret, or the Festival of Conclusion (Leviticus 23:36; Numbers 29:35-38). This is the last of the Seven Days of Remembrance, proclaimed by YHWH.

Here,the prescribed offerings are one bull, one ram, seven male year old unblemished lambs, and one male goat for a sin offering. (Numbers 29:35-38)

****

When we look closely at these special times, there is much to be discovered. Far more than just the primitive expression of gratitude and fear of a nomadic nation before an impersonal deity, these appointments speak to all men,of all nations, at all times.

Within these set apart meetings between YHWH and His people, can be found not just an agricultural history, but the most precious jewel in the crown of all History, the One Who is the Essence of the redemption of the elect of national Israel, spiritual Israel, and all humankind.

The Scriptural year begins in the spring, in the first month known as Aviv or Nisan. It is the season of renewal, and the time of planting for another year, and the early harvest. Although its first day is set apart as a commemorative of the New Moon, known in the Hebrew as Rosh Chodesh, it is not until the 14th day (Passover) that the first of the seven

Days of Remembrance, is celebrated. On the 10th day of that first month, the year old unblemished kid (lamb) was chosen for that fateful night, when salvation would come to Israel on the 14th through the blood of the (kid) lamb as ordained by the Almighty.

The 'civil' year begins in the autumn, in the seventh month, known as Tishrei. Its first day is Yom Teruah, the Day of Trumpets. It is a day that calls us to repentance, a reminder of the covenantal relationship Israel enjoys with the Eternal, and a heavenly proclamation to all nations to turn to the only true YHWH Elohim.

Passover in the spring, and Trumpets in the autumn, are both proclaimed memorial days. Though seasons apart, they both reflect the beginning of redemption, one for the early harvest of spring, and the other, for the late harvest of autumn.

On the 10th day of this seventh month is Yom Kippur, the Day of Atonement.

Recall the chosen lamb on the 10th day of the first month, and consider the profound message proclaimed on this Day; that the lamb of the Passover, the sign to Israel and to YHWH for salvation from death and destruction, and the 'Kippur" (covering or atonement) of Yom Kippur are symbolically one. The salvation first revealed in the springtime is reflected richly and profoundly in the atonement of the autumn.

Indeed, the one goat (kid) that appears in every new moon and festival offering as a sin offering for atonement directs our eyes to the one kid (goat or lamb) that had to die for each household at dusk on the 14th of Nisan, over three thousand years ago, on the night when Israel was redeemed from Egypt.

On the 15th day of the first month, is the Feast of Unleavened Bread. It begins on a full moon. It is the start of the wilderness journey of redeemed Israel from Ramses to the shores of the Sea of Reeds (Red Sea), through which Israel will receive her complete deliverance from Egypt seven days later. The removal of leaven portrays not only the haste with which the Israelites departed from Egypt, but the total (seven symbolizes completeness) separation from sin (symbolized by leaven) that they are called to. As one of the three elements of the annual Passover commemoration [roasted lamb, unleavened bread, and bitter herbs], the eating of unleavened bread daily for seven days directs the heart and the mind to the Passover lamb [the Pesach], through which the blood redemption and deliverance was wrought. In the Messianic Scriptures, Yahoshua the Messiah makes this identification of matzo (unleavened bread) with the sacrificial lamb of Passover, prophetically picturing [the Messiah] Himself, sure. [Luke 22:19, Matthew 26:26, Mark 14:22]

On the 15th day of the seventh month is Sukkot, the Feast of Booths or Tabernacles, the Final Harvest of Ingathering. It, like the Feast of Unleavened Bread, celebrated on the 15th day of the first month, also begins on a full moon. It too commemorates a journey in the wilderness that will culminate with arrival in the Promised Land.

Both Chag HaMatzos (Unleavened Bread) and Sukkot reflect the scriptural truth that we are strangers in the cultures and civilizations of this earth, and pilgrims enroute to another, far better place, the Kingdom of the Eternal YHWH.

The joining of the 4 species in the lulav and esrog, like the two loaves and two lambs waved at springtime's Pentecost (Firstfruits), the autumn Festival of Ingathering, (Sukkot, Booths or Tabernacles), with its offering of 70 bulls, portrays Israel as the intermediary between the Almighty and the nations, awaiting the final redemption. The salvation of the early and latter harvest is reflected in these days of remembrance.

Pentecost, coming 50 days after the first weekly Sabbath of Passover-Unleavened Bread completes the spring cycle of mo'edim [appointments or sabbaths of Yahweh] that portray His plan of salvation. Seven weekly Sabbaths are counted in what is known as the "Counting of the Omer", beginning the day after the first Sabbath after Passover. For 49 days, seven weeks complete, the omer or barley sheaf, directs the heart and the mind of the obedient faithful, to the first omer lifted up and offered the first Sabbath after Passover, celebrating the hope of new life joined with the lamb. [Leviticus 23:10-12]

Each one of the weekly sabbaths counted in the omer pictures the annual sabbath year of remission of debts and release of the Hebrew bondman [Deuteronomy 15:1]; and rest for the land [Leviticus 25:4].

As Pentecost is the culmination of the Seven Sabbath Omer, the Jubilee (Yovayl in Hebrew) is the culmination of the count of seven sabbaths of years. [Leviticus 25:8-55]. In this 50th year, a trumpet blast on the Day of Atonement proclaims "liberty throughout the land to all the inhabitants thereof"[Leviticus 25:9-10]. It is the year of redemption, remission, release, restoration, and renewal.

Pentecost and Jubilee are intimately connected.

Both come at the conclusion of seven cycles of seven sabbaths.

Pentecost marks the 50th day; Jubilee, the 50th year.

As '50' is 7 cycles of 7+1 [49+1], it denotes a new beginning, which may be thought of as a picture of a new creation week, starting with Pentecost or Jubilee.

Pentecost crowns seven weeks of seven sabbaths with the hope of a new life redeemed, as it began on Passover. It is the spring harvest, picturing the resurrection hope for all Israel, sealing Yahuweh's covenant with Abraham, in whose seed all the nations would be blessed, and confirming the Torah of Yahuweh, given through Moses at Sinai. [Acts 2:1-47]

In the autumn harvest, "Shemini Atzeret", the final "8th Day of Assembly" perfects this vision, crowning the seven days of Tabernacles with the hope of a new life redeemed, as it began on Trumpets [Yom Teruah-Rosh Hashana] and The Day of Atonement [Yom Kippur], for Israel and the nations, pointing to 'The World to Come' [Olam Ha-bah in the Hebrew].

On this 50th day [or 50th year], the cycle of remission and redemption is complete.

****

All the Days of Remembrance, the Set-apart Appointments with Yahuweh, move us toward the Festival of Conclusion, Shemini Atzeret, the Eighth Day of Assembly. It is distinct from Sukkot, the Festival of Booths, that immediately precedes it; yet it is intimately connected to it.

From the atonement and redemption that is portrayed in the lamb of the first Passover, to the lamb of the first barley harvest, to the blood of goats, and bulls, and rams throughout all of Scripture, to the Anointed Redeemer of Israel and the Nations, the goal of all History is this Last Great Day.

The Torah boldly proclaims that blood is the means by which the people may fully meet with YHWH. This scarlet thread of redemption, the very fabric of salvation and atonement, first appears in the Garden of Eden, when YHWH Elohim graciously made garments of skin for Adam and his wife and clothed them, after their sin of disobedience was made known. A moment's reflection will reveal that an innocent animal had to be killed for the sake of Adam and his wife. When its blood was shed, Adam symbolically died too. The Hebrew word for blood is 'dom' or 'dam'; and is the core of Adam's name (Adom), the very seat of his life. When the animal died in Eden, indeed, whenever any animal died before the altar of YHWH, Adam, and every child of Adam "died" too.

This is the essential truth of substitutionary or vicarious atonement.

> "For the life of the flesh is in the blood; and I have given it to you upon the altar to make atonement for your souls; for it is the blood that maketh atonement by reason of the life."
>
> **(Leviticus 17:11)**

From the Tabernacle in the wilderness to the Temple in Jerusalem, there was always the 'Korban', commonly called the sacrifice, but more accurately signifying the means by which the people would draw near to YHWH, their Heavenly Father. Through its blood, where life itself resided, purity and sinlessness would be imputed to the offerer, and as he or she had symbolically died, forgiveness of sin would be granted, atonement given, and life would be restored to the offerer of the korban.

From the very first, all creation has awaited this Feast of the Eighth Day, a number that symbolizes not simply conclusion, but something totally and entirely new.

This will complete the redemption of a broken creation; it will mark the final victory over the spiritual forces of darkness, death, and sin.

Israel, the nation appointed to be a light to the Gentiles, will at long last, be that fully redeemed people, ruled by her beloved Messiah from the New Jerusalem.

The Messiah of Israel appears in every offering ordained in Torah. He is prophetically pictured as 'suffering servant', in the daily, sabbath, new moon, and festival offerings. He is seen in the slaughtered unblemished yearling male kid of Passover, the lamb offering of the first barley harvest, the broken (matzoh) of the Passover seder*, the seven days of sinlessness in the Feast of Unleavened Bread (matzo symbolizes sinlessness), the wave offering of the first of the harvest (the omer rayshees) after the first Sabbath of Passover- Unleavened Bread, the splendid harvest of the First Fruits of the Pentecost, and the Atoning instrument throughout the autumn days of remembrance.

> "And He said, It is too light a thing that you should be my Servant to raise up the tribes of Jacob, and to bring back the preserved ones of Israel! I will also appoint you for a light to the nations, (so) that my salvation may reach to the end of the earth."
>
> **(Isaiah 49:6)**

The Servant Messiah is at once Prophet, Priest, Judge, Saviour, and King. The Anointed and Appointed One of Yahuweh Elohim is our Passover, (1Corinthians 5:7), and the first fruits of those who are asleep.

> "But now Messiah has been raised from the dead, and has become the first fruits of those having fallen asleep."
>
> **(1Corinthians 15:20)**

Over the centuries many words have been written about The Servant-Messiah.

But what is also true, is that the people and nation of Israel are essential elements in this vast eternal plan of salvation.

"For unto Me the children of Israel are servants; they are My servants whom I brought forth out of the land of Egypt; I am Yahuweh your Elohim."

(Leviticus 25:55)

"And He said to me, "You are my servant, Israel, in whom I will show my honor."

(Isaiah 49:3)

"But thou, Israel, My servant, Jacob, Whom I have chosen, the seed of Abraham, My friend;
Thou, whom I have taken hold of from the ends of the earth,
And called thee from the uttermost parts thereof,
And said unto thee: " 'Thou art My servant',
I have chosen thee, and not cast thee away",
Fear thou not, for I am with thee,
Be not dismayed, for I am thy Eternal,
I strengthen thee, yea, I help thee,
Yea, I uphold thee with My victorious right hand."

(Isaiah 41:8-10)

For too many years, a wall of separation has divided humanity, Israel and the nations, Jew from Gentile. Religion, with its man made traditions and humanly inititiated quest for the ideal has done little to bring us together.

The servant of Yahuweh called Israel, as ordained in the Torah,and the Servant of Yahuweh called Yahoshua, the Messiah, as ordained in the Torah, have a common purpose; the redemption of all people to the ends of the earth.

> "But now in Messiah Yahoshua, you who were once
> far off have been brought near by the blood of
> Messiah. For He is our peace, who has made both
> one, (and) having broken down the partition of the
> dividing wall."
>
> **(Ephesians 2:13,14)**

The Word of the Eternal, the Torah, and the Living Torah, the Messiah, will go forth. As it is written:

> "Out of Zion shall go forth the Torah, and the Word
> of Yahweh from Jerusalem."
>
> **(Isaiah 2:3)**

Yahuweh's great Plan of Salvation, for all peoples, for all time, is pictured here in these 'Seasons of Reflection'.

In these last days, as we approach the time of the Final Redemption, a witness such as this will surely abide.

---

*The broken Matzo of the annual Passover seder meal, is known as the "Afikomen". While half is kept on the Passover table, before this household of Israel, the other half is wrapped in white linen, hidden during the annual ritual of the telling of the Passover Redemption, and only upon its "discovery" can the seder be considered complete, and thus, conclude.

This Greek word (afikomen), curiously found in the Jewish home ritual of the Haggadah (telling) of the Passover story, is thought by some to mean, "I HAVE COME"

If this broken matzo, this unleavened bread as sinless symbol, is to be understood as the Suffering Servant Who "has come", by way of His Resurrection from death to life, the conclusion we may draw as to His identity is at once startling and splendid. Indeed, as often as we do this, that is, observe in remembrance, the Redemption of YHWH at Pesach (Passover), as ordained in the Torah, we do it, in remembrance of Him, the Messiah of Israel. (Luke 22:19; 1Corinthians 11:24-26).

PART V:
The Messiah and The Passover

CHAPTER 22

The Cup of Praise

It is the last of the four cups of the 'fruit of the vine' in the Passover meal celebration known in Hebrew as the seder. It remained on the table, untouched by the Messiah Yahoshua, when He celebrated His final Passover with His beloved Jewish disciples on the eve of the 14th of Nisan, after the dusk of sunset and before the darkness of night, obedient to His Father's commandments to the last, just as it is written in His Word [Exodus 12:24-27;Leviticus 23:4,5; Matthew 26:18-20].

In the Garden called Gethsemane, Messiah in anguish, prayed and accepted the will of His Father three times when He said:

> "My Father, if it is possible, let this cup pass from Me; yet not as I will, but as Thou will."
> **(Matthew 26:39)**

> "My Father, if this cannot pass away unless I drink it, 'Thy will be done'."
> **(Matthew 26:42)**

> "And He left them again, and went away and prayed a third time, saying the same thing once more."
> **(Matthew 26:44)**

The first three cups of the Passover seder meal, in which the telling ('haggadah' in Hebrew) of the mighty and miraculous deliverance of Israel from Egypt to freedom is retold each year, according to the commandment, symbolize:

1. the cup of sanctification
2. the cup of instruction
3. the cup of redemption

Messiah, at His last Passover meal, drinks from all three.

Messiah, in His earnest prayer in Gethsemane, symbolically partakes of all three.

Here, Yahoshua is ultimately sanctified [set apart] as:

1.Anointed Son of Man and Son of Elohim ("God"), the Messiah ('Moshiach' in Hebrew).
2.Supreme Teacher of Torah and Rabbi of Righteousness.
3.Saviour and Redeemer of Israel and all Mankind.

But neither symbolically, nor actually, does He take from the final fourth cup.

This cup is poured before the door is ritually opened for Elijah the Prophet*, who will appear just before the Great Day of Judgement of the Gentile Nations who have presumed to thwart the Plan of the Almighty and have relentlessly hurt the Chosen of YHWH, His people Israel.

After His Righteous indignation is visited upon the Nations who did not know Him, and bruised the "apple of His eye" (Zechariah 2:8), will Messiah come (again), and the Eternal Kingdom be set up.

> "And in the days of those kings, the Elohim ['God'] of Heaven will set up a kingdom which will never

be destroyed, and that kingdom will not be left for another people; it will crush and put an end to all these kingdoms, but it will itself endure forever.
Inasmuch as you saw that a stone was cut out of the mountain without hands and that it crushed the iron, the bronze, the clay, the silver, and the gold, the great Elohim has made known to the king what will take place in the future; so the dream is true, and its interpretation is trustworthy."

(Daniel 2:44-45)*

"For all the nations have drunk of the wine of the passion of her (Babylon's) immorality, and the kings of the earth have committed acts of immorality with her, and the merchants of the earth have become rich by the wealth of her sensuality.
And I heard another voice from heaven, saying, "Come out of her, my people, that you may not participate in her sins and that you may not receive of her plagues; for her sins have piled up as high as heaven, and Elohim has remembered her iniquities."

(Revelation 18:3-5)

"And the seventh angel sounded; and there arose loud voices in heaven, saying,:
'The kingdom of the world has become the Kingdom of our Elohim Yahuweh ['Lord'] and of His Messiah, and He will reign forever and ever.'"

(Revelation 11:15)

With the Kingdom finally established, all creation will declare His honor, and sing praises unto Him.

These psalms of praise, known in the Hebrew as the 'Hallel', are now recited.

Only now, the fourth cup, all ready poured, is taken.

This is the cup of praise. This is the Hallel cup.

It is the cup of the Kingdom.

****

Christianity acknowledges that the Messiah, whom they call "Jesus Christ" has come, but that the Torah has been nullified and abolished.

Judaism embraces and obeys the Torah, but does not acknowledge that Messiah has come.

Islam, founded on the teachings of their prophet Mohammed, and their 'Holy Koran', deny both Torah and Messiah.

And so it is, that these three great monotheistic religions have led the whole world astray.

The cups of these three faiths await to be filled with the true fruit of the vine: Torah AND Messiah Yahoshua together!

When this wondrous Truth is finally known, we, with the Eternal Father and His Anointed Son, Yahoshua ha-Moshiach [the Messiah], shall together drink from the fourth cup, "The Cup of Praise", just as He had promised. (Matthew 26:29).

On that great day, Passover, the festival of Freedom and Redemption, will be fully realized by all nations, and at long last, the Truth will set us free. (John 8:31,32)

*[The interpretation of the dream of Nebuchadnezzar, king of Babylon, by the Hebrew prophet Daniel reveals that earth's history will progress through 4 world empires, ruled by Gentile kings. Beginning with Babylon, they are followed in succession by Medo-Persia, Greece, and finally Rome.

The Roman empire is still very much with us, geopolitically in the configuration of the present day European Union of nations, and religiously, in the form of the Roman Catholic Church and her daughters, the Protestant faith(s). [Revelation 17:5, 14-18]

The cup of Elijah is understood by many to be the "5th" cup of the Passover meal. Indeed, the great prophet Elijah, (or one who comes in the spirit of Elijah, as did John 'the Baptizer') will precede the final coming of the Messiah King. Intimately tied to the Redeemer's rule and reign, the "5th" cup of Elijah proclaims the "5th" Kingdom, that is, The Kingdom of Elohim, which will triumph over the 4 preceding kingdoms that flow from earthly Babylon, and forever establish the Kingdom of Heaven, on earth!]

CHAPTER 23

The Passover Redemption

The Torah's teaching is most perfectly understood when the Word of YHWH is allowed to interpret itself. Any other principle of Scriptural interpretation (hermeneutic), although intellectually gratifying, may lead one astray, far removed from His message of Truth. While allegorical, homiletical, or mystical meaning may, at times, be gleaned from the text, these must never supersede Its plain or literal meaning. Indeed, unless symbolic or figurative language is clearly intended, seeking any meaning other than the plain sense may lead the reader to nonsense!

Only by using that principle, can we be assured of the clearest, truest, and best understanding of Yahuweh's eternal message to us.

Torah's third book, Leviticus, was originally known as Torat Kohanim, the Teaching of the Priests, and the priestly nation. Today, in the synagogue, this book is known as "Vayyikra", Hebrew for "And (He) called". Within this book is instruction on sacrifice and the purity of life.

In the twelfth chapter of Leviticus, in the portion called 'Tatzria' in Hebrew, the seminal event of childbirth and delivery is addressed.

Upon the birth of a son, the mother is deemed unclean for seven days, "as in the days of the impurity of her sickness, she shall be unclean" (Leviticus: 12:2). Curiously, if she bears a daughter, then she shall be unclean for two weeks (fourteen days) as in her impurity (Leviticus 12:5).

After 33 days of purification for her son, and 66 days of purification for her daughter, she is commanded to bring burnt offerings and sin offerings to the priest to make atonement before YHWH, and she shall be cleansed from the 'fountain of her blood'.

The fact that the birth of a little girl demanded a period of uncleanness and purification twice as long as that of a boy (eighty days vs. forty days) has troubled and puzzled commentators for centuries. Surely, this cannot mean that a female child is inherently more unclean than a male, and therefore twice in need of purification. Yet the Torah appears to teach that this is exactly the case.

But on closer examination, the Torah does not teach this at all.

When allowed to interpret itself, the Scripture reveals it is not the gender of the child who is born, but the blood of the mother, as in the days of 'the impurity of her sickness' (Lev.12:2) that determines the time of her uncleanness.

A male child will never have a monthly bleeding cycle (menstrual period) as does a woman. The teaching of "Separation and Purification", known in the Hebrew as "Niddah and Taharah", can apply then only to the female (Leviticus 15:19, 18:19). It is here that the transcending principle of substitution is played out in the most basic of all relationships, that of a mother and her newly born little girl. It becomes the duty then, of the mother, to 'cover' her daughter's biologically ordained monthly bleeding cycle (menses), as her loving and devoted personal representative before the priest and YHWH Himself. As a woman is unclean for seven days at the time of her period, so too shall her daughter be, when she comes of age. It is in this anticipation that the Torah calls upon the mother to initiate and secure the process through which purification and atonement is attained, and makes clear why an additional seven days of uncleanness and 33 days of purification was commanded.

Passover, or Pesach in the Hebrew, ordained in Torah to be a memorial for all time, commemorates the salvation of Israel on the eve of the fourteenth day of Nisan, the first month of the year, according to Scripture.

If Nisan is the month of Israel's redemption from bondage, marking the beginning of the year, why didn't YHWH save Israel on Nisan's first day? Why did He wait until the fourteenth day to bring about their deliverance and His redemption?

If we can agree that nothing in the Master's Design happens without reason, and that there is nothing haphazard or purposeless about His perfect plan of deliverance, then we must seek to earnestly determine why YHWH chose to wait until the fourteenth day of Nisan to break the chains of Egyptian bondage and bring Israel to salvation.

When we consider the teaching on "Purification and Atonement", I believe the answer becomes both plain and compelling.

As Israel had dwelled in a culture permeated by polytheism, paganism and a perverted preoccupation with death, Israel herself had become stained and tainted by such uncleanness and impurity.

Consequently, a time of (ritual) impurity prior to Israel's deliverance had to be defined and dealt with. The Jewish sons and daughters of Israel were about to come out of the darkness of Egypt into the Light of Torah at Mount Sinai, and a new covenantal purifying relationship with YHWH.

As was true for the natural birth of the individual Israelite, so it was for the national birth of the whole people of Israel. Therefore, fourteen days had to transpire before this newly born nation could be brought to their place in time and space of 'Separation and Purification'.

In YHWH's grand design, atonement with Him is the ultimate purpose and goal of life. Through Yahoshua, the Atoning Messiah Who died and rose from the grave at Passover, the sovereignly elected people of Israel, and all nations, would be saved from this world of sin and death, symbolized by Egypt and Rome, and delivered into Yahuweh's Kingdom of righteousness and eternal life.

The end of the matter is this.

It is by way of substitution, representation, identification, vicarious atonement, separation, and purification from and through a 'fountain of blood', that both physical and spiritual redemption are united in the Passover; first for Israel, but ultimately for all who are called.

CHAPTER 24

The Memorial for All Time

For the Jewish people, Passover, known as Pesach in Hebrew, has always been the defining moment in their history. In fulfillment of Torah prophecy, it commemorates their liberation from the bondage of slavery in Egypt, and the commencement of a unique and eternal covenantal relationship with their Redeemer Yahuweh.

The annual observance of Passover and the Days of Unleavened Bread (Chag ha-Matzos in the Hebrew) reminds the faithful Israelite of the miracle of consecration, deliverance, and redemption wrought by Yahuweh in the life of His chosen nation. It is then, no small matter, as to which day is the proper day of its observance.

Jewish tradition, for more than two millenia marks the Passover with the seder meal at dusk, as the 14th of Nisan ends and the 15th of Nisan begins. But it hasn't always been that way. Within the Jewish community, when the Second Temple still stood, there was lively debate as to whether observing Passover at dusk, as the 13th of Nisan ended and the 14th of Nisan began, was really what the Torah had commanded. With the destruction of the Temple, rabbinic (Pharasaic) Judaism triumphed, and this debate was largely silenced. Fortified by centuries of the rabbinic affirmation, Judaism has been averse to considering the unsettling possibility that the rabbinic traditional way may not be the right way.

The language of the Torah, as the only authority of correct observance, will help resolve this ancient conflict.

In Exodus (12:3-6), each household in Israel is instructed to take an unblemished year old lamb or goat on the tenth day of Nisan and keep it UNTIL ('ad' in the Hebrew) the fourteenth day of Nisan, when it would be killed at dusk. The Hebrew word 'ad' may be translated as 'until', 'even unto', or 'as far as'; it could not mean that the lamb would be kept through to the end of the 14th, but only until, or as far as, or even unto the beginning of the 14th of Nisan.

At twilight, at the start of sunset, when the fourteenth was about to begin, the lamb was to be slaughtered immediately at dusk, the twilight hour.

In Exodus (12:7-8) each household is commanded to put the lamb's blood on the door's sideposts and lintel, and eat the roasted flesh of the lamb with unleavened bread (matzoh), and bitter herbs on that very night, the night that is the 14th of Nisan.

> "For I will go through the land of Egypt in that night,
> and will smite the first born in the land of Egypt, both
> man and beast; and against all the gods of Egypt will
> I execute judgements, I AM YAHUWEH."
> (Exodus 12:2)

At midnight, on the 14th of Nisan, on the very evening the Pesach (the lamb) was killed, was when the Redeemer went through Egypt in judgement and deliverance. If Israel had waited until the end of the 14th of Nisan to slay the lamb, their firstborn would, without the covering of its blood, be killed, just like the Egyptians.

> "And this day shall be unto you for a memorial, and ye shall keep it a feast to Yahuweh, throughout your generations ye shall keep it a feast by an ordinance forever."
>
> (Exodus 12:14)

So it was in this way that the first Pesach (Passover) was observed. Fearfully, apprehensively, but faithfully, the obedient Israelite dared not leave their homes that awesome night; their houses had been passed over, as Yahuweh had assured them, and at daybreak, on the morning of the 14th, they would leave their houses to burn the left overs of the Pesach (the Passover lamb). (Exodus 12:10,22)

Daylight was now the time they could move, tend to their flocks, gather up their belongings, and leave Goshen for Ramses, taking with them in haste, their dough before it was leavened. At Ramses, all Israel congregated in joyful anticipation, preparing to leave at sunset AT THE BEGINNING OF THE FIFTEENTH OF NISAN. (Numbers 33:3) On the 15th of Nisan (also called Aviv or Abib), the first month of the Scriptural year, on a full moon, redeemed Israel begins her journey for the Promised Land.

The narrative that is known as the Passover Hagaddah retells each year the miracles of our Mighty King and Redeemer, but the source and inspiration for the Exodus story is the Torah where the evidence for the proper time of observance is cogent and compelling. A teachable spirit, an open heart, and a willing mind are the essential ingredients to receive Truth. The Message for Israel comes from The Author and Finisher of our Faith, the Eternal King of Heaven, and is revealed in His Torah.

It is here, and not in the customs and traditions of men, no matter how learned or wise they claim to be, that we must put our confidence and our trust.

Observe therefore, and remember, that Passover, the day of our miraculous redemption from bondage and death, is to be commemorated at dusk on the 14th of Nisan; and the Feast of Unleavened Bread, marking the beginning of our journey is to be celebrated, the next day, at evening, on the 15th of Nisan.

As a people called to be His servant, Israel must be a light to the nations. And it all began at Passover, which is, according to Yahuweh's commandment, a memorial for all time.

CHAPTER 25

Who Let the Jews Out?

The Messiah of Israel in the Passover

The story of the Passover (Pesach in the Hebrew) is the signal central event in the life of the covenant people of Israel. The liberation of the Jews from Egypt was much more than just a national unshackling from physical bondage; but a crucial release from a vastly more insidious kind of slavery.

The lashings and stripes of this cruel oppression was not felt and seen only upon the backs and shoulders of this broken people, but even more so, within their hearts and minds. Deeply scarred by the fixed and false Egyptian beliefs about all of life (and death), these unwitting heirs of Yahuweh's promises to Abraham, Isaac, and Jacob would likely be swallowed up into the swampy and dark waters of Egyptian delusions about false gods, the immortality of the soul, and the complex world of the dead. All of these beliefs, so repugnant to YHWH, could not go unjudged and unpunished for ever. And so it was that the Passover and the Exodus marked the remarkable liberation of this people, for whom the ancient promises had to be fulfilled.

Crushed by centuries of despair, and numbed by hopelessness, the expectation for a better life was held only by a desperate few. And while there were many figures playing on this critical historical stage, one in particular would stand out.

His name was Moses.

Saved from Egyptian sponsored genocide in his infancy, raised in the courts of his people's oppressor, and keenly aware of his Hebrew roots, this unique individual married the daughter of a Midianite priest, lived out much of his life as a shepherd, and reluctantly answered the call of the Elohim ('God') of his people Israel, when he first encountered the Voice from the burning bush.

Moses, drawn out of the waters as a child, was destined to pass through the waters again, as an aged man, at the Reeds Sea (Red Sea) affecting the complete escape of the Jewish people from Egypt on the seventh day of Unleavened Bread, an ordained annual day of commemoration according to the Scriptures.

But first, Moses would have to confront Pharaoh, (Pahraoh in Hebrew translates as the mouth [peh] of Rah, [the sun god]), the ruler of Egypt, and demand the freedom of the Hebrew slaves so that they may serve Yahuweh in the wilderness, summed up in that familiar timeless refrain; "Let my people go".

This was a confrontation between two determined men, to be sure. Both were leaders of their people, but only one had the full force of a mighty army and an earthly throne. And if this were only a disagreement between men, the outcome would be obvious; the Hebrew people would remain slaves and never leave Egypt. But leave Egypt they did, and in a most spectacular and extraordinary way.

Pharaoh represented Rah, the supreme deity of Egypt.

Moses represented Yahuweh, the supreme deity of Israel and all creation.

Would the god of the ruling oppressor, Rah, be able to withstand the Power of YHWH, the "God" of the oppressed.

Would the great fiery sun god be defeated by the Invisible Deity of the Hebrews, known to Pharaoh only by the words of two elderly men, Moses and his brother Aaron.

Yes.

Yes, indeed!

Rah and all of his pagan associate gods would lose this great war. After a series of lesser battles, illustrated as 'plagues', the tenth and final battle would be the death blow to Rah, his spokesman Pharaoh, and all Egypt.

The crushing defeat came not on a battlefield, nor by a massive uprising and rebellion. It did not play out in intellectual debate, religious disputations, or diplomatic persuasion.

Rather, the victory of Yahuweh, His servant Moses, and the Jewish (Hebrew) people, came by way of the blood of a year old unblemished lamb (or goat), and the active redeeming work of the Eternal Himself.

Moses, himself a shepherd, and YHWH's representative, had instructed all the congregation of Israel to take a lamb for a household, where it would live within the Jewish home from the 10th until the 14th day of Nisan. (Exodus 12:3-7) In a very real sense, this creature of the grassland and the field, would now be a part of the family. The transformation of a slave people to a redeemed flock, to be led by YHWH's shepherd and redeemed by YHWH as Shepherd, had begun.

At midnight, on the 14th of the month of Nisan, the firstborn of all the Egyptians, and all who did not have the lamb's lifeblood on their doorposts, were killed.

To be sure, the agent of this judgment and its execution was, in the ultimate sense, Yahuweh (YHWH). But His instrument is identified clearly only in the Hebrew words of the Torah's account of that wondrous night.

> "For YHWH will pass through to smite the Egyptians; and when He sees the blood upon the lintel, and on the two sideposts, YHWH will pass over (pesach or posach in the Hebrew) the door (pesach in the Hebrew), and will not suffer the 'destroyer' (ha-mashichiys) to come in to your houses to smite you."
> **(Exodus 12:23)**

That 'destroyer' was the instrument used by Yahuweh to bring about His final plague and judgement on Egypt.

It is classically thought of as a "destroying angel" or the "angel of death".

Yet the Hebrew word for angel is 'malach' and it is not present in the Hebrew original text.

Rather than 'malach', a different, and remarkably unique word is used.

It is "ha-mashichiys", composed of the Hebrew letters:

"hey-mem,shin,ches, yod,sof"

The root of this word is 'mem,shin,ches, yod', the elemental letters that compose the Hebrew word for anointed, or MASHIACH . This is well illustrated in the liturgy of the Seventh Day of Unleavened Bread (popularly called "Passover"), where we read in IISamuel 22:51:

> "A tower of salvation (yeshuos)* is He to His King,
> And showeth mercy to His anointed (mashiach)*,
> To David and to his seed, for evermore."

*yeshuos is the Hebrew word for salvation, as in "Yeshua"

*mashiach is the Hebrew word for anointed, as in "Messiah"

Thus, the agent of judgment and execution for pagan Egypt, and the agent of mercy and salvation for Hebrew Israel, is not an ordinary angel.

It is ha-Mashiach, the Anointed Messiah of Israel.

His role as Judge and Redeemer is proclaimed at this momentous event, the first Passover.

In this role and responsibility assigned to Him by Yahuweh Elohim, He redeems the Jewish people who faithfully and obediently apply the lifeblood of the unblemished year old lamb to the doorposts and lintel of their homes, saving them from the death of the first born.

But wait! There is more; for the Hebrew word for 'passover' (spelled pey,samech, ches) and for 'door' (spelled pey, sof, ches) are both "pesach"!

So then, whereas faith comes by hearing the written word spoken, 'passover' and the 'door', both "pesach" in the Hebrew, share an essential connection.

The One Who said:

> "Truly, truly, I say to you, I am the door (pesach) of
> the sheep."
>
> **(John 10:7)**

also proclaimed,

> "I am the door (pesach); if anyone enters through Me,
> he shall be saved, and shall go in and out, and find
> pasture."
>
> **(John 10:9)**

And He is also the passover (pesach), as it is written;

> "For Messiah (Mashiach), our Passover (Pesach), also
> has been sacrificed."
>
> **(ICor5:7)**

And He is also the lamb, as it is written,
"He was oppressed and He was afflicted,
Yet He did not open His mouth,
Like a lamb that is led to slaughter,
And like a sheep that is silent before its shearers,
So He did not open His mouth."

(Isaiah 53:7)

Thus the Anointed One, the Mashiach, is at once Judge, Redeemer, Passover, Door (to salvation), and the Lamb.

As the congregation of Israel was to become like sheep so as to be led by the Shepherd, so the Messiah was to become like a lamb, to be like Israel; and as one of us, to die for us, to deliver us, and to ultimately lead us, as Shepherd, through the Door (which is Himself) to salvation.

This stunning and awesome act, on behalf of Israel, Yahuweh's son, and His first-born, (Exodus 4:22), through the agency of His Mashiach, Yahuweh's Son and Only Begotten, leads to the exodus, saving the Jews not just from perpetual slavery in Egypt, but from the death that comes from the sin of participating in Egypt's paganism, and her rejection of the One and Only True Elohim, Yahuweh.

Who, then, let the Jews out?

Well, after much persuasion, and powerful plagues, Pharaoh did finally "let" them go.

And after that fateful Passover night, the opportunity arose, the "door" opened, and Moses finally "got" them out.

But in the final analysis, Yahuweh (YHWH) orchestrated the whole event so as to bring about His Plan of Redemption, vindicate His Righteous Name and Character, and fulfill His promises to Abraham, Isaac, and Jacob.

He did this by giving His Mashiach, the Messiah, the job of Judge and Executioner to the Egyptians, and the exalted role of Deliverer, Liberator, Redeemer, and Saviour for the Jews.

In the last days, before the establishment of the Kingdom of Yahuweh here on earth, all nations will be judged, as Egypt was on that first Passover.

The Messiah, will again serve Yahuweh Elohim as Judge and Redeemer, as it is written in the Book of Revelation 20:11-22:5.

So then, the Messiah "let" the Jews out; and the Messiah "got" the Jews out.

And at the end of days, He will do it again.

> "And it shall come to pass in that day,
> That the Eternal (Adonai) will set His hand again the
>   second time,
> To recover the remnant of His people,......(sic.)
> And He will set up an ensign for the nations,
> And will assemble the dispersed of Israel,
> And gather together the scattered of Judah,
> From the four corners of the earth."
>   **(Isaiah 11:11,12)**

> "Therefore prophesy, and say unto them:
> Thus saith (Adonai) Yahuweh:

Behold, I will open up your graves, and cause you to
come up out of your graves, O My people; and I will
bring you into the land of Israel.
And you shall know that I am Yahuweh, when I have
opened up your graves, and caused you to come up
out of your graves, O My people.
And I will put my Spirit in you, and you shall live, and
I will place you in your own land;
And you shall know that I, Yahuweh, have spoken,
and performed it,
says Yahuweh."

(Ezekiel 37:12-14)

"And so all Israel will be saved, as it is written:
'The Deliverer will come from Zion;
He will turn godlessness away from Jacob.
And this is My covenant with them,
When I take away their sins.' "

(Romans 11:26,27)

PART VI:

Revelation vs. Religion

CHAPTER 26

Torah and Talmud: Truth and Tradition

The Jews are a unique, peculiar, and remarkable people. Often vilified, sometimes praised, yet always significant, they have defied the forces of history, and remain alive to this very day. Unlike any other people, they can be secure, not because of protected national boundaries, great wealth, or a mighty army, but simply, solely, and completely, because their future is promised by the Eternal Elohim ['God'].

It began with the call of Abraham, the son of a Chaldean pagan idol merchant, who heard the literal, external, audible, and actual voice of the Almighty. From the time of Creation, from everlasting, this was the call of the One and Only True King of the Universe........and Abraham, by the grace of the One Who calls, was spoken to, personally, by Him.

Abraham was told to leave his country for a place that "I will show you" (Genesis 12:1); and Abraham did. Later, a child was born unto Abraham and his wife Sarah in their old age, a time well beyond their reproductive years, a miracle birth indeed. Yet when his beloved 'only son' Isaac became a young man, Abraham was commanded to return him to Elohim, Who desired that he be lifted up as an 'olah' (a burnt offering), upon a mountain in the land called Moriah.

And Abraham would have done just as he was commanded, except for the saving intervention of the Almighty Himself, Who appeared as 'malach Yahuweh', the messenger-angel of Yahuweh. (Genesis 22:11-12)

The life of Abraham is the story of one man's exodus from the familiar to the unknown; dramatically foreshadowing what the lives of his children would be like. For Isaac, his son, for Jacob, his grandson, and in every generation of Israel, there have been Jews who would heed the call of Yahuweh, and go forth as He commanded.

From Egypt to Canaan to Assyria to Babylon to Greece to Rome to Europe to the 'New World' to the Middle East to the modern state of Israel, the Jews have been the ultimate survivors; a survival that came at a price, measured in not just the loss of their sovereignty and lives, but in the purity of their message and mission.

In their ambivalence and zeal about participation in the surrounding cultures, the Jewish people were challenged to protect and preserve the legacy of their covenant with Yahuweh. Sensitive to the influence and sometimes even seductive attraction of the ways of the nations in which Israel found herself, the rabbis ultimately created a written 'safe zone', or a 'fence around the Torah'.

These writings, of which there are many, most notably took the form of an extraordinary composite work known as the Talmud. According to orthodox Judaism, the Talmud is believed to be the "Oral Torah [Oral Law of Instruction]", received by Moses at Sinai, and given as a charge to Joshua and the elders of Israel.

As an oral tradition, it was not to be reduced to the written word or taught in public, but 150 years after the destruction of the Second Temple in Jerusalem by the Roman general Titus, the great Rabbi Judah ha Nasi (Rabbi Judah, the prince) put pen to paper and arranged 35 generations of scholarly interpretations, explanations, discussions and dicta of these sages known as the 'Tanaaim' into orders and tractates and chapters. This voluminous work came to be known as the Mishnah [meaning "repetition", circa 200 C.E.].

This was a time of great turbulence for the Jewish people. As subjects of the Empire, the powerful religions and philosophies of Rome, Greece, Persia, and Babylon, could have conspired with the destruction of the Jerusalem Temple, the epi-center of Jewish life, and prove to be too great a force to overcome. The disappearance of Jews, Judaism, the Revelation of Torah, and its message of Truth was too real a possibility. The rabbis believed that the very survival of this people, their future, and the hope of the nations, was at stake.

Out of this desperate environment, Rabbi Judah and his peers sought justification for the decision to write the 'Oral Torah', and they found just that in the 119th Psalm of David, verse 126, which says:

"It is time to act for YHWH, they have broken thy Law (Torah)".

Having initiated the process, it would now be easier for future generations to contribute to Jewish "Holy Writ" in order to preserve the whole. About 300 years later [circa 500 C.E.], this indeed is precisely what happened.

The 'Amoraim', a group of scholars who studied the Mishnah, found themselves, at times, in conflict with the 'Tanaaim', the sages of the Mishnah, regarding accuracy, reasoning, principles, and perceived errors in this oral tradition. Together, the Amoraim composed a repository of instruction, doctrine, law and narrative of their own, taught by thousands of sages over the centuries, and called it Gemarah [meaning "completion"].

The Mishnah and Gemarah together make up the Talmud. Interestingly, the Gemarah itself is comprised of a Babylonian and a Jerusalem 'edition'. Both written in Aramaic, the Babylonian Talmud is elaborate and extensive, while the Jerusalem Talmud is more abbreviated and concise. Typically, it is the Babylonian Talmud that is the universal document of study amongst orthodox Jews worldwide.

The Talmud, the Torah Shebe'al peh, (Hebrew for oral Torah), had become a mobile homeland for the Jewish people in exile. This powerful 'constitution' for the Jews in "galut"(exile) would insure their integrity, insularity, and survival as the Chosen people of "The Book".

This was achieved, in no small measure, by elevating a now transcribed oral tradition to the level of the Written and Revealed Torah.

And although the Heavenly Authority for such a claim is not evident, perceived historical necessity afforded the ascent of the Talmud to, (at least for some), the level of the written Word of Torah. Over the centuries, the plain teachings of Torah would be seen through the lens of Talmud and tradition. Ultimately, it was concluded that Torah could only be understood in this way. This would prove to be in contrast with the Torah message as being open to all, requiring neither a trained segment of society, nor a manual of interpretation.

The Scripture proclaims:

> "Yahuweh is near to all who call upon Him, to all who call upon Him in truth."
>
> **(Psalm 145:18)**

Furthermore, in the 5th Book of Torah, Deuteronomy, the Almighty declares:

> "You shall not add unto the word which I command you, nor shall you diminish aught from it; that you may keep the commandments of YHWH, your Eternal, which I command you."
>
> **(Deuteronomy 4:2)**

The gnawing fact that Talmud and tradition are both forged on the template of human experience creates a dilemna. Seeking to keep the Jewish nation uncontaminated and pure from the intrusion of foreign ideas, philosophies, and religions, the Talmud and tradition (unintentionally and regretfully) undermined this very goal.

Like the mysterious Red Heifer of Torah, it both purified and contaminated. But unlike Torah, whose author is Yahuweh, the Eternal Ruler of the Universe, the Talmud is a human composition, and bears the signature of any human product;

ambivalence, uncertainty, error, and conflict. Furthermore, the Talmud, and tradition, is externally motivated; that is, formed, (at least in part), as a response to perceived external threats and the internal insecurities and fears of its authors. In its development, it inadvertently incorporated the symbols and ideas of the civilizations the Jewish people found themselves living in along the way.

One such example is the "Hebrew" month of Tammuz, appearing on the secular calendar around July or August. According to history, Tammuz was the Sumerian god of fertility, named after an actual 'shepherd-healer' who produced ewe's milk and tended lambs. In the words of the prophet Ezekiel, the vision of the abomination of Tammuz is one of several sober admonitions to Israel. (Ezekiel 8:12-16).

Both the Talmud and tradition are rich in content and insight, giving abundant texture and substance to Jewish life. But they have the potential to threaten the very integrity of the essential Torah message by inviting a pagan deity named Tammuz into the sacred space that is the revealed Torah (Tanakh) given by YHWH Himself. (Exodus 20:3; Deuteronomy 6:14)

This is the dilemna Judaism finds itself in, taking "as commandments the traditions of men". (Isaiah 29:13)

Paved with good intentions, the religion of Israel has taken an unintended detour on the road to the 'Promised Land' and the Kingdom of YHWH.

****

It has been said that the enemy of the 'best' is not the 'worst', but the 'good'. The Talmud and tradition contain indeed much that is good....and that may be just the problem.

You see, "Religion", at its best, is the noble pursuit of the truth, the ideal, the utmost, and the highest. Such a goal is sublime, exalted and lofty. But the means to reach this pure vision is inherently flawed, for it originates and is sustained in the reprobate and broken heart of man.

"Revelation", on the other hand, is the gracious disclosure of all of these by Yahuweh, the Source of Reality Himself, Who dwells supernaturally above all, and by Whose will, inspired wisdom has been made known to His chosen and sovereign elect throughout the ages. Flawless and perfect, such exquisite knowledge originates, is sustained, and is fulfilled in the pure and perfect Mind of our heavenly Father and His Messiah.

So then, at the end of the day, and in the final analysis, the Torah is paramount, for it is the supreme and unchanging Word of Yahuweh Elohim.

This ultimate revelation was spoken by the One we know as Creator, Sustainer, and Redeemer:

Who called Abraham, Isaac, and Jacob;

conmmissioned Moses and the prophets;

sovereignly chose Israel and the Jewish people;

and proclaimed the Gospel of Salvation and the Kingdom to Israel and the Gentile elect of all nations.

His revealed, transcribed Word we know as Scripture, is right, just, and true.

As it is written:

> "All Scripture is inspired by Elohim ['God'], and profitable for teaching, for reproof, for correction, for training in righteousness."
> **(2 Timothy 3:16)**

> "Forever, O Yahuweh, Thy Word is settled in heaven."
> **(Psalm 119:89)**

****

The Talmud and Tradition have earned an honorable place in the lore of the Jewish people. Over the centuries, together they have woven a rich and resilient fabric of identity and practice. But it must never be forgotten that while their role may have been to illuminate the Word of Elohim, they can never replace, supersede, or supplant It.

For only in His written Word, the Torah, and in His Living Word, the Messiah, is our life, the length of our days, and our abiding hope.

CHAPTER 27

When Milk and Meat "Meet"

The observant Jew, according to custom, tradition, and scriptural provision will never consume milk (dairy) and meat at the same meal.

According to Dov Rosen in his book "Shema Yisrael: Judaism-The Belief and the Belonging":

> "This law is a novelty, and is above human understanding. Here are two foods. Taken separately, each is permissible. Brought together they are forbidden."
>
> **(volume 1, p.26)**

Despite this, over the centuries, various explanations have been proffered, including protection against superstition and idolatry, or the cultivation of tender-heartedness, compassion, and humane sensitivity.

The basis of this uniquely Jewish doctrine is derived from three verses in the Torah: Exodus 23:19, Exodus 34:26, and Deuteronomy 14:21 where (in all) the transliterated Hebrew reads as:

"Lo tivashale gidee ba-chalave eemo."

This is translated, in the English as:

"Thou shall not seethe a kid in its mother's milk."

The verses in Exodus follow the Eternal's instruction regarding the three annual festivals dedicated to Him. They are:

1. The Feast of Unleavened Bread (Passover-Chag ha Matzos)
2. The Feast of Harvest-First Fruits (Pentecost-Shavuos)
3.The Feast of Ingathering (Tabernacles-Sukkos)

(The verse from Deuteronomy appears at the conlusion of the repetition of the dietary laws.)

In Exodus 23:18 the faithful Jewish pilgrim is commanded: "Thou shall not offer the blood of My sacrifice with leavened bread: neither shall the fat('chaylev' in Hebrew) remain all night until the morning."

In Exodus 34:25, using slightly different words, the essential elements remain. It reads: "Thou shall not offer the blood of My sacrifice with leavened bread; neither shall the sacrifice of the feast of the Pesach (Passover) be left unto the morning."

These commandments clearly refer to the first pilgrim annual festival of Passover-Unleavened Bread. They are intended to commemorate the first Passover in Egypt, where in Exodus 12:(9,10) the 'whole assembly of the congregation of Israel are commanded to eat the lamb not raw, nor sodden (boiled or seethed) ("oovashale mivooshal" in Hebrew) with water, but roasted.

In this context, is the traditional law of milk and meat separation plainly commanded in Torah?

Using the sustaining hermeneutical principle of allowing Scripture to interpret itself, what deeper insight might we glean?

At issue is the proper understanding of the Hebrew word 'chaylev', translated as fat, and 'chalave', translated as milk.

Both words are constructed of the same three consonants: 'ches, lahm-ed, and vays'. It is important to note that the Hebrew manuscript of the Torah scrolls is written by trained scribes without vowels.

The vowels change the meaning of the word in the succeeding verse from fat (chaylev) (Exodus 23:18) to milk (chalave) (Exodus 23:19). Furthermore, the Hebrew root, "vashale", meaning seethe or boil, appearing in Exodus 23:19, Exodus 34:36, and Deuteronomy 14:21 compels us to look back to Exodus 12:9,10 where "vashale" first appears in this context.

These three verses may be better translated as:

> "Thou shalt not seethe a kid in its mother's fat."

Repetition of a word, a frequent occurence in Torah, reinforces and enhances the essential teaching. Here it serves to confirm for posterity the proper observance of the annual pilgrim Festival of Passover-Unleavened Bread.

To further lend support to this position, one need only look to Leviticus (3:16,17), where it is written:

> "kol chaylev l'Yahuweh" meaning "all fat is Yahuweh's".

and

> "kol chaylev v'kol dom lo toechayloo" meaning "all fat and all blood you shall not eat".

The remembrance of Passover, and its annual commemoration is at the core of Israel's identity.

In the Messianic Scriptures, this same memorial meal is ordained by Yahoshua the Messiah, at His last Passover supper, and will serve to focus our faith on Him and His finished atoning work, until He comes again.

All "sanctifying" commandments flow forth from Yahuweh's redemption of Israel from Egypt, from sin and from death. In our obedience, we honor Him and His saving Work, and proclaim our faithfulness and trust in Yahuweh Elohim and His Messiah as our Savior.

Just a change of a dash or a dot, or not mindfully attending to words in context, can change the meaning of a word or a phrase, and alter our understanding of Torah, and guide for centuries the beliefs and practices of a people. Rather than an orderly and internally harmonious flow toward further enlightenment and deeper understanding, traditional interpretation can become an awkward intrusion upon the Teaching that is Torah.

To be sure, critical exposition, interpretation, and explanation must be the foundation of legitimate Scriptural exegesis. And while this principle clearly applies to the whole of Scripture, it is especially pertinent here.

****

Perhaps it is time for the tradition of the separation of milk and meat to be prayerfully and humbly re-examined.

To be sure, the Kingdom of Yahuweh is not eating and drinking, but knowledge of the Truth is Its enduring foundation.

In Deuteronomy 4:2 we are commanded to neither add to nor diminish from the Word He has given us, so that we may keep His commandments. This is our high and heavenly calling....and to it may we ever be faithful.

*("Shema Yisrael" by Dov Rosen, published by Peli Printing Works Ltd., Jerusalem,Israel, 1972)

CHAPTER 28

The Right Stuff

People have always had a certain fascination with mixing various elements together so as to bring about new and better products. Indeed, modern civilization owes much to natural and synthetic combinations, producing benefits in clothing, construction materials, foods, pharmaceuticals, fuels, and even life forms. And in music and the visual arts, the mixing of an almost infinite number of tones, melodies, shapes, and colors have enriched the lives of us all.

It might seem odd to us then, that the Scriptures are quite clear in proclaiming that not all combinations are good.

Of course, the average person would acknowledge that undisciplined chemical mixtures can lead to dangerous and even disastrous results, when one, for example, considers the risks of biological, chemical, or nuclear catastrophe.

And now, in this age of modern genetic engineering, splicing genes with dissimilar DNA can potentially produce ecological and human catastrophies, when one considers resistant mutations and the risk of novel, unknown "creations".

But such 'common sense' is notoriously, 'uncommon'.

Indeed, if man was left to his own imaginings and designs, such undisciplined experimentation could potentially lead to our own extinction, through famine, disease, pestilence, or thermonuclear destruction.

The Creator of the Universe has given humanity a remedy for this tragic flaw, this inclination to follow our own desires: that is, our heart, our conscience, our will, or our passions, called by Paul in Romans chapters 6-8 the carnal or fleshly nature, and by the rabbis as "ha-yetzer ra", [the inclination to sin or evil].

The solution is found in His Torah and in His Redeemer.

At the heart of the Torah, (the Pentateuch of the Hebrew Scriptures commonly referred to as the "Old Testament"), is the 19th chapter of Leviticus, known in the Hebrew as "Kedoshim", or "holiness", better translated as "set-apartedness" for that is what "Kadosh" truly means.

The chapter's overarching message is proclaimed in Lev.19:2, where YHWH commands:

> "Kedoshim teehiyu ki kadosh Ani YHWH Elohaychem"; which translates as:
>
> "You shall be set apart ["holy"], for I, YHWH, your Elohim, am set apart ["holy"]."

The chapter goes on to teach us how to be set apart, how, as it were, to be "holy"-----how to be like Yahuweh(YHWH). Its instruction on parental reverence, sabbath observance, idols, ritual sacrifice, consideration for the poor, honesty, righteousness in judgment, gossip, hatred, forgiveness, love, sexual purity, prohibition of eating blood, harvest precepts, divination, heathen customs involving hair and flesh, just weights and measures, proper child rearing, respect for the aged, and honor and love for the stranger is far-reaching and plain-spoken...no area of human existence is untouched by the righteous Teaching of Yahuweh and His Torah.

But halfway into chapter 19 is the 19th verse which begins reasonably enough with instructions about animal husbandry and agricultural techniques, but concludes, somewhat inscrutably, with the law of mixed materials (italicized):

> "You shall keep My statutes. You shall not breed together two kinds of your cattle; you shall not sow your field with two kinds of seed, *nor wear a garment upon you of two kinds of material mixed together.*"
> **(Leviticus 19:19)**

This mixing or mingling of materials is known in Hebrew as 'shaatnez'.

The statute of mingled materials, or shaatnez, is more fully elucidated in Deuteronomy 22:11, which declares:

> "You shall not wear a mingled stuff, wool and linen together."
> (Deuteronomy 22:11)

The statute of shaatnez has traditionally been understood as a command for which no reason has been given, and must be obeyed just because it is given by YAHUWEH.

Indeed, obedience to the commands of our Heavenly Father is the charge of the person of faith.

But if there is a reason for this statute that Scripture reveals, should we not endeavor to discern it?

Consider the following:

The prohibition that is shaatnez, in its fullest elucidation, speaks of not just any two materials, but specifically of WOOL and LINEN.

What, according to Torah, makes these two materials unique?

Linen, a cloth made from flax, was used in the construction of the garments of the Levitical priests (Exodus 28), and the curtains and veil and screen (Exodus 26) of the tabernacle, and the clothing of the Levitical singers (2Chronicles 5:12).

In the Messianic scriptures, linen is spoken of figuratively, as pictures of righteousness and purity. (Revelation 19:8,14).

Wool is the material derived from skin of the lamb (sheep), the animal that figures boldly in the Passover and Temple sacrifice. Ezekiel notes that the Levitical priests, clothed with linen garments, shall not wear wool.(Ezekiel 44:17). In the sign of the fleece, wool pictured Israel's deliverance (Judges 7:36-40). In Isaiah's prophecy, it, like white snow, is the assurance of sins forgiven (Isaiah 1:18). To Daniel, the hair of the Head of the Ancient of Days is like pure wool (Daniel 7:9), seen also by John in Revelation 1:14.

Linen and wool are both profoundly involved in the themes of priest and sacrifice, righteousness and forgiveness, purity and deliverance.

And it is precisely for this reason that they must not be mingled together by man.

The mysterious rite of the 'red heifer', the 'parah adumah' in the Hebrew, simultaneously pictured sanctification and defilement, purifying obedient Israel from contact with the dead. This "mingling" of pure and impure in one creature, pictures the Messiah, in Whom righteousness and sin, priest and sacrifice mingled, and became the one perfect "Korban" (Hebrew for "that which brings near"), the Atonement.

The statute of shaatnez, that prohibits the mingling of linen and wool is really no mystery after all.

When the Torah is read with the Mind of Yahuweh Elohim, the goal of atonement permeates all of Scripture. After all, only through atonement can "kedoshim" ["holiness"] ever be attained.

In the final analysis, the mingling of linen and wool has been done for us by Yahuweh Himself. Through His ancient and eternal plan, He has woven the whitest wool, and the finest linen together, to create the purest and most perfect garment of Righteousness, the Messiah Yahoshua.

CHAPTER 29

The Scriptures: New Insights on the Good Book

Law vs. Grace

Whatever happened to the Creator's Law?

Most Christians have been taught that now that we live under 'grace', we are no longer bound by the Law (Torah or teaching instruction) of our Creator. Since we are saved by 'grace', and not by keeping the Eternal's Torah, the Torah then is of no effect; it cannot save, and therefore it has been done away with.

But what do the Scriptures really say on this subject?

What does the Messiah, the Anointed One of Israel and Yahuweh say? What do the words of Yahoshua the Messiah tell us about the Torah?

The answer will surely surprise many.

Look at the Gospel of Matthew 5:17-20 in the Messianic Scriptures:

> "Do not think that I have come to abolish the Torah or the Prophets; I have not come to abolish them but to fulfill them. I tell you the truth, until heaven and earth disappear, not the smallest letter, not the least

stroke of a pen, will by any means disappear from the Torah until everything is accomplished.

Anyone who breaks one of the LEAST of the commandments and teaches others to do the same will be called LEAST in the Kingdom of Heaven, but whoever PRACTICES and TEACHES these commands will be called great in the Kingdom of Heaven. For I tell you that unless your righteousness surpasses that of the Pharisees and the teachers of the Torah, you will certainly not enter the Kingdom of Heaven."

When you take the plain words of Messiah Yahoshua and hold them up against the traditions and teachings of the religion built around Him, what we see before us is startling!

Look at what the Apostle Paul has to say in the book of Romans:

"We know that the Torah is spiritual; but I am unspiritual, sold as a slave to sin."
(Romans 7:14)

"So then, the Torah is set apart [holy], and the commandment is set apart [holy], righteous and good."
(Romans 7:12)

"For in my inner being, I delight in Elohim's Torah, but I see another law at work in the members of my body, waging war against the law of my mind and making me a prisoner of the Law Of Sin at work within my

members. What a wretched man I am! Who will
rescue me from this body of death?

Thanks be to Elohim, through Yahoshua Messiah, our
Master.

So then, I myself in my mind, am a slave to the Torah
of Elohim, but in the sinful nature, to the Law of Sin.

(Romans 7:22-26)

****

For even the casual reader, this must be an eye opener. You
see, there is not one law, but two!

One is the 'Law of Elohim': the Torah.

The other is 'the law of sin': the carnal, fleshly, unregenerate
nature of man.

Take another look at Paul's words:

"For sin shall not be your master, because you are not
under law but under grace."

(Romans 6:14)

Which law is it that we are not under?

Is it the first one, that is, the 'Law of Elohim', or the second,
'the law of sin'? The answer is obvious. It is the law of sin
that we are not under; from this law we have been rescued
by Messiah, who took upon Himself the full penalty of its
punishment, through His Atoning Death in what should
have been rightfully our place. Paul makes this brilliantly
clear when he concludes:

"Therefore there is no condemnation for those who are
in Messiah Yahoshua, because through the Messiah

the Law of the Spirit of Life set me free from the law of sin and death.........The mind of sinful man is death, but the mind controlled by the Spirit is life and peace, because the sinful mind is hostile to Elohim.

IT DOES NOT SUBMIT TO ELOHIM'S TORAH, NOR CAN IT DO SO.

Those controlled by the sinful nature cannot please the Eternal.......Therefore, brothers, we have an obligation--but it is NOT to the sinful nature, to live according to it. FOR IF YOU LIVE ACCORDING TO THE SINFUL NATURE YOU WILL DIE; BUT IF BY THE SPIRIT YOU PUT TO DEATH THE MISDEEDS OF THE BODY, YOU WILL LIVE, BECAUSE THOSE WHO ARE LED BY THE SPIRIT OF ELOHIM ARE SONS OF ELOHIM."

(Romans 8:1,6,12-13)

"For the wages of sin is death, but the gift of Elohim is ETERNAL LIFE in Messiah, our Master."

(Romans 6:23)

Now let's look at what John has to say on this subject.

In 1John we read:

"Everyone who sins breaks the Torah (Law), in fact SIN IS TORAHLESSNESS (LAWLESSNESS).
But you know that He appeared that He might take away our sins. And in Him is no sin. NO ONE WHO LIVES IN HIM KEEPS ON SINNING. NO ONE WHO CONTINUES TO SIN HAS EITHER SEEN HIM OR KNOWN HIM."

(1John 3:4-6)

Finally, let's return to the Gospel of Matthew to hear the words of Yahoshua, the Messiah; perhaps in a way we have never heard them before.

> "Not everyone who says to me Master, Master will enter into the Kingdom of Heaven, but only he who DOES THE WILL of my Father Who is in heaven.
> Many will say to me on that day; 'Master, Master, did we not prophesy in your Name, and in your Name drive out demons and perform many miracles?
> Then I will tell them plainly, 'I NEVER KNEW YOU. GET AWAY FROM ME, YOU WHO WORK TORAHLESSNESS (LAWLESSNESS)"
>
> **(Matthew 7:21-23)**

The Scriptures have a great deal to say on the subject of the Torah of Elohim. It is the Royal Law (Teaching), the set apart [holy] Law (Instruction) of Life.......it is the Eternal Law (Teaching), given to mankind by the Eternal Elohim, Whose Will and Character is revealed in its' precepts.

It is a Way of Life so precious and valued by our Creator, that only the sacrifice of His Son, our Anointed Redeemer, could pay the price for breaking it.

Can we, nay.....dare we, value it any less than our Heavenly Father? By now the answer should be plain.

****

There are many 'teachers' out in the world who would object to the claim that the Torah of Elohim is still binding and is the Law of Life for the redeemed children of the Eternal.

Some of them; indeed most of them, claim to represent the Saviour, the Author and Finisher of our Faith.

Listen to what 1John says:

> "Dear friends, do not believe every spirit, but test the spirits to see whether they come from Elohim, because many false prophets have gone out into the world.......Dear friends, if our hearts do not condemn us, we have confidence before Elohim, and receive from Him anything we ask, because we OBEY HIS COMMANDS, and do what pleases Him. And this is His command: to believe in the Name of His Son Yahoshua Messiah, and to love one another as He commanded us. Those who obey His commandments live in Him, and He in them."
>
> **(1John 4:1 and 3:21-24)**

The final book of the Scriptures seals this message with the assurance of Yahuweh's Eternal Truth. It appears in the Book of Revelation; here's what it says:

> "This calls for patient endurance on the part of the saints who obey the commandments of Elohim and remain faithful to Yahoshua."
>
> **(Revelation 14:12)**

****

Well, there you have it. For most of you, the inescapable conclusion reached here will make you think.

But for those of you who believe you have been truly called to take on the yoke of the Kingdom of Heaven, may you be moved to transform your lives so that they will be set apart (holy) and living sacrifices to Him Who loved us enough to die for us, and Who lives, so that we may also live for Him.

> "Enter through the narrow gate. For wide is the gate and broad is the road that leads to destruction, and many enter through it. But small is the gate and narrow the road that leads to LIFE, and only a few find it."
>
> **(Matthew 7:13-14)**

> "Blessed are those who hear the Word of Elohim and obey it."
>
> **(Luke 11:28)**

May your will and His will be ONE.

CHAPTER 30

The Christian Controversy: Grace vs. Law

It is certain, though not generally well known, that the earliest founding members of the Messianic faith were almost entirely Jewish. The Gospel message was embodied and communicated by a Jewish rabbi to Jewish disciples in a Jewish land, in Jewish synagogues, and a Jewish Jerusalem Temple, in a way that was truly in harmony with the Jewish Scriptures, namely the Torah and the Prophets and the Writings. Although some of the writings of Paul may suggest that faithful and loving obedience to the Torah's instructions, in commandments, statutes, ordinances, and judgements (The Law) was nullified "at the cross", such a conclusion is entirely unwarranted and completely untenable in light of the words of the Messiah Himself and the whole of Scripture.

Yet, amazingly, that is exactly what the Christian faith has done. From its earliest beginnings, the Torah observant Messianic Jewish community suffered the enmity of Rome and the excommunication of the synagogue. Exceedingly small in number, their members were quickly overwhelmed by the massive infusion of Gentile converts to a religion that had morphed through syncretism into a hybrid faith.

Steeped in pagan beliefs and customs, the nascent Jewish followers of Israel's Messiah were effectively silenced, and the power and influence of Roman and Greek culture successfully infused the 'church', leading her away from the Jewish Rabbi Messiah Yahoshua to 'Jesus Christ', a different Messiah with a different gospel.

Through clever arguments, a "bully pulpit", pervasive anti-Jewish sentiments, and doctrinal decrees, a false controversy was set up; placing commandment keeping and grace in opposition. Obedience to the Jewish Torah, Sabbath observance, eating only clean foods (kosher); indeed all things Jewish were maligned. On the other hand, acceptance of the teaching of the Gentile church fathers, rejection of the Torah, which they demeaned as "The Law" and legalism, Sunday observance, eating pork and all unsanctified foods, and believing on the "Lord Jesus Christ" was elevated and exalted.

In a very short time, the doctrines of the Christian church triumphed and were formalized in a series of Councils, the most significant being the Council at Nicaea in 325 A.D. (C.E.), when the Emperor Constantine changed the official day of worship to Sunday. Just about forty years later, at the Council of Laodicea (363 C.E.), the following directive was sent forth:

"Christians must not "Judaize" by resting on the Sabbath, but must work on that day, rather honoring the Lord's Day (Sunday)....But if any shall be found to be Judaizers, let them be anathema (cursed and excommunicated) from Christ."

Today, virtually all of Christianity has been alienated from its Torah heritage, believing that Christians live under grace and are no longer bound by the "Law" (the Torah). Being of no effect; this Torah cannot save, and has therefore been done away with.

However, when we carefully search the Scriptures, "rightly dividing the Word of Truth", with a sharp, critical mind and a discerning spirit, we must reach an entirely different conclusion.

What does the Messiah Himself say about the Law (Torah)?

Here is what He says:

> "Do not think that I have come to abolish the Torah or the Prophets; I have not come to abolish them but to fulfill them. I tell you the truth, until heaven and earth disappear, not the smallest letter, not the least stroke of a pen, will by any means disappear from the Torah until everything is accomplished. Anyone who breaks one of the least of these commandments and teaches others to do the same will be called least in the Kingdom of Heaven, but whoever practices and teaches these commands will be called great in the Kingdom of Heaven. For I tell you that unless your righteousness surpasses that of the Pharisees and the teachers of the Torah (Law), you will certainly not enter the Kingdom of Heaven.
>
> (Matthew 5:17-20)

The words of Paul the Apostle, and the Word incarnate, Yahoshua the Messiah Himself, bring searing and revealing light to the distortion that has become a central dogma of Christianity: that the Torah has been nullified, abolished and done away with.......and that faith and grace have replaced it.

In this contrived controversy, The Scripture proclaim an essential doctrine of truth; and it is this: The Torah is the Royal Law, the Holy Law of Life. It is the eternal Law given to mankind in love by the Eternal Elohim and Father of the Messiah, who's will and character is revealed in its precepts and teachings.

> "Blessed are those who hear the Word of 'God' and obey it."
>
> (Luke 11:28)

Obedience to the Law of 'God', the Torah, the very foundation of His government as Sovereign of the Universe is obtained not through human efforts, but through the Life of the Resurrected Messiah, Who now lives in the surrendered lives of His redeemed. Through His Spirit, we may:

> "Enter through the narrow gate. For wide is the gate and broad is the road that leads to destruction, and many enter through it. But small is the gate and narrow the road that leads to life, and only a few find it."
>
> (Matthew 7:13,14)

In the end, it may be said that a masterful deception has led the whole world astray.

In truth, there really is no controversy between grace and law.

For the Scriptures reveal that both law and grace work together to achieve a redeemed people and a redeemed creation that the Eternal Father and His Son, the Messiah, had ordained from the very beginning.

CHAPTER 31

The Monotheists

There are three major religions in the world which can trace their origins from the Abrahamic faith of the Hebrew Torah Scriptures that proclaim the "One God". They are Judaism, Christianity, and Islam.

First to appear, and most senior of this company, is Judaism, followed by Christianity, and then Islam.

Judaism, fortified in its historic system of faith and doctrine, has never yielded its unshakeable belief in the absolute and indivisible unity of 'God', despite challenges to obscure or mitigate this foundational dogma over the centuries.

The central confession of Judaism is declared in Deuteronomy, the Fifth Book of the Torah:

> "Hear O Israel, the 'LORD' is our 'God', the 'LORD' is ONE."

[Many respected and reliable translators and scholars have proposed that the central confession of Judaism, called the greatest commandment by the Messiah, known as the "Shema", may also be translated:

"Hear O Israel, the LORD (Yahuweh) is our GOD, the LORD (Yahuweh) alone"

affirming that only the Hebrew deity, Whose Name is YAHUWEH, is the "GOD" of Israel.]

which in the Hebrew reads:

"ShemA Yisrael YHVH Elohaynu YHVH EchaD."
(Deuteronomy 6:4)

It is only in the original Hebrew, the pure and exclusive language of The Torah, that the full depth and breadth of this (or any) verse of Scripture can be properly understood. Exegesis of a translated text, whether it be Israel's Greek Septuagint, Rome's Latin Vulgate, Germany's Guttenburg, Switzerland's Geneva, England's King James, or America's New International, American Standard or new KJV version(s) of the "Bible", can never convey completely or correctly, the pristine, undefiled message critically discernible only in the Hebrew exegetic.

The six Hebrew words of this 'confession of faith' merit the most careful scrutiny; for upon them, the central Being of proper (Jewish) worship, devotion, and covenant relationship is defined.

In previous chapters, YHVH, (or YAHVEH, YAHUWEH, YAHUVEH), the Memorial Name of Elohim ('God'), has been carefully and comprehensively presented and discussed.

YHVH appears twice in this single verse. But first we are commanded to listen or hear, which in Hebrew we read as:"Shema[Hear or Listen up]Yisrael [Israel]"

so that we may be taught:

> 1. YHVH is "our God" - in Hebrew we read it as, YHVH "Elohaynu".
> 2. YHVH is "ONE"- in Hebrew we read it as, YHVH "EchaD".

In the actual preserved and transcribed Hebrew text of The Torah, the last letter of the first word of the verse, 'Shema', (spelled with 3 Hebrew letters as "shin-mem-AYIN") the word for Hear or Listen up, is the letter 'ayin', and is WRITTEN LARGE. It resembles most closely the English letter 'y', but WRITTEN LARGE.

Additionally, the last letter of the last word of the verse, 'echaD', (spelled with 3 Hebrew letters as "aleph-ches-DAHLID"), the word for ONE, is the letter 'dahlid', and is WRITTEN LARGE. It resembles most closely the number '7', but WRITTEN LARGE.

Why are these letters "WRITTEN LARGE"?

When we look at the word 'echaD', the LARGE DAHLID (pronounced like 'D' but looks like a LARGE '7' is meant to distinguish the word 'echaD', which means 'one' (spelled in Hebrew as: aleph-ches-dahlid) from 'achar' (spelled aleph-ches-raysh) which means 'another' or 'other'. In fact, 'raysh', (which is pronounced like 'R', and also looks like a '7'), the last letter of the Hebrew word 'achar', is WRITTEN LARGE in Exodus 34:14 which states:

"For you shall bow down (worship) to no 'OTHER god' (l'ayl achar in Hebrew), for YHVH, Whose name is Jealous, is a Jealous 'God'."

If 'achar' were read as 'echad', this verse would present an untenable contradiction to all of Torah, and would read: "you shall not bow down to the ONE God."

If 'echad' were read as 'achar', the "Shema" would declare the blasphemous contradiction that YHVH is not ONE but another!

Since the 'dahlid' and 'raysh' closely resemble each other in Hebrew transcription, the reason for the 'dahlid' WRITTEN LARGE, in Deuteronomy 6:4, is manifestly plain. The word that means 'one' (or alone) must not be misread to mean 'another'!

But what about the large Hebrew letter 'AYIN'?

The reason for the 'ayin', the last letter of the first word 'Shema' (spelled 'shin-mem-AYIN' in Hebrew), WRITTEN LARGE, is not so evident. There is another Hebrew word 'Shema', (spelled shin-mem-aleph), which means "perhaps". However, an 'ayin' and an 'aleph' do not look at all alike, so distinguishing these two written words from each other, (as was the case between 'echad' and 'achar'), cannot be a reasonable explanation.

(Coincidentally, the 'aleph' and the 'ayin' are the only two silent letters of the Hebrew alphabet.)

Therefore, our search for truth cannot be confined exclusively to this verse, but must be sought elsewhere in Torah Scripture, for the most precise answer to this question.

Still, the first clue to the LARGE AYIN is indeed within the verse itself; for when you put these two LARGE letters together (AYIN-DAHLID), the word "AD", meaning "WITNESS" is formed. To be sure, Israel is called to be a WITNESS to YAHUWEH before all nations, and for all time.

However, the most sublime truth of this "confession of faith" can be rightly discerned, only by returning to the recognition of Who YHVH is, by studying His Own Word about Himself.

To do so, we now must turn to the call and commission of Moses, in the third chapter of Exodus. Here, the angel-messenger-manifestation of YHVH, Who in this case is YHVH Himself, calls from the midst of the burning bush.

[Compare Exodus 3:2 with Exodus 3:4, which illustrates an interchangeable allusion to YHVH that occurs throughout the Torah. Specifically, sometimes YHVH appears as the "malach YHVH", (the angel-messenger of YHVH), and other times as YHVH Himself, showing both to be YHVH, and not another (created) being.]

It is further along in this encounter that the nature of the 'ONE GOD' is revealed.

Having heard the call and the commission as Elohim's chosen human agent of Israel's deliverance, Moses now asks:

> And Moses said unto 'God' (Elohim): 'Behold, when
> I come unto the children of Israel, and shall say unto
> them: The 'God' of your fathers (Elohay avotaychem)
> has sent me unto you: and they shall say to me:
> What is His Name?
> What shall I say to them?
> And 'God' (Elohim) said unto Moses:
> "I AM THAT I AM";
> and He said, ' Thus you shall say to the children of
> Israel:
> "I AM" has sent me to you.'
> And 'God' (Elohim) said moreover to Moses:
> Thus you shall say to the children of Israel:
> "YHVH", the 'God' (Elohay) of your fathers, the Elohay
> of Abraham, the Elohay of Isaac, the Elohay of Jacob,
> has sent me to you; THIS (YHVH) is MY NAME for
> ever, and THIS (YHVH) is MY memorial unto all
> generations."
>
> (Exodus 3:13-15)

Observe that Moses asks two questions of Elohim, who further describes Himself as the 'Elohay' avotaychem ('God', the 'God' of your fathers).

[Recall that Elohim, the Creator in Genesis is a plural form of El, and means "Mighty Ones". Still, the unity of Elohim is inescapable, since the singular verb for the word 'created' ('bara' in Hebrew) is declared at the very outset in Genesis 1:1. Furthermore, in this encounter (Exodus 3), the plural Elohim is the same Elohay of the fathers, Abraham, Isaac, and Jacob.]

In His answer to Moses' inquiry, Elohim first says

"I AM THAT I AM", proclaiming "I AM" twice, but then immediately follows this by saying:

to the children of Israel, you shall say "I AM", (just once, NOT "I AM" twice) has sent me to you.

Why would the two great "I AM"s audible to Moses, be followed by the single "I AM", specifically intended for the children of Israel.

Indeed Moses had heard the Voice of YHVH Elohim from the midst of the bush, when the Voice called out to him:

"Moses, Moses"
(Exodus 3:4)

At another time, in an earlier age, the patriarch Abraham has heard the Voice of YHVH Elohim at the binding of his son Isaac, when the Voice from heaven called out to him:

"Abraham, Abraham"
(Genesis 22:11)

And finally, when Jacob learned that his beloved son Joseph was not dead, but alive, and invited him and his entire household into Egypt, YHVH Elohim spoke to Israel in the visions of the night, to confirm the covenant and assure his redemption from Egypt, and said to him:

"Jacob, Jacob"
(Genesis 46:2)

Why then, would Moses and Abraham and Jacob hear the Voice of YHVH Elohim call out their names not once, but twice?

The answer to these questions is wondrously revealing and splendidly sublime.

To His chosen servants, Abraham, Moses, and Jacob, YHVH Elohim made Himself more fully known.

In His fulness, He indeed is I AM, (that) I AM!

But this is not just a statement of self existence and eternality; because if that is all that it was, saying "I AM" once, would have sufficed. The two "I AM"s must be understood in the light of the Voice of YHVH Elohim calling out the names of his chosen servants Moses and Abraham and Jacob, not once, but twice!

Furthermore, the two "I AM"s must be understood in light of the "uni-plurality" (or "plural unity") of Elohim.

YHVH Elohim, which translates as "YHVH the Mighty ONES", is concurrently Elohay avotaychem (the El ['God'] of your fathers).

These two Voices are the Voices of the Two "I AM"s that co-exist and make up the One Elohim.

YHVH Elohim commanded to Moses that only One "I AM" (of the Two "I AM"s) be made known to the children of Israel. Indeed, this One Personal Spirit Being was all ready known to the children of Israel for He is the very One

Who was active in Creation, present in the Garden of Eden, visited Abraham and Sarah, appeared as Melchizedek, stood by Jacob in his dream of a ladder with the ascending and descending messengers of Elohim (malachay Elohim in the Hebrew) at the place Jacob called Beth-El (Genesis 28:12,13), met Jacob as "malachay Elohim" at the place Jacob called "Machanayim" meaning "the Pair (two) of camps or companies"(Genesis 32:2,3), wrestled as a Man with Jacob at the ford of Jabbok (Genesis 32:25-31), delivered Israel from Egyptian bondage, was the Rock that gave water in the wilderness, gave the Ten Commandments, met with Moses and his company on Sinai, and appeared to Joshua before Israel's entry into Canaan, the Promised Land.

That One "I AM" is the pre-incarnate WORD, the One Who would, in the fulness of time, be YHVH as Messiah, YHVH incarnate, YHVH as YAHOSHUA. The other "I AM" is His Father. Both share the Name YHVH; Both are ONE. Both are perfect in Unity. (John 14:9-11; 17:21-23)

This then, is the final clue as to why the last letter of 'Shema', the Hebrew word for Hear or Listen up, the letter 'AYIN', is WRITTEN LARGE.

Ayin is the last letter of the Name of the Messiah, YAHOSHUA, and the Hebrew word for salvation, 'Yeshua', the incarnate "I AM" of YHVH, (Whose Hebrew Name, means Salvation of Yah and is spelled in Hebrew as 'Yod-Hay-Vav-Shin-AYIN')!

Testifying to Yahoshua, 'Shema's' (last) silent letter "AYIN", proclaims that He would come as Savior the FIRST time, humbly and meekly, as a Suffering Servant; almost silently, perhaps like the other silent Hebrew letter, "Aleph", the FIRST letter of the Hebrew alphabet, and the FIRST letter of the Word that would become flesh and dwell amongst us, "ET".(Recall Genesis 1:1 and John 1:1)

Yahoshua is the Person of YHVH Who is revealed from Heaven, and He is ONE with His Father in YHVH Elohim (YHVH , the Mighty ONES)!

> [Incidentally, the Hebrew word "echad", found in Deuteronomy 6:4, does not necessarily mean absolute, indivisible unity; but may be used to describe a unity composed of members, as in one nation, one people, or one family. In the context of the Shema, as previously stated, "echad" may also convey exclusivity of worship and devotion to Yahuweh]
>
> The Hebrew word "yachid" is the word for indivisible, absolute unity.]

****

The monotheism of the Christian witness is the Trinitarian confession: that the one 'God' exists eternally in 'three' Persons: a Father, a Son called Jesus Christ, and the Holy Spirit. This non-Scriptural, paganly derived doctrine, can find support neither within the TaNaKh ('T'orah, Prophets ['N'evi'im], and Writings ['K'etuvim], the so-called Old Testament), nor the Messianic Scriptures (the so-called New Testament).

The monotheism of Islam is firm and absolute regarding the indivisible unity of 'God', but the god of Islam, is another (god), whose name is Allah. Such a proposition is not only alien to the Teaching of Torah, but blasphemous. Plainly put, YHVH is the Only true Elohim ['God'], and demands absolute loyalty. (Exodus 34:14; 20:3-7)

But YHVH is neither a mysterious trinity, nor a rigid, indivisible, and absolute other ["achar" in Hebrew] unity.

Of the three, the monotheism of Judaism has been most faithful to the revelation of Torah; but its purest and truest expression is derived, as we have seen, only through the most careful and diligent exegesis of the Hebrew.

Therefore, the proper interpretation and explanation of: "ShemA Yisrael YHVH Elohaynu YHVH EchaD"

> ("Listen up Israel, YHVH IS our 'God', YHVH IS One!")
>
> > (Deuteronomy 6:4)

is this:

YHVH is the Memorial Name for ever of Elohim, the Great "I AM" that "I AM". Revealed to Moses and Abraham and Jacob as the God (Elohim) with Two Voices, only one "I AM" has been visible and audible to the children of Israel and all nations throughout Scripture.

To Jacob, Elohim reveals Himself as an extraordinary stone ("ehben" in Hebrew, meaning 'Father and Son')(Genesis 28:11-22), and as the Messengers of Elohim (Malachay Elohim) in that 'Place' (makom) Jacob named Paired Companies or Camps ("machanayim" in Hebrew)(Genesis

32:2,3), when ALL THE TRUTH and all the mercies were shown unto this servant (Jacob). (Genesis 32:11)

In every appearance of YHVH in Torah, only one "I AM" of this eternal union of TWO Spirits that comprise Elohim, in a sublime inscrutable unity and oneness, has been revealed.

Both the Hebrew Torah and The Messianic Scriptures proclaim:

> "And He said: "You cannot see My face, for man shall not see Me and live."
>
> (Exodus 33:20)

and

> "No man has ever seen Elohim ('God'), the only begotten Son, Who is in the bosom of the Father, He has explained Him."
>
> (John 1:18)

The "I AM" Who created the heavens and the earth, and Who met the patriarchs and prophets in Person and in visions, is the same One Who said: "Before Abraham was, "I AM""; "He who has seen Me has seen the Father"; and "I and My Father are One".

He is the same "I AM" Who came to seek and to save the called out and elect of Israel and the nations.

Finally, He is the same "I AM" Who will come again to redeem all of creation and establish His Eternal Kingdom, starting in Jerusalem, right here on earth.

This is the teaching of Yahuweh Elohim, as told to Moses, as written in The Torah, and ultimately revealed in the Person of Yahoshua the Messiah.

****

The paradigms of the three monotheistic religions must be re-visited. In the final analysis, when all the Scriptural challenges are considered, the Revelation and Truth of Torah and Messiah will be victorious.

Ultimately, this is the pure Torah proclamation to Israel, and the true 'confession of faith' in the "Shema" of Judaism. This is the Hebrew witness to all the world, for all time:

> "Now it will come about that in the last days, the mountain of the house of Yahuweh will be established as the chief of the mountains, and will be raised above the hills; and all nations will stream to it.
> And many peoples will come and say, "Come, let us go up to the mountain of Yahuweh, to the house of the Elohay ('God') of Jacob, that He may teach us concerning His ways, and that we may walk in His paths.
> For the Torah will go forth from Zion,
> And the Word of Yahuweh from Jerusalem."
>
> (Isaiah 2:2.3)

> "And Yahuweh will be King over all the earth; on that day Yahuweh will be One, and His Name will be One!"
>
> (Zechariah 14:9)

CHAPTER 32

The "Blessed Holy Trinity" and the Destiny of Humanity

Winston Churchill, the honorable leader of Great Britain during the Second World War, once said:

"Men occasionally stumble over the truth, but pick themselves up and hurry off, as if nothing had happened."

No observation among men has been more on the mark than this, especially when we carefully study the Scriptures, and "rightly divide the Word of Truth".

In the very first verse of the very first Book of the Scriptures, we know as Genesis, [or B'reishis in Hebrew, meaning "Beginnings"], the third word, in the original Hebrew, proclaims "WHO" in the beginning, created the heavens and the earth.

> "B'reishis bara ELOHIM et ha-shamayim v'et ha-aretz."

which has been translated as:

> "In the beginning GOD created the heavens and the earth."
>
> [Genesis 1:1]

The English translation identifies this Creator as "GOD"; but that 'generic' title, which itself may be traced back to the name of a pagan Teutonic deity known as "GAD", does not begin to properly, accurately, or honestly define the true nature of "ELOHIM".

Although Elohim gramatically points to the plural form of the Hebrew "El", [meaning 'Mighty One'], it most emphatically does not speak of multiple, separate, and distinct 'gods', but rather comprehends and unites all the forces of infinity and eternity in Him as ELOHIM. Indeed, the singular conjugated form of the Hebrew word 'bara' [meaning 'created'] precludes any idea of an ordinary plurality.

The testimony of all of Scripture proclaims that this ELOHIM IS ONE!

Still, while ELOHIM may not be any ordinary or common plurality, neither is He an absolute and indivisible unity.

In fact, early on in Torah, (the Hebrew Scriptures commonly known as the Old Testament)., ELOHIM refers to Himself as "us" and "one of us".

> "And ELOHIM said: Let Us make man in Our image, after Our likeness........"
>
> [Genesis 1:26]

> "And YAHUWEH ELOHIM said: Behold the man is become as one of Us......."
>
> [Genesis 3:22]

"Come, let Us go down, and there confound their
language......."

[Genesis 11:7]

Hence, ELOHIM, while self-existent as ONE, appears, by
His own self disclosure, to be composed, extraordinarily,
and supernaturally, of more than an absolute and indivisible
One.

And it is at this critical juncture that the Christian doctine
of 'the blessed Trinity' would take hold. The Christian
creed and confession would declare that Elohim is a
mysterious triune deity, made up of three divine Beings,
manifest in the Persons of "the Father, the Son, and the
Holy Spirit (Ghost)", all co-equal, yet with different roles
and personalities, maintaining the cryptic dogma of 'God
in Three Persons, "three-in-one", the blessed trinity.

It will surprise many that neither the word trinity, nor the
doctrine of the tri-unity, is any where to be found in either
the Messianic Scriptures (New Testament)*, or the Hebrew
Scriptures (Torah and Tanakh).

*(Careful scrutiny and unbiased scholarship has shown that the verses found
in 1John:5:7,8 are absent in the original manuscripts, and were later added by a
Roman Catholic monk scribe in the 4th century. Such gives truth to the words of
the prophet Jeremiah, where it is written:

"How   can   you   say   we   are   wise,   and
the   Law   of   Yahuweh   is   with   us?
But behold, the lying pen of the scribes has made it
into a lie."

[Jeremiah 8:8])

The trinity is the flower of human reasoning, founded in abstract metaphysics, pagan mythology and religion, political expedience, and the anti-Torah, anti-Jewish sentiments of the early Christian Church. Numerous and prevalent variations of triad deities [three-in one gods] existed long before the Christian era.

In Egypt, they were worshipped as Osiris (whose lineage may be traced to Nimrod-the first ruler of Babylon), Isis (whose lineage may be traced to Semiramis-the mother and wife of Nimrod), and Horus (the son and reincarnation of his father Nimrod).

In Babylon, these three were known as Ninas, Ishtar, and Tammuz. Centuries later, in Rome, this trio of gods were known as Jupiter, Fortuna, and Mercury. All heathen religions, from ancient times the world over, shared a triad deity or trinitarian theology. Even Hinduism has its three in one god known as Trimutri, consisting of Brahma the creator, Vishnu the preserver, and Shiva the destroyer.

Indeed, long before the formalization of Christian dogma and belief, apostasy occurred even in the earliest Messianic faith, within the first 100 years of her existence. [See II Thessalonians 2:7; II Corinthians 11:13-15; I John4:1; Jude 3.]

In due time, the Church fathers turned this Christian apostasy into Christian orthodoxy.

Greek philosophy and gnosticism largely supplanted the Word of Elohim to Moses in Torah, the Teaching of the Hebrew prophets, and the Message and Person of the Jewish

Messiah Yahoshua in the Gospels and 'New Testament' writings. With this evolution of thought and belief, the nature of Elohim became susceptible and subject to the pervasive and deceptive false teaching of the doctrine of the trinity. Allegory, philosophy, mysticism, esoteric and secret knowledge, revelation, and wisdom, strongly and deeply influenced the interpretation of Scriptures in the minds of these false teachers, theologians, and "Christian apologists".

For the Church, the mystery of the Trinity had become the supreme expression of her greatest human minds, fashioning Scripture and Revelation to fit their vain and worldly, ill-conceived and heathen, worthless intellectual notions about ELOHIM. [Colossians 2:8]

Contrarily, The Scriptures instruct the obedient and faithful to "prove all things, and hold fast to that which is good." [I Thessalonians 5:21]

Furthermore, in The Scriptures, any and all "so-called mysteries" are resolved and revealed. [See Mark 4:11; I Corinthians 15:51; Ephesian 1:9; Colossians 1:26]

If the "Holy Spirit" was a Person, that is, one member, as it were, of a triad deity, a tri-unity, then "He" would be the Father of the Son, Yahoshua the Messiah, Who was also Immanu-El, meaning El ['God'] with us.[see Matthew 1:20, Luke 1:35]

Yet, Yahoshua the Messiah never addresses, worships, or prays to such a being. In all of His allusions that illuminate

His relationship with Elohim, He speaks only of His Father.[see John 1:14; John 17:1-26]

Indeed, all the called out and chosen of Elohim are begotten by the Father Elohim [Elohim the Father]. [I Peter 1:3]. But, unlike the Saviour's miraculous birth, the called out sovereignly chosen mortal believer is begotten after a physical and natural birth, not before.

The Person of Elohim Who Fathers the First Born Son and Saviour, is the same Father who begets the many brethren of the First Born Son. [Romans 8:29; I Corinthians 15:20-23; Hebrews 2:10, 11; I John 3:1-2, 5:1-18; Matthew 12:48-50; John 1:12-13, 17:21-23; Ephesians 1:23, 5:30, 3:15; IIPeter 1:4; IPeter 1:3, 23]

The term 'Holy Spirit' is derived from the Hebrew "Ruach Ha-kadosh". Ruach, also means wind, and makes its first appearance in Genesis 1:2 as the 'Ruach Elohim', or Spirit of Elohim, as it hovered over the face of the waters. The Greek word 'pneuma', similarly may be translated as breath or wind, and appears in the Greek manuscripts for the Spirit of Elohim. While assigning gender to 'pneuma', a noun, [as he or him] may be linguistically correct in the Greek language, it wrongly confers personhood on the power or spirit of Elohim. The Spirit has been called comforter; not because it is a person, but because of what it does, emanating from the Source of comfort Himself: Elohim.

In addition, another spirit is spoken of in Scripture: that of the spirit in man. [see Job 32:8; I Corinthians 2:11]

No theologian would suggest that such a spirit is a separate person from the man himself.

As it is true for the human spirit, so too, it is true for the 'divine' Spirit of Elohim.

Furthermore, Scripture declares the pouring out and filling of the "Holy Spirit" on Pentecost. [Acts 2:4], an event that will occur again, in the last days. [Joel 2:28,29; Ezekiel 39:29]

Persons can neither be poured out, nor fill another person.

Unlike the Spirit, Elohim as Father, and Elohim as Son, are never described as being poured out. They are Persons in Elohim; the Spirit is not!

Finally, if the Spirit were co-equal with the Father and the Son, why would blaspheming the Spirit be the only unpardonable sin?

> "Therefore I say unto you, any sin and blasphemy shall be forgiven men, but blasphemy against the spirit shall not be forgiven. And whoever shall speak a word against the Son of Man, it shall be forgiven, but whoever shall speak against the holy spirit, it shall not be forgiven him, either in this age, or in the age to come."
>
> [Matthew 12:31-32; Luke 12:10]

Clearly then, the Spirit of Elohim is not just another member of a trinitarian godhead, but the very mind and power of Elohim that draws and enables one to come to the Father through the Son. Blaspheming against such a power, the very Mind of Elohim, would effectively shut the door to any hope of atonement and forgiveness.

****

The doctrine of the Trinity is based on false wisdom, convoluted reasoning, and sinister deception; a legacy of the Babylonian Mystery Religion. It is another clever contrivance of the adversary Satan, clothed in the language of the pious and religious, a heathenish corruption syncretically joined to the Messianic faith.

Its closed, static, mysterious, and indefinable and incomprehensible triad deity; what Christianity calls "the holy blessed trinity", effectively blinds humanity to its ultimate destiny.

For this is the destiny of humanity:

The quintessential purpose of the Messianic redemption, and the goal of the salvation of mankind, is to bring forth and raise up new immortal members, adopting them into the Family of the eternal Elohim, currently composed now exclusively of Two Spirit Beings:

> 1.The Father,
> 2.and the Word [NOT the Greek 'logos', but the Hebrew "ET" as in ELOHIM-ET in Genesis 1:1], Who has been revealed to the world as The Son of the Father, The First and the Last ["ET" as the Hebrew first letter Aleph and the Hebrew last letter Tav], Immanuel (El ['God']with us), Yahoshua the Messiah. [John 1:1-5, 11-14; John 10:33-36].

"I said you are elohim [gods],
And all of you are sons of the Most High."
[Psalm 82:6]

Yahoshua answered them, "Has it not been written
in your Torah, 'I said, you are elohim [gods]'?"
[John 10:34]

At the end of days, upon the establishment of the Kingdom of Yahuweh on earth, the redeemed of Elohim, will change from mortal to immortal, either translated in life or resurrected from death, like the Saviour Son; and through the power of the spirit of Elohim, are destined to share the throne of the King of Kings, to rule and reign with Him throughout all eternity.

[Revelation 3:21, 2:26, 5:9-10, ICorinthians 6:2-3, John 17:22, 1:11-12; IJohn 3:1-2; IITimothy 2:12; Romans 8:14]

PART VII:
The Way, The Truth, and The Life

CHAPTER 33

The Mystery of the Kingdom

It was proclaimed nearly two thousand years ago by a rabbi who studied under the tutelage of the great Jewish scholar, Rabbi Gamaliel, but it was unknown to Gamaliel. And while it may be discerned in the words of the Torah and Prophets after its proclamation by Rabbi Sha'ul, (Paul, the apostle), the faithful servant of Yahoshua the Messiah, it was a mystery until it was revealed in his writings to the faithful and obedient Gentiles in Rome.

In the eleventh chapter of the Book of Romans in the Messianic Scriptures*, he says:

> "Brothers, I do not want you to be ignorant of this mystery, so that you may not be conceited; Israel has experienced a hardening in part, UNTIL THE FULL NUMBER OF THE GENTILES HAS COME IN.
> **(Romans 11:25)**

Rabbi Sha'ul understood that the Sovereign of the Universe, no respecter of persons, had done this before, as a means to bring honor and esteem (kavod) to Himself, through deliverance and His purpose in election.

Consider the drama of the redemption of Israel from Egypt as recorded in these verses from the second book of the Torah, Shemos [Exodus]:

"So Yahuweh said to Moses, "See, I have made you a 'mighty one' (elohim) to Pharaoh, and Aaron your brother is your prophet. You shall speak all that I command you, and Aaron your brother shall speak to Pharaoh, to let the children of Israel go out of this land. BUT I AM GOING TO HARDEN THE HEART OF PHARAOH, AND SHALL INCREASE MY SIGNS AND MY WONDERS IN THE LAND OF EGYPT".

(Exodus (Shemos) 7:1-3)

"But Yahuweh hardened the heart of Pharaoh, and he did not listen to them, as Yahuweh had said to Moses."

(Exodus(Shemos) 9:12)

"And Yahuweh said to Moses, Go in to Pharaoh, for I have hardened his heart and the hearts of his servants, so that I shall show these signs of Mine before him".

(Exodus)Shemos 10:1)

"However, Yahuweh hardened the heart of Pharaoh, and he would not let them go".

(Exodus)Shemos 10:27)

"And I shall harden the heart of Pharaoh, and he shall pursue them. But I am to be esteemed through Pharaoh and over all his army, and the Egyptians shall know that I am Yahuweh".

(Exodus)Shemos 14:4)

"And for this reason I have raised you up, in order to show you My Power, and in order to declare My Name in all the earth".

(Exodus)Shemos 9:16)

The Sovereign Elohim, according to His will and purpose, modified the will of Pharaoh and his servants, replacing their imperfect will, with His own.

On another occasion, Yahuweh intercedes to not harden the heart, but to cloud perception and impair understanding. But this time He does it with Israel.

> "And Moses summoned all Israel and said to them; "You have seen all that Yahuweh did before your eyes in the land of Egypt to Pharaoh and all his servants and all his land: the great trials which your eyes have seen, those great signs and wonders. Yet to this day Yahuweh has not given you a heart to know, nor eyes to see, nor ears to hear".
> **(Devarim)Deuteronomy29:4)**

> "For Yahuweh has poured over you the spirit of deep sleep, and has closed your eyes; over the prophets, and your chiefs, the seers, He has cast a veil.
> **(Isaiah 29:10)**

In the grand scheme, the purpose and will of the Sovereign Master of the Universe 'trumps' everything else. Even the adversary and accuser of Israel, Satan, is subject to His will. (Job 1:6-12; Isaiah 14:12-20).

When we return to the eleventh chapter of the book of Romans, Sha'ul (Paul) further illuminates the 'mystery of the Kingdom' with these salient points:

> 1. Yahuweh did NOT reject His people Israel whom He foreknew. (verses 1,2)
> 2. At the present time, there is a remnant chosen by grace. (verse 5)

3. The elect (chosen) receive what Israel has sought, but the rest were hardened. (verses 7,8)

4. These (hardened) stumbled, not to fall beyond recovery, but in order that the Gentiles would come to deliverance. (verse 11)

5. Their fall, and their loss means riches for the Gentiles; their rejection means reconciliation of the world. Their fullness will bring greater riches; their acceptance (of Messiah), will be like life from the dead. (verses12, 15)

6. Not only is the first fruits of Israel (the believing chosen remnant) set apart for the Almighty's purpose, but so too is the whole of Israel, root and branch. (verse 16)

7. The branches of Israel were broken off by HaShem (YHWH) so that Gentiles, chosen by His grace, may be grafted in. Born outside of Israel, these strangers to Yahuweh's promise are warned not to boast in their redemption. (verses 17-24).The gifts and call of the Eternal are irrevocable. The election of Israel, as the chosen servant nation, is irrevocable.

Israel did not accept the gospel or Messiah FOR THE SAKE OF THE GENTILES. (verses 28,29)

8. All men have been bound over to disobedience, so the Almighty may have mercy and compassion on all. (verse 32)

9. The deep and rich wisdom and knowledge of Elohim, His unsearchable judgements, His untraceable ways cause us to stand in awe and wonder. (verse 33)

10. AND SO ALL ISRAEL SHALL BE SAVED, (WHEN) THE DELIVERER WILL COME OUT OF ZION. (verse 26)

The 53rd Chapter of the Hebrew prophet Isaiah speaks of a 'suffering servant'. Although classical Jewish thought and

Christian writers have acknowledged this servant as an individual redeeming and atoning Person, modern Jewish scholarship interprets this figure as the nation of Israel. It may be that both views are correct.

The mystery of the Kingdom proposes a suffering Messiah and a suffering Israel. The story of both Yahoshua the Messiah and Yisrael (Israel the Nation and People) resounds with the truth of this claim.

Both the Jewish Messiah, and the Jewish people have been chosen by Yahuweh to redeem the nations.

Now, as then, the secret of this mystery, all ready made plain, remains hidden to the vast majority of Jews and Gentiles.

But the Scriptures assure us that this mystery, like all of Yahuweh's Truth, will ultimately be uncovered, perfectly according to His plan, at exactly the right time.

> "And He will destroy on this mountain the face of the covering which covers all the people, and the veil that is spread over all the nations.
> He will destroy death forever; and Yahuweh Elohim will wipe away the tear from all faces; and the shame of His people will He remove from off all the earth, for Yahuweh has spoken it. And men will say on that day: This is our Elohim, for Whom we have waited that He would help us. This is Yahuweh for Whom we have waited. Let us be glad and rejoice in His deliverance."
> **(Isaiah 25: 7-9)**

CHAPTER 34

The Plan of Salvation

The Hebrew Scriptures we know as Torah contains history, allegory, prophecy, wise instruction, inspiration, redemption, epiphany, and revelation.

While not always plainly evident, its essential, over-arching message of personal and national salvation actually permeates all of Torah in word and in spirit.

Although hidden and concealed to so many for so long, the three pilgrim festivals of Israel powerfully portray the Eternal plan of salvation, elegantly and exquisitely.

To Jerusalem, three times a year; at Passover, Pentecost, and Tabernacles, they would come and gather and worship. (Exodus 23:14-17)

From every corner of this Promised Land, the sons of Israel would come to the Great Temple for their appointment with YHWH, the Creator, the Redeemer of Israel.

Intimately tied to the times of planting and harvest, on first appearance, they seem to be agricultural festivals and nothing more.

But on closer examination, they are something else, and so much more.

In the first month of the Scriptural year, in the month of Aviv (Nisan), on the fourteenth day, is the Passover of YHWH (Pesach l'YHWH as found in Exodus 12:11 and Leviticus 23:5).

This is the first pilgrim festival.

It is a day of momentous import, when the Eternal Himself entered into history to redeem His people from death, and deliver them from the bondage of Egyptian slavery and spiritual darkness.

The Passover day is immediately followed by the seven day Feast of Unleavened Bread (Chag ha-Matzos l'YHWH as found in Leviticus 23:6). It begins with a 'sabbath' (a day of rest and no work, and distinct from the weekly 7th day Sabbath), on the fifteenth day of this first month and ends with a 'sabbath' on the 22nd day.

On the day after the first weekly 7th day Sabbath after Passover, during the week of Unleavened Bread, is the offering of the first fruits, waved by the priest as the sheaf or omer of barley.

From this day onward, Israel is commanded to count seven complete Sabbaths (49 days or 7 weeks (Shavuot) to the 50th day, the day after the seventh Sabbath. On this 50th day, two loaves baked with leaven are presented as a new grain offering to YHWH.

As the barley and one year old unblemished male lamb was waved and offered on the first day of counting, so too are two loaves and two yearling male lambs waved and offered on this 50th day of counting. This 50th day, the Pentecost, is known variably as Yom ha-Bikurim, the day of First-Fruits or harvest, as Shavuos or "Weeks", and in Talmudic literature, as Atzeret or the "concluding festival" to Passover.

This is the second of the three pilgrim festivals.

So, at the very begining of the year, in the spring and early summer, the redeemed people of YHWH, are commanded to commemorate one day of Passover, 7 days of Unleavened Bread, one day of First Fruits of the harvest with the barley sheaf or omer, the counting of the 7 Sabbaths (the 49 day counting of the omer), and the 50th day of the count known as Shavuos, Pentecost, Yom ha-Bikurim, or Atzeret.

That these days signify agricultural events is self evident. That there is deep spiritual significance is not as plain, but it is surely there.

Passover is, at its very core, the deliverance of a people from death to life.

> "and the blood shall be a token to you upon the houses where you are; and when I see the blood, I will pass over you and there shall no plague be upon you to destroy you."
>
> **(Exodus 12:13)**

The Festival of Unleavened bread is a complete (that is, 7 day) removal of leaven from this redeemed people. Throughout the Scriptures, **leaven**, which puffs up through fermentation, represents **sin.**

During this week of separation from sin, the omer (sheaf) of the first fruits of the harvest is offered with one male lamb. Seven Sabbaths, or seven weeks, are counted from this day. During this cycle of seven weeks, comprised of seven Sabbaths and seven days each, the redeemed people are completely imbued with the fullest realization that the first fruit of the spring harvest is not their accomplishment, but the Eternal's. The cycle concludes with the 50th day offering of two leavened loaves and two male lambs.

Within the first week of Unleavened Bread, the First Fruit (barley) is brought forth, according to the plain words of Torah Scripture, on the day after the weekly [7th day] Sabbath that follows Passover (and not the day after the first day of Unleavened Bread, a 'festival sabbath' as conceived by rabbinic interpretation and practiced by traditional Judaism). By joining this wave offering of the omer of barley with a one year old unblemished male lamb, we can "see" again, the Pesach or Passover lamb reappearing. The blood of this lamb saved Israel from the destroying angel and death. But in this event, the lamb is symbolically alive again, on the day after the Sabbath, with the freshly born omer (barley sheaf) of the first fruit of the harvest.

This Jewish ritual, commanded in Torah, and practiced over and over again, in each and every year, prophetically pictured the Messiah Who died to save, only to live again.

He is the first fruits of those that are asleep, and vividly portrays the future resurrection in the Great Plan of Salvation. (1Corinthians15:20, 36-38, 42)

On Shavuos (Pentecost), the 2 lambs and 2 leavened loaves symbolize the Redeemer of Israel and the Nations, the Saviour of Jew and Gentile alike. As leaven represents sin, these loaves are an accurate picture of the condition of all humankind.

[The loaves may also picture the double portion of Manna, the heavenly bread given to Israel in the wilderness, before the Sabbath.]

The greatest Sabbath is yet to come, when all humanity will come to know the Redeemer of Israel, the Creator of Heaven and Earth, and the King of Kings, Who will reign for all eternity.

As we temporally travel across the dry terrain of the hot and arid landscape of summer in this Promised Land, we look forward to the third and final pilgrimage festival as ordained in the Torah, Chag ha-Sukkos, the Feast of Booths, or Tabernacles (Lev. 23:34).

It commences on the 15th day of the seventh month at the full moon. In like fashion, it is the autumn image of Chag ha-Matzos, the springtime Feast of Unleavened Bread, which begins on the 15th day of the first month at the full moon.

On the first day of Tabernacles, at this Feast of Ingathering at year's end (Exodus 23:16), on this day of no servile work, this festival 'sabbath', the people are commanded to rejoice. With the fruit of beautiful and goodly trees, palm branches, boughs of thickly leafed trees, and willows of the brook, they are to rejoice before YHWH and dwell in booths for seven days. (Lev. 23:39-44)

On these seven days of Sukkos (Tabernacles), the Temple bullock sacrifices numbered 70, intended as an atonement for all the nations. This unique commemoration, rooted in the typical atonement ritual of Temple sacrifice, casts the priests of Israel into the role of intermediary for not just the Jewish nation, but for all nations. This separation from sin parallels the separation portrayed in the Festival of Unleavened Bread.

Interestingly, it is not the seventh day of this Festival that is reckoned as a 'day of assembly' and rest, after Tabernacles is ended, but a separate day, known as "Yom Shemini", the Eighth Day.

As the atoning day of Passover precedes and propels the sanctifying and commemorative days that follow it (Unleavened Bread, First Fruits, and Pentecost or Atzeret [the Feast of Conclusion]); the Day of Trumpets (Yom Teruah-"Rosh Hashana") and Atonement (Yom Kippur) precede and propel Tabernacles (Sukkot) and the Eighth Day of Conclusion or "Shemini Atzeret".

The year end harvest at this Festival of Ingathering is at once both agricultural and spiritual. The Torah, with its command to rejoice with the land's bounty, and to offer the 70 bullocks in the Jerusalem Temple show this plainly.

As Pentecost was and is the "Atzeret" or conclusion to Passover and the spring festivals, so too is Yom Shemini, (the Eighth Day), Shemini Atzeret, the conclusion to the Day of Atonement and the autumn festivals.

The Plan of Salvation appears and reappears throughout all of Scripture.

The sabbatical years, the yearly cycles of 7, and the (50th) year of Jubilee mirrors the annual 49 days of counting the omer and the Pentecost. (Lev. 25, Deut. 15:1). These years are marked by rest for the land, remission of debts, and the ultimate return of the land to its rightful owner.The land is not to be sold permanently, for we are but aliens and sojourners with YHWH, and the land belongs to YHWH and to Him alone. (Lev. 25:23).

They culminate the Torah's rhythm and refrain, beginning with Sabbath on the 7th day of the week, Pentecost at the end of 7 Sabbaths, the 7th month of the year, abundant with special days of remembrance, and concluding, at last, with the Eighth Day.

On this Last Great Day, this Eighth Day of Conclusion, Yahuweh's plan of salvation has reached its fullest culmination.

Israel's atonement, and his separation from sin, is pictured in the first harvest of spring, and the Messianic redemption.

The latter harvest of autumn is for all nations. It gloriously ascends to the ultimate purpose of the Plan of Salvation: the return of all the earth to its rightful owner, the Redeemer of Israel and the Nations, the Righteous Messiah and King.

In the majestic sweep of these three great pilgrim festivals, the city of Jerusalem is always the focus, and ultimately the destination of all humanity.

Passover and Unleavened Bread commemorate the miraculous salvation and separation of YHWH's people Israel, from slavery and death and sin. In the Pesach, which is Hebrew for the lamb that was sacrificed, is pictured the Suffering Servant of Israel, the Messiah Who must die to bring redemption.

The Festival of First Fruits and the Pentecost reflect the great bounty of YHWH and the gift of His Torah. In the days known as Yom ha-Bikurim (Day of First Fruits) and Shavuos (Weeks or Pentecost) we see the Resurrected Messiah and and the outpouring of His Spirit, the Ruach ha-Kodesh.

Finally, in Tabernacles and the Eighth Day of Conclusion and Assembly, we are reminded again of the Presence of the Eternal in all that we have, in all that we do, and in all that we are.

Prophetically, these last days of the pilgrim's ascent to Jerusalem point to the conclusion of the plan of salvation, and the ultimate dwelling of the Almighty Eternal King and Messiah with His people........ in the New Jerusalem, on the new earth.

The great confession of Scripture is this:

"Hear O' Israel, YHWH is our Elohim ('God'), YHWH is ONE.

(Deut. 6:4)

Blessed be His
honored Kingdom forever and ever."

This is the sublime message of the pilgrim festivals of YHWH.

It is the heart of the Gospel taught by the Messiah.

Indeed it is the message of all of Torah.

Its call resounds in the hearts and minds of the willing and the chosen continually.

It is the resonant melody of the universe.

****

The final movement of this wondrous symphony is just about complete.

What an awesome opening night that will be!

P.S. The Hebrew Prophet Daniel speaks of a prophecy of 70 weeks of years, when there will be an end to sin, atonement will be complete, and everlasting righteousness will come. (Daniel 9:24).

Here, the prophetic word of Scripture proclaims the pattern of the plan of salvation that pervades all of Torah.

CHAPTER 35

"The New Cre-8-tion"

The Scriptures proclaim in its opening verse, unequivocally, and without apology, that the Almighty Elohim is the Creator of heaven and earth.

For six days the Eternal Elohim, in the Power of His Word alone, created on the first day: light; on the second day: the firmament or sky; on the third day: sea, land, and vegetation; on the fourth day: heavenly bodies to give light by day and by night, and the stars; on the fifth day: sea creatures and birds; and finally, on the sixth day: land animals and penultimately, man, that sole part of creation made in the image and likeness of Elohim.

The work of Creation was now completed, supernaturally performed in six days; but Elohim was not finished, for it is the 'seventh day' that culminates the creation process.

> "And on the seventh day, Elohim finished His work which He had made, and He rested ("shabbot" is the Hebrew for rested) on the seventh day from all His work which He had made. And Elohim blessed the seventh day, and set it apart; because that in it, He rested from all His work which Elohim created to make."
>
> **(Genesis 2:2-3)**

The goal of Elohim's creation, on the surface, appears to be just a day of rest from the other six days of toil and labor. But the seventh day is much more than that. Firstly, it is not described like the other days, which conclude with the phrase: "And there was evening, and there was morning, the 1st, 2nd, 3rd, 4th, 5th, or 6th day.

Secondly, and most importantly, the 7th day is the only day that is blessed by Elohim, and set apart by Him. While the Creator invites, indeed, commands us (to) rest on the seventh day, as He did, so as to grow in His likeness and image, this blessed and consecrated day, points our spiritual vision to the future. (Exodus 20: 8-11, Isaiah 56:1-8, Hebrews 4:9)

The blessed seventh day, instituted at creation, establishes a pattern that repeats throughout all of Scripture; that pattern is the 'cycle of 7's'.

This is no more evident than in the twenty-third chapter of Leviticus which proclaims the appointed seasons and convocations of Yahuweh.

But within this chronological scheme of appointed times and consecrated assemblies is also a template that may reveal yet another pattern, which may be thought of as a 'cycle of 8's'. Careful and diligent scrutiny will enable us to see how this unfolds.

After the account of the weekly sabbath, to be observed on the 7th day, follows (the proclamation of) the annual convocation of the Passover, to be observed on the 14th day (a cycle of two 7's) in the first month, followed by the 7 Days of Unleavened Bread, which begins on the fifteenth day of the first month (two cycles of '7' + 1, followed by "the waving of the sheaf of First Fruits" on the "morrow after the sabbath" (one cycle of '7' + 1), followed by the counting of seven sabbaths (sheva shabbatot in the Hebrew, culminating in the day after the seventh sabbath known as Pentecost, the 50th day) (seven cycles of '7' + 1), followed by the first day of the 7th month, the day of horn blasts (observed as "Rosh Hashana" also known as "Yom Teruah").

At this point, for one unique day only, the pattern changes; the next convocation comes on the tenth day of the seventh month, Yom Kippur, the central and supreme Day of Atonement.

But the pattern is resumed once again, as Yom Kippur is followed by the first day of the Feast of Tabernacles, which comes on the fifteenth (day) of the seventh month. Tabernacles is observed for seven days, and like the Feast of Unleavened Bread, begins on the 15th day of the (seventh) month, (two cycles of '7' +1).

****

The last convocation is distinct, and boldly breaks with the pattern of 7's. It is the final and concluding 'assembly of the "Eighth Day" (Shemini Atzeret) (Leviticus 23:36, 39), and in its uniqueness, may be declaring a new pattern for a New Creation (Cre-8-tion). It is also, the Eighth consecrated convocation of solemn rest in the series of appointed seasons of Yahuweh, that began with the weekly "7th day sabbath", when no work was to be done, and culminates with the yearly "8th day sabbath" ('va-yom ha-shemini shabbaton' in the Hebrew).

Following the 7th day of Tabernacles, which itself came to be known as an echo of the Day of Atonement in later times, this 8th day opens the door to the World to Come (Olam Habah).

The present order reflects the plan of creation as recorded in Genesis, and the pattern of seven (and multiples of 7 as in "70") permeates its very being, appearing in social customs (Genesis 29:20,27;33:3;50:10; Judges 14:12,17; 1Samuel 31:13), historical events (Genesis 41), nations (Genesis 7:1), prophecy (Daniel 9:24-27), sacrifice (Leviticus 23:18), blood sprinkling (Lev. 14:16), jubilee years (Lev. 25:8), prophetic symbols (Revelation 1:4, 5:1, 8:2, 13:1, 15:6, 15:7, 17:10), Messiah's utterances in the final moments of His earthly life (Luke 23:34, 43, 46; John 19:26, 28, 30; Matthew 27:46), appointed elders (Exodus 24:1,9), disciples (Luke 10:1), and in forgiveness (Matthew 18:21,22).

The new order, reflecting the pattern of the new heaven and new earth in the world to come, is hinted at in the Hebrew Torah, especially in Leviticus 23.

The First Day of Unleavened Bread, the 15th day of the first month, is celebrated, in effect on the 8th day, following the pattern of two cycles of 7. It marks the beginning of sinlessness as symbolized by unleavened bread (matzoh).

The beginning of the spring harvest celebration of "First Fruits" is observed on the morrow after the sabbath of the week of Unleavened Bread, which in effect, is an '8th day'. It symbolizes new life from the ground and may picture the first fruits of the resurrection, as in the life of the Messiah, appearing after His Sabbath resurrection on the

8th day. (Lev. 23: 9-14,; Exodus 34:26; Deuteronomy 26:3-10; Romans 11:16; 1Corinthians 15: 20, 23; James 1:18).

The last day of the seven day Feast of Unleavened Bread is the 8th day after Passover. It may symbolize the completed separation from sin, as pictured by eating only that which is without leavening.

Pentecost, or the 50th day, is observed on the day after the seventh sabbath, and is, in effect, an 8th day, following the cycle of seven 7's. It marks the completion of the spring's barley harvest, and is commemorated in part, by the presentation of two leavened loaves, symbolizing Israel and the gentile nations (Lev. 23: 17, 20), and the coming of the Spirit of Elohim upon the Jewish pilgrims in Jerusalem marking the beginning of His new creation (Acts 2:1-47).

Similarly, the Jubilee, or the 50th year, is observed in the year after the seven sabbaths of years, following the sabbatical year and the cycle of seven 7's, and is, in effect, an 8th day (Leviticus 25:8). The Jubilee year, this type of 8th day, is a time proclaimed by the sound of the horn (shofar) on the Day of Atonement, and is observed by emancipation, redemption, homecoming, justice, and return. Freed from the slavery to sin, full redemption in this new birth is now possible; and in the pattern of the new creation, it is consecrated and ordained.

The seventh day of Tabernacles, or Sukkot in the Hebrew, the final day in the annual commemoration of the latter harvest, was a time of profuse gratitude and thanksgiving to the Eternal. But it was also characterized by the Temple priesthood's fulfilling the ordained offering of the total sum of 70 bullocks of sacrifice at the altar, corresponding to the 70 nations of the world, representing an atonement for the whole of mankind.

The Eighth Day of Assembly vividly and dramatically presents the possibility of yet another Creation narrative. The seeds of the story of a wonderful new future began with the Resurrection of Israel's Messiah, the Redeemer of all nations. It is veiled in the pattern of this present order, but will be plainly revealed in the world to come.

In that splendid and wonderful (8th) Day, all things will be made new.

> "Remember these things, O Jacob,
> And Israel, for you are My servant; I have formed you to be My servant,;
> O Israel, you will not be forgotten by Me.
> I have wiped out your transgressions like a thick cloud,
> And your sins like a heavy mist.
> Return to Me, for I have redeemed you."
> **(Isaiah 44:21,22)**

> "And Yahuweh (the LORD) of hosts will prepare a lavish banquet for all peoples on this mountain;
> A banquet of aged wine, choiced pieces with marrow, and refined aged wine;
> And on this mountain He will swallow up the face of the covering which is over all the peoples,
> Even the veil which is stretched over all nations.
> He will swallow up death for all time,
> And Yahuweh Elohim (the LORD God) will wipe tears away from all faces,
> And He will remove the reproach of His people from all the earth;

For Yahuweh has spoken.
And it will be said in that day,
Behold, this is our Elohim for whom we have waited
that He might save us.
This is Yahuweh for Whom we have waited;
Let us rejoice and be glad in His salvation.

(Isaiah 25:6-9)

"And I saw a new heaven and a new earth; for the first
heaven and the first earth passed away, and there is
no longer any sea.
And I saw the holy city, new Jerusalem, coming down
out of heaven from the Eternal, made ready as a bride,
adorned for her husband.
And I heard a loud voice from the throne, saying,
"Behold the tabernacle of the Eternal is among men,
and He shall dwell among them, and they shall be
His people, and the Eternal Himself shall be among
them.
And He shall wipe away every tear from their eyes,
and there shall no longer be any death; there shall no
longer be any mourning, or crying, or pain, the first
things have passed away."
And He Who sits on the throne said, "Behold, I am
making all things new."

(Revelation 21:1-5)

The Creator of the Universe is also its Redeemer.

As a sign of the everlasting covenant between Abraham, and
his descendants, and Yahuweh Elohim, the circumcision
was commanded on the eighth day. (Genesis 17:12; Romans
2:29, 4:11; Deuteronomy 10:16, 30:6; Colossians 2:11)

On the eighth day, the day after His sabbath, there will be
a New and Greater Sabbath for all creation. A universe

that is healed from all brokeness and decay, all sorrow and corruption, all sadness and death, will be the New Order [of things].

It is to this New Creation that all Sabbaths, all prophecy, and all of Scripture point.

It is the essential message of the Gospel of the Kingdom spoken of by the Messiah.

It is the ultimate purpose of the Eternal's plan, revealing His perfect, just, and righteous character.

****

The Good News of the World to Come is the Hope of Israel and the Nations; and when it does come, it will come as "The New Cre-8-tion".

Epilogue:
The World to Come

CHAPTER 36

The Final War

A Unified Theory of Theology and History

> "'I am Yahuweh, and there is none else.
> There is no Elohim ('God') besides Me.
> I will gird you though you have not known Me. That
> men may know from the rising to the setting of the
> sun that there is none but Me. I am Yahuweh, and
> there is no other.
> Forming the light and creating darkness; making
> peace, and creating evil; I Yahuweh do all these
> things."
>
> **[Isaiah 45:5-7]**

The purpose and workings of Elohim since Creation and throughout history has been carefully planned, assiduously arranged, and strategically ordained. Nonetheless, there is a common belief (wish) that 'God' is incapable of the things attributed to Him in the words of Isaiah the prophet. According to this misguided teaching, anything man does not perceive as personally beneficial, meaningful, gratifying or good, cannot be of 'God'', and therefore must be of the 'devil' (Satan, the adversary and accuser). Yet, those who hold to this concept insist that this 'God' is all knowing, all powerful, and that:

> "by Him all things were created and made, both in
> heaven and on earth, visible and invisible, whether
> thrones or dominions or rulers or authorities-all

> things have been created by Him and for Him. And
> He is before all things, and in Him all things hold
> together."
>
> **[Colossians 1:16,17]**

Isaiah 14:12-32, Ezekiel 28:2-19, and Luke 10:18 all proclaim that the created being Satan, who rules the nations (Ephesians 6:11-12), finds his origin from heaven itself.

It is intellectually untenable and theologically inconsistent to believe that the Omniscient and Omnipotent Creator Elohim could not have foreseen the defective flaw of character in this diabolical being.

Yet, that is just what traditional popular religion believes.

The Scriptures reject dualism completely and categorically.

There can be no truth to the claim that the forces of good and evil are in constant conflict because such powerful opponents of Elohim ['God'] might actually win the battle and the war.

The instigator of this broken and fallen world did not catch Elohim ['God'] unaware and off guard. And the remedy for its chaos and despair, through the Torah and the Messiah, was not an afterthought. Indeed, the players and the play on the world's stage were all conceived in the Mind of Elohim before creation. There was nothing unforeseen, nothing contingent. All was known by Him who sees the end from the beginning.(Revelation 21:6).

From the purposeful placement of Adam and Eve with the deceiving adversary Satan in Eden's Garden, to their expulsion into the wilderness of an unknown world, to Cain's jealousy leading to his brother Abel's murder, to sibling rivalries, to tribal conflicts, to wars between nations, to nuclear catastrophes, to worldwide epidemics, to poverty, injustice, slavery, oppression and disease, to anti-Semitism and the holocaust, to the death of the Messiah, and the death of every man, Elohim knew it all from the beginning.

Why did He allow it to go forth?

Why didn't he stop it?

How can we reconcile this apparent dilemma of a "good 'God'" who is ultimately responsible for a seemingly corrupt and evil creation?

We can; and the reason we can is because the answer is found in His written Word.

All of it, from the beginning, was part of the Master's Plan!

His supreme sovereignty surely gives 'God' the right to do whatever He pleases, but this does not adequately explain it.

Hence, fatalism, nihilism, and despair is not the answer.

Traditional apostate religion offers sentimental nostrums, or retreats from the challenge, calling it all a great impenetrable mystery.

Therefore, none of these are satisfactory, for they fail to apprehend the revelation of Elohim ['God'] plainly written in His Word.

****

The trials and tribulations of humanity are not haphazard, incidental, inadvertent, or unintended. While the forces of spiritual darkness are exercised within the domain of the Adversary and his rebellious partners (both human and "demonic") in their hopeless efforts to win control of this earth, the ultimate source of their sustained battle is Elohim Himself.

It has to be; it cannot be otherwise; "for in Him all things were created and made, and in Him all things are held together!"

This view of Elohim and history forces us to relinquish our perception of creation and The All-Mighty as unfortunate victims of a brilliant and powerful army of renegade spirits led by Satan. In its place, we embrace the true nature and character of Elohim as revealed in His Word, to champion a Scripturally based muscular theology, where Yahuweh is in control every step of the way.

When bad things happen, we can come to know that these do not happen in a vacuum, but are the result of sin, the transgression of the "Law of Elohim". [1John 3:4]

Turning away from sin in repentance (teshuvah in the Hebrew), and running into the "arms" of Elohim, we find atonement, and unite with the Ruler of the Universe. Out of suffering and slavery in this world, will come (potentially), surrender and submission to the yoke of the Kingdom of Heaven, and the development of the character of Yahuweh Elohim in his creation, man. In this way, Yahuweh's strategy of 'tough love' will have achieved its intended purpose.

> The most important lesson to be learned in life is this:
> "Trust in Yahuweh with all of your heart (will), and lean not on your own understanding,
> In all your ways acknowledge Him,
> And He will make your paths straight.
> Do not be wise in your own eyes;
> Fear Yahuweh and turn away from evil.
> It will be healing to your body,
> And refreshment to your bones."
> **(Proverbs 3:5-8)**

All of Scripture, indeed, all of human experience leads us to these inescapable conclusions:

To win the battle and secure victory in the final war:

Man alone is insufficient.

Elohim ['God']Alone is Self-sufficient.

Elohim ['God'] and man together, according to His Master Plan, will be all-sufficient.

And so the sufferings we endure now will be counted as nothing when compared to what splendor lies ahead, vindicating the Name of Yahuweh, and establishing His Kingdom on this earth.

****

"For I consider that the sufferings of this present time are not worthy to be compared with the splendor that is to be revealed to us.

For the anxious longing of the creation waits eagerly for the revealing of the sons of Elohim ['God'].

For the creation was subjected to futility, not of its own will, but because of Him who subjected it, in hope that the creation itself also will be set free from its slavery to corruption into the freedom of the splendor of the sons of Elohim ['God']".

(Romans 8:18-21)

"And we know that Elohim causes ALL things to work together for good to those who love Elohim, to those who are called according to His purpose."

(Romans 8:28)

CHAPTER 37

Come Out of the Wilderness, Come into The Light

Epilogue

From his earliest recorded memory, man has sought to understand his identity, place, and purpose in the universe. But by rejecting his Creator's perfect will and untainted revelation as irrelevant or insufficient, he has instead formed humanly engineered religions as the means to answer his deepest yearnings. While some might argue that these efforts have ennobled the human spirit and elevated civilization, they have, on the whole, missed the mark. Whether inspired by natural inclination or spiritual deception, they have failed to liberate man from the twin prisons of his sinful nature and his own mortal end, offering only delusions and false hopes about his earthly existence and life in the hereafter. And even where Revelation can be found, syncretism leading to concession, compromise, alliance, and collusion with heathen beliefs has resulted in the adulteration of every faith man has ever known.

The story of Israel's centuries of bondage and oppression in Egypt, his miraculous redemption, his wandering in the wilderness, and the many wars he fought to gain entry into the Promised Land is familiar to anyone who has read the Hebrew Scriptures. Struggling with his destiny as a peculiar people, as a nation set apart, as a chosen race, his special relationship with The Eternal has been both a boon and a burden to him. At times, he would falter, and join with his neighbors in faith and practice, losing sight of the One True Deliverer, Yahuweh Elohim-but a remnant of Israel would be forever preserved to repent and return, so as to remain steadfast and true to the Covenant faith.

****

The story of Israel is the story of all people of all nations who are called and chosen to join this forward guard of the Almighty. [Matthew 22:14]

Today, people of every stripe, sense that history is at a cross road, a turning point. Some even say that history, as we know it, is at an end. No one can know this with certainty.

But if we are in the last days of 'business as usual', it would not be unreasonable to look beyond the ordinary and fallible, to the extraordinary and transcendent, for the way out of this dark and deluded world. Indeed, the time is long overdue to be liberated from cleverly contrived customs, corrupted creeds, deceptive dogma, and disparate doctrines, (all) masquerading as 'truth'.

False prophets, and the apostate religions of men, have led too many of us astray.

****

"The Light in the Wilderness" champions the premise that perfect righteousness, enduring truth, and redemption unto everlasting life, can be received solely and uniquely through Revelation and Election.

This is the pattern plainly portrayed throughout the Scriptures. In essence, it is the only journey that every called out and chosen servant of the Kingdom of Heaven must take.

If you hear His voice, it is never too late to begin.

We have all waited in stupor long enough.

It is time to come out of the world's darkness.

It is time to come out of the wilderness and into His light!

Appendix:
Meeting the Author

My Personal Journey:

The Discovery of Truth

Norman Martin Wolk

We all travel our own path. We would like to believe that most of the time, and for much of the way, that we, in our conscious choices, have created a unique map.

Yet our personal journey reflects much more than the sum of all the logical decisions of our lifetime. Beyond the emotional and subconscious influences that move us, and far distant from the familiar internal and external environments in which we live and breathe, there is a Transcendence that leads to wonder. We look in awe at such a Power.

Still, the natural mind bristles at the possibility of this, for it defies the most elegant methods of observation and measure. If it cannot be observed or measured, it cannot be real. If it does not cooperate with the principles of scientific validation, it is relegated to the realm of the "soft" sciences of sociology or psychology. Whatever "truths" are derived from this Transcendent Power are personal and subjective; tainted, as it were, by the culture, the community, the family, the unique signature and neurobiology of the proclaimer. Such declarations of "truth" may be embraced by countless others. They become the religious truths......

useful, meaningful, valuable, cherished.....but ultimately personal.

Their worth is limited by the container in which they are preserved.

So we have Christian truth, Jewish truth, Hindu truth, Moslem truth, Buddhist truth, and many, many others.

"What is true for you is not necessarily true for me" says the Jew to the Christian to the Moslem to the Buddhist to the.... Well, you get the idea.

What if there is a Truth that transcends the religious containers in which it has been deposited? And what if this Truth, while not measureable or observable according to the natural repeatable principles of science remains True nonetheless? Indeed, the possibility of science, with its foundation of observation and repeatability postulates, albeit by inference, an order to the universe......cosmos and not chaos!

Such a Truth does exists! It is a Truth that is infinite, and therefore, immeasurable. A Truth that is spiritual, and therefore, super-natural. It is resistant to the rules of engagement of the natural mind.

Infinite and Spiritual, it defies classification, and is diminished by the 'religious containers' into which it has been placed.

The wall of partition between 'science' and 'religion' has been constructed not by this Transcendent Power, but by humanity.

And now, in the 21st century, the wall seems almost insurmountable.

We are a people divided, not just from one another, but from ourselves. We compartmentalize in our minds the Reality of the One Who can take down this wall.

This book is about the observations and conclusions of a gentile "Christian" and a "Jew" who have discovered, separately and together, the Power that can dissolve the forces that divide us from each other and from ourselves.

And while each of us will undoubtedly continue to travel our own unique journey, we are confident that all the time, and all along the way, He was, is, and will always be there.

You see, the infinite, immeasurable, spiritual, super-natural, transcendent Power is not just a forceful influence, but [is] a Person. The record of His dealings with us and His universe are recorded in the Scriptures (the Torah, the Prophets, the Writings, the Gospels, the Letters), proclaiming events that happened in real time to real people.

Even today, on our own path, He is there.

In truth, my personal journey has never been a solitary adventure. Indeed, whether we believe it or not, we never walk alone!

A VIEW FROM ABOVE

Personal Reflections of the Author

<u>Norman Martin Wolk</u>

<u>My Testimony of Faith</u>

Looking backward in time, across 55 years of lifetime experiences, it is a genuine challenge to filter out the significant events from the mundane, the life changing from the ordinary. While the task is difficult, it is not impossible. What I have chosen to write has been through the "refiner's fire" many, many times.

So, the accounts recorded here will be only the essential framework upon which the Master has designed His message.

I was born in Beth El Hospital in Brooklyn, New York on September 26, 1950, the middle of three children, and the second son of my mom and dad. Raised in a secure, traditional, and observant Jewish home, I began my formal religious education when I was eight. At Congregation B'nai Israel, a modern orthodox synagogue and school, I was trained in Torah, Talmud, Hebrew language, Jewish history and heritage. My world view and self concept was being shaped in deeply powerful ways, although my young mind was not fully aware of it. The Book of Proverbs declares:

"Teach a child the way he should go, and when he is old, he will not depart from it."

These words were inscribed on my 'Hebrew school' report card, and reminded me every few months that the Potter was molding His clay.

My religious studies continued up to and beyond my 13th year, the year of my Bar Mitzvah, when a Jewish young man is reckoned an accountable adult before the community.

Before leaving for university, I studied with a young Hasidic orthodox rabbi. It was here that I asked about the dominant religious faith of our nation, Christianity. It was 1967, and his response was almost prophetic in its broad tolerance.

Rather than dismissing my question, he respected my sincere quest for truth. And while I had only attended afternoon and Sunday school for five years, and not yeshiva (all day religious parochial school), I was well grounded in my ancestral faith.

The rabbi's answer was both comforting and unsettling. He said that the Christian faith was true for the Gentiles, but not for us. As Jews, we could be secure in knowing that Judaism was our heritage, and our truth. The existence of mutually exclusive claims of authenticity did not resonate well for me. Still, at least for then, it would have to do.

I began college when I was 16 years old. I read the 'New Testament' for the first time. At the same time, I read two popular books by Dr. Hugh Schoenfeld of Britain's Oxford University; "The Passover Plot", and "Those Incredible

Christians". I yielded to the scholarship of Dr. Schoenfeld, and became convinced that the Hasidic rabbi had answered me wisely.

Still, contact with people of faith, always important to me, became all the more so, in the secular, and revolutionary culture of college in the last years of the 1960's. I joined the Lutheran Club, the Newman Club(Catholic), an Interfaith Forum, and Hillel (Jewish). The experiences were richly rewarding, and enhanced my college years greatly. Nonetheless, despite sincere testimony from zealous and dedicated Christians, my belief and commitment to Judaism was unshakeable. I celebrated their faith, as I did my own.

I lived out the political correctness of tolerance long before it was in vogue.

I achieved a life long dream when I was accepted to the University of Southern California School of Medicine in Los Angeles. Twenty one years old, and 2500 miles from home, all kinds of products in the marketplace of ideas were available to me. Despite the distance from the familiar, I earnestly sought the familiar in this new place. I became a regular congregant at Temple Sinai in Westwood, the largest Conservative Jewish synagogue in the Western United States.

In 1973, Evangelical Christians had embarked upon an ambitious program of evangelization called "Key '73". Within their ranks was a group called by the unlikely name "Jews for Jesus".

I met with their leaders and members, and was persuaded that my co-religionists had lost their way. The thought of conversion to the dominant Christian faith was unconscionable, and personally untenable.

As a response to this movement, I founded a group at Temple Sinai called 'Involvement'. It attracted hundreds of Jewish young adults seeking a deeper understanding of their faith and heritage.

The threat of a vanishing Jewish generation disturbed me greatly, and the remedy had to be education and increased Jewish knowledge.....or so I thought.

Upon graduation from USC, I moved to Denver to intern at the University of Colorado Medical Center. Witnessed to by many sincere Christians, I remained true to my faith.

My career as a physician began after that one year in Colorado.

I chose to practice as a 'locum tenens' M.D., covering different clinics and hospitals throughout the United States.

In 1979, in Longview, Washington, I was given the book "The Late Great Planet Earth" by author Hal Lindsey. I was about to complete my locum assignment and was to spend Yom Kippur in Salt Lake City, Utah. These were the days between Rosh Hashanah (the Scriptural Feast of Trumpets, the Jewish New Year), and Yom Kippur, (The Day of Atonement), known as the Yom Ha'moraim, the Days of Awe.

It was on an Amtrak train, around midnight, somewhere in the Northwest, with one lone reading light, in an otherwise "sleeping" car, that I met the Living Moshiach (Messiah).

The author Mr. Lindsey spoke of the 'Paradox of Israel', that the Messiah came to his own Jewish people and they would not receive Him. Such an idea was familiar to me. I had considered it thoughtfully over the years and concluded that the Hasidic rabbi back in 1967 was correct. But this time, it was different.

In the summer of 1979, I happened to be outside a Manhattan synagogue near New York's Lincoln Center. It was the time of the rabbi's Sabbath sermon, and the door of the sanctuary was open. He quoted the words of King David in his psalm that said:

"A broken spirit, and a contrite heart, these are the sacrifices you will not reject."

These words, and their profound meaning, spoke to my heart.

In this one verse was the summation of the best of Judaism; the means of atonement, the goal of life, and the way of reconciliation with the Almighty.

The **authentic** Messiah of the Christian, was after all, a Jew. This Man was not only the triumphant, victorious human, political redeemer formulated by rabbinic Judaism. He was a meek and suffering servant. He did not bring about a restoration of the Jewish kingdom. He did not bring an end to earthly suffering, sorrow, persecution, or injustice. But in fact, in the name of Jesus Christ, the Christian messiah, some of the most terrible and murderous acts against the Jewish people had been committed.

And in the end, He died the death of a sinner.

Yet, at that moment, everything changed. All of the arguments against His true Jewish identity as Messiah, when properly understood, were swallowed up by His role as the 'Suffering Servant'. He was completely and fully the atoning figure described by the prophet Isaiah in the 53rd chapter of his book. He was the perfect Personification of One with a broken spirit and a contrite heart. He held the Key to the Kingdom of Heaven and Atonement with HaShem (Yahuweh Elohim).

I physically trembled at the possibility that the Messiah was Yahoshua.

How could almost 2000 years of Jewish scholarship have overlooked this?

Who was I to presume a superior understanding of the Scriptures? After all, the great rabbis and sages of the last two millenia have faithfully guarded our heritage and helped to preserve our people.

I could not leave my Jewish faith. I had spent much of my life persuading other seekers of its complete truth. I had to know that this was not just a powerful emotional or psychological event that would alter my self concept and world view.

How would I know the Truth?

There was only one possible answer. I would seek the Truth from the Revealer of Truth Himself.

Where would I find Him?

In the synagogue, of course.

And so, on Yom Kippur in 1979, I worshipped with the Jewish people of Salt Lake City, Utah. At the end of this "Holiest of Days", as the sun began its descent in the Western sky, the portion of the worship service known as Ne'eilah or the 'closing of the gates of repentance' had begun.

I fervently prayed to HaShem (Yahuweh) for forgiveness and shalom (peace) for myself, my family, for Israel, and for all the world. But this time I prayed also for the Truth of the Moshiach (Messiah).

If what happened on that train was a quirky orchestration of memory, emotion, subconscious desire for assimilation, or some other psychological need, I wanted none of it.

But if it was really true, that Moshiach (Messiah) had come as the Jewish Rabbi Yahoshua, the Perfect Suffering Servant, I wanted it all.

****

As the sun set in the West, and the synagogue service had come to its conclusion, I had the Answer I was seeking.

The Rabbeinu shel Olam (Our Master of the Universe), had given me an Answer I waited for all my life, an Answer that resonated with Authenticity and Truth.

Moshiach had come to Israel and the Jewish people just as He had promised in the Torah.

Moshiach came first to suffer as our "Korban" (that is, that which brings a person near to Yahuweh Elohim, and usually translated as 'sacrifice'). And while He died a sinner's death, He was restored to life by the resurrection.

He lives eternally, having tasted mortal death, and overcoming it, He holds the Key to Eternity.

From the very beginning, Yahuweh, my Heavenly Father, has directed my steps to that fateful moment of encounter with His Son, Yahoshua the Messiah.

His view from above, has become my view from here.

Then, and now, we are one in purpose, and one in destiny.

And in the future world to come, when Yahuweh and His Name shall be one, we shall be as One indeed.

THE STORY OF THE CLOUDS, SUNBEAMS, AND STARS

My Personal Testimony

Norman Martin Wolk

When I was very young, I remember staring up at the sky, watching the beams of sunlight pierce through the soft silence of the great white clouds, and thinking that there must be more to our lives than what we think we know.

For a six year old lad, relaxing on a wooden slat bench in Brooklyn, such thoughts seemed greater than my brief life, so far, needed to entertain. But they wouldn't just go away; and so began a life long journey of my search for meaning.

My Jewish faith and my strong identification with the 'people of The Book' began at home, where my mother and father lived out the great and noble way of life we call Judaism. For six days a week,(except on Saturday, the 7th day Sabbath) from age eight to thirteen, I attended Hebrew school and was taught by the rabbis and teachers at our orthodox synagogue Torah, Talmud, Jewish history and heritage, and the Hebrew language.

It was only in the arena of public school that I had any contact with people of a different faith, and even that was rare.

Each winter at Christmas, and each spring at Easter, I was reminded that most of the world outside of my own, celebrated holidays that were alien to me, and I needed to know why. As the years went by, I would read the 'New Testament', speak to Catholic priests, Protestant ministers, Christians of all denominations; and return securely, confidently, and serenely, to my Jewish faith.

From college in Queens, (New York), to medical school in Los Angeles, to internship in Denver, I would be challenged by the 'truth claims' of Christianity, and still would remain steadfast in my ancestral faith. Indeed, I would even establish a club at my West Los Angeles synagogue to combat the rising tide of heresy within our own ranks known as 'Jews for Jesus'.

So at the age of 29, I found myself in a world where two great monotheistic religions were each still claiming that they are the only true religion.

They say the more things change, the more they stay the same; and it's true, for the world had not changed much at all from when I was just a kid. The 70's in America were surely not the '50's; the Vietnam war, racial strife, feminism, the drug and secular revolution had left their searing marks, and they remain with us today. And the chasm between Judaism and Christianity was as wide as ever.

So now, after about two decades, I came to realize that people generally believe what they are taught to believe when they are young. In fact, most (people) don't ever really seriously question their beliefs at all.

My search for meaning could have ended there, but it didn't. I could have settled back comfortably into what "I knew to be true", but I didn't.

For in September 1979, around midnight, somewhere in the Pacific Northwest, on an Amtrak train, I encountered the Messiah of Israel, the One Who claims to be "the Way, the Truth, and the Life". (John 14:6)

Suddenly, in the stillness of that speeding train, on that star filled autumn night, during the 'days of awe' between Rosh Hashanah and Yom Kippur, I 'heard', as it were, the words of the psalmist, David the King, and the prophet, Isaiah, who both proclaimed this abiding truth:

> "The sacrifices of the Eternal are a broken spirit;
> A broken and a contrite heart, O Elohim, Thou
> will not despise."
>
> **(Psalm 51:17)**

> "But to this one I will look,
> To him who is humble and contrite of spirit, and
> who trembles at My Word."
>
> **(Isaiah 66:2)**

Within these inspired proclamations was the summation of the essence of Judaism, the means of atonement, the goal of life, and the way of reconciliation with HaShem (Hebrew for "The Name of YHWH").

The Messiah of the "Christian" was, after all, a Jew; not a Greek speaking Hellenized Jew, but a Torah observant, commandment keeping son of Israel, son of Man, and Son of HaShem (YHWH). He came this time to His people as a meek and suffering servant, and not as the triumphant, victorious, human redeemer expected by rabbinic Judaism. He did not bring an end to earthly suffering, sorrow, persecution, or injustice. In fact, in "His Name", some of the most terrible, heinous, and murderous acts against the Jewish people had been committed. And in the end, according to Messianic Scripture, He died the death of a sinner.(Deuteronomy 21:22)

How then, could this first century itinerant Jewish carpenter and rabbi really be Moshiach (Hebrew for Anointed One or Messiah), the promised and long awaited Messiah of Israel?

Was such a thing even possible?

Suddenly, at that fateful moment, everything changed (for me). All of the arguments against His identity as Messiah were swallowed up by His role as the Suffering Servant, utterly and perfectly fulfilling the role of "Korban", the Atonement that lets us draw close to HaShem (YHWH). This Anointed Redeemer, prophetically proclaimed by Isaiah, (especially in his 53rd chapter), and in numerous places in the Tanakh, with His broken spirit and contrite heart, held the keys to the Kingdom of Heaven.

I literally trembled at the possiblility that Yahoshua was the Moshiach. I thought that I had already rejected the Messiah of Christianity....and indeed, I had; for this

Messiah (Yahoshua) kept His Father's Commandments, and lived and died totally, completely, and perfectly, as a Torah (observant) Jew.

But what about the great rabbis and sages of the last two thousand years, who helped to faithfully guard our heritage and preserve our people; how in heaven's Name could they have overlooked this?

Where would I go for the answer?

Where would this life long quest for meaning be found?

It would be found where I always sought the truth; it would be found in the synagogue.

And so, on Yom Kippur, 1979, in Salt Lake City, Utah, towards dusk on this Day of Atonement, that part of the worship service known as "Ne'ilah", ("the closing of the gates"), had begun.

I fervently prayed to HaShem for forgiveness, and peace, and to be written and sealed in His book of life; not only for myself, but for my family, for the Jewish people everywhere, for the nation of Israel, and for all nations.

But on this Yom Kippur, I also prayed that I would know with certainty whether Messiah had come; and if He had, Who was He?

When the sun had fully set, and the Day of Atonement had ended, I had the Answer I was seeking, an Answer that resonated with authenticity and Truth.

The Messiah had come to Israel and to the Jewish people, just as He had promised He would in Torah. He came first to suffer as our 'Korban', and die. And though dead, He would be revived to life by His Resurrection. Having tasted a mortal's death, and overcoming it, in the Power of YHWH, He lives eternally, to justify and to save. And He came in His Father's Name, Yahuweh; and His Name is Yahoshua, meaning the salvation of Yah.

It is Yahoshua the Messiah, Who holds the Key to the Gates of Heaven, Redemption, and Eternity.

My search for meaning in life had been found. I realized that it comes by knowing and loving the true Eternal Creator of the universe, Yahuweh Elohim, and His chosen Messiah, Yahoshua, and obeying His commandments.

The six year old lad, twenty three years before, on that wooden slat bench, had met His Redeemer, exactly on schedule, according to the Creator's will and sovereign choice.

But in truth, the search for meaning, at least in this life, had only just begun.. Still, now, the One Who dwells on High, far beyond the clouds, the sun, and the stars was palpably, powerfully, and personally, my Rabbi, my Teacher, my Redeemer, my Judge, and my King. And one future day, He promises that:

> "Hereafter, you shall see the Son of Man sitting at the right hand of Power, and coming on the clouds of heaven."
>
> **(Matthew 26:64)**

****

On that Yom Kippur night, while walking home from the synagogue, I would look up into the brilliant evening sky, and quietly whisper, "thank you, HaShem" for inviting me to glimpse beyond the clouds, the sun, and the stars; for inviting me to see You.

A Glossary

Yom Kippur: one of the seven "Festivals of Israel", a day to 'afflict' one's soul, a day set aside for atonement with HaShem.

HaShem: Hebrew for "The Name", that is, the traditionally ineffable Name of the Eternal, that appears in Scripture as YHWH (Yahweh, Yahuweh), used synonymously with Almighty, Eternal, Creator, Adonai, Elohim

Moshiach: Hebrew for Messiah, that is, the Anointed One, the Redeemer of Israel

Torah: The Pentateuch, the Five Books of Moses of the Hebrew Scriptures

Tanakh: an acronym for Torah, Nevi'im, Ketuvim.

Nevi'im is Hebrew for the Prophets;

Ketuvim is Hebrew for the Writings.

These three, when taken together (Genesis, Exodus, Leviticus, Numbers, Deuteronomy(the Torah), the Prophets, and the Writings(Psalms, Proverbs, Ecclesiastes, Job, Song of Solomon, Ruth, Lamentations, Esther, Ezra, Nehemiah, Chronicles) make up the revealed and written Word of YHWH.

Bibliography

References and Sources

1.THE HOLY BIBLE, translation revised by Dr. I.M. Rubin (New York: Star Hebrew Book Co., 1928)

2.THE HOLY BIBLE, New International Version, New York International Bible Society (Grand Rapids, Michigan: Zondervan Bible Publishers, 1978)

3.THE NEW AMERICAN STANDARD BIBLE, The Open Bible Edition, The Lockman Foundation, La Habra, California (Nashville: Thomas Nelson Publishers, 1977, 1979)

4.THE PENTATEUCH AND HAFTORAHS, 2nd edition, Joseph H. Hertz, editor (London: The Soncino Press, 1988)

5.THE SCRIPTURES, Institute for Scripture Research (PTY) LTD., Johannesburg, South Africa, 2nd edition (New York: Port City Press, 1998, reprinted 2000)

6.THE PRAYER BOOK, translated and arranged by Ben Zion Bokser (New York: Hebrew Publishing Company 1957, 1961)

7. Dr. C.J. Koster, COME OUT OF HER MY PEOPLE, Institute for Scripture Research (PTY) LTD., revised edition (Johannesburg, South Africa: The Rustica Press, R.R. Donnelly and Sons, Co., 1996; reprinted 1998)

8. SHEMA YISRAEL, Judaism: The Belief and the Belonging, by Dov Rosen, translated from the fourth Hebrew edition by Leonard Oschry, (Peli Printing Works Ltd., Givatayim, Israel, distributed by Zion Talis Book Division, New York, 1972)

"I HEARD THE CALL.... AND OBEYED"

"Now Yahuweh said to Abram: Get out of your country,
and from your kindred, and from your father's house,
to the land that I will show you"

[Genesis 12:1] "

After these things I saw another angel coming down from heaven, having great authority, and the earth was illumined with his splendor. And he cried out with a mighty voice, saying, "Fallen, fallen is Babylon the great! And she has become a dwelling place of demons and a prison of every unclean spirit, and a prison of every unclean and hateful bird. For all the nations have drunk of the wine of the passion of her immorality, and the kings of the earth have committed acts of immorality with her, and the merchants of the earth have become rich by the wealth of her sensuality."

And I heard another voice from heaven , saying,
"Come out of her, My people, that you may not participate in her sins and that you may not receive of her plagues; for her sins have piled up as high as heaven, and Elohim ('God') has remembered her iniquities."

[Revelation 18:1-4]

****

Thousands of years ago, a man from Babylon, who would become Abraham, a father to many nations, patriarch to Israel, father in faith, and friend of Elohim was commanded to "get out of Babylon".

The Babylon of Abram was not just a place, but a world of spiritual darkness and deception.

The source of that deception remains constant; he is a spirit being opposed to Elohim, His Torah, and His Messiah Yahoshua. He is revealed in the Hebrew Scriptures as an 'adversary and a liar' whose name is 'Satan'.

As he worked to lie and deceive in ancient Babylon, he has worked throughout the ages, in all nations that have been scattered across the earth since the destruction of the Tower of Babel, finding his greatest impact and success in the religions of man. Here, by cleverly combining truths and lies, he would create powerful systems of counterfeit belief, leading the whole world astray.

And so it is, even in today's advanced civilizations, where knowledge abounds, humanity remains in the stranglehold of this master of deceit.

At this juncture in history, the nations of the earth are trying to cope with the overwhelming challenges of terrorism, intolerance, religious fanaticism and bigotry, in what may very well become a cataclysmic clash of Judeo-Christian and Islamic world views.

Yet, of these three great and noble religious traditions of mankind, none are pure and undefiled; all are stained by errors that have been subtly, cunningly, and deceptively introduced by the Adversary.

Indeed, despite our sincere wish and belief to the contrary, these, [and all religions], are kingdoms divided against themselves, and estranged from the Elohim ['God'] of Abraham. Honest and diligent scrutiny would reveal that all, in some way, carry the legacy of Babylon, "walking to the course of this world, according to the prince of power of the air, of the spirit that is now working in the sons of disobedience." [Ephesians 2:2]

Nevertheless, such discernment and wisdom is not to be found in the abundant knowledge of this world, since Satan, the deceiver, continues to remain in control; and will continue to deceive, until the Return of Israel's Messiah and the establishment of the Kingdom of His Father on earth.

Except for sake of the called and elect of Elohim, all of humanity would be led astray.[Matthew 24:24; Mark 13:22; Luke 18:7]

(For) it is only through His chosen servants, that the ability to discern between the spirit of truth and the spirit of error is given. [1John 4:6]

"He who has ears to hear, let him hear."
[Matthew 11:15]

****

[Essays written by Angela M. Parisi have been modified and edited by the book's author.]

Just over a half century ago, a child of Italian-American parents was born. Her name was Angela Mary. Although earnestly and devoutly reared in the Roman Catholic Church, Angela, having received the spirit of discernment, came to recognize the errors of her ancestral faith.

Like the Gentile Moabitess Ruth, in whose lineage would come King David of Israel, and Israel's Messiah, Angela would come out of the Babylon of Christianity, and find in Torah and the Messianic Scriptures, Israel's Yahuweh Elohim and Yahoshua the Messiah as "The Light in the Wilderness".

It gives me great pleasure to include the writings of Ms. Parisi, as a testimony to her personal walk of faith. May the reader be blessed in their reading, as I have been blessed in knowing their author.

****

"I will raise up a prophet from among their countrymen like you, and I will put My words in His mouth, and He shall speak to them all that I command Him."

[Deuteronomy 18:18}

"I am He Who bears witness of Myself, and the Father Who sent Me bears witness of Me."

[John 8:18]

****

Angela Mary Parisi invites the reader to consider her thoughtful reflections on Christian tradition and practice.

****

Babylon and Christian Belief

The Babylonian Mystery Religion began about 400 years after Noah, with his great grandson King Nimrod, his wife, Semiramis, and their son, Tammuz. These three desired to be gods, and as objects of man's worship, became the central figures of religious systems throughout the world.

In the Mesopotamian city called Babel [Babylon], when the whole earth used the same language and words, a tower was built, whose top would have reached into heaven, and its builders would have made themselves a name so they would not be divided apart. [Genesis 11:4]

But divided they were, "....because there Yahuweh confused the language of the whole earth; and from there Yahuweh scattered them abroad over the face of the whole earth." [Genesis 11:9]

Nevertheless, despite this [divine] strategy of 'divide and conquer', the deceptions of this Mystery Religion of Babylon did not go away. Indeed this triad of counterfeit gods, originating with Nimrod, Semiramis, and Tammuz, would take on many and varied forms throughout history, appearing in every religion of man, save one, the religion of Torah Judaism and the Messianic Faith in the Jewish Messiah.

Christianity, the dominant faith of the Western world for two thousand years has not been spared; for essential features of this powerful system of belief may be traced back to their ancestral origins in Babylon.

Indeed, the legacy of the Mystery Religion permeates all of Christian creed and practice.

Among the many false traditions and beliefs, consider these:

1. The celibate priesthood
Here, unmarried men, fully devoted to Nimrod and Semiramis, were distinguished by black robes. Their celibacy assured total allegiance to King Nimrod and his wife.

The celibate priesthood of Christian Roman Catholicism carries on this ancient practice of Babylon's religion.

2. The Pontiff or Pontifex Maximus
This was the title conferred upon the high priest, or Nimrod himself. Pontifex means bridge; Nimrod was believed to be the 'bridge' between the world of the living, and the world of the dead. Their priestly garb included a head dress that resembled the open mouth of a fish; such adornment is worn by Christian clergy today.

Furthermore, the head of the Roman Catholic Church is called Pontiff, Pope, and Vicar of Christ.

3. The Cardinals
This council of twelve, dressed in scarlet and red, aided Nimrod in running the affairs of state in his empire. Known as "priests of Baal", their initiation included shaving the corners of their beard, so as to create a ring of hair on their scalps, symbolizing the halo around the sun. The sun, of course, was the central object of worship for the Babylonian

Mystery Religion. Certain monastic orders of the Church have perpetuated this initiation rite, characterizing it as an emblem of asceticism.

Furthermore, Cardinals hold positions in the Church throughout the world, assisting the Pontiff from Rome, in the affairs of his Church.

It is noteworthy that Yahuweh's chosen nation, Israel, were warned neither to observe the customs of the pagans, nor imitate their idol worship, in 'deifying' the sun.

> "Do not learn the way of the nations, and do not be terrified by the signs of the heavens although the nations are terrified by them:
> For the customs of the peoples are delusion......."
> [Jeremiah 10:2,3]

and

> "Ye shall not round the corners of your heads, neither shalt thou mar the corners of your beard."
> [Leviticus 19:27]

4. The Nun

The nun was origininally "a daughter of Nimrod", a vestal virgin, dedicated to the service of the celibate priests of Babylon.

The history of this tradition has been littered with innocent victims of abortion and infanticide.

5. The Sacraments

The sacraments were "divine secrets" possessed by Semiramis, and given to those who qualified, beginning with 'baptism' and ending with prayers for the dead. Such secrets were the sole path to salvation.

6. Purgatory
This was a 'holding area' for the dead, before their admission into heaven. This powerful deception effectively held the surviving family member hostage to the priesthood. Through additional sacrifices, penance, and indulgences [as gifts of money or land] to the priesthood [Church], the entry of the departed to heaven was 'hastened and assured'.

7. Confession and Penance
Semiramis felt she would have better control over her devotees if she knew their secrets or 'sins', since she was ever vigilant for discontent that could lead to uprisings within the empire. The confessional booth was most effective, for a non-confessor may lose his salvation.

8. IHS
These three initials were used by Egyptians to signify, Isis [I], Seb [S], and Horus [H]; signifying the initials of Semiramis, Tammuz. and Nimrod, the names of the original Babylonian triad deity in Egyptian.

In the 'Mass' and Eucharist of the Roman Catholic and Christian Church, "IHS" is imprinted on the communion wafer, representing the "Body of Christ", and appears on furnishings within the Christian church the world over.

9. The Cross
Faithful adherents of the Mystery Religion of Babylon would make the sign of the "T" for Tammuz across their chests, and bow in obeisance. Christianity absorbed this practice,

and perpetuates it in the custom of genuflecting before the altar, a crucifix, a graven image [statue, idol] of the "holy family", a saint, 'Christ', or as a matter of superstition to assure good luck, and ward off 'evil spirits'.

10. Lent and Easter

This spring period of 40 days memorialized the death of Tammuz, who was said to have been killed by a wild boar, and was characterized by sorrow and weeping. It preceded the joyful return of Tammuz in a 'resurrection' from the dead, celebrated as "Ishtar".

This time of rejoicing would feature the eating of ham, to symbolize victory over the pig that killed Tammuz, facing the east to honor the rising of the Sun-god, the exchanging of colored eggs to symbolize rebirth, and baking cakes marked with the "T", a cross, for Tammuz and the 'queen of heaven'.

(The burning yule log and evergreen tree find their origins in this pagan myth.)

> Even the children of Israel were not immune to this powerful delusion, causing Elohim to send His prophets to issue strong admonitions against such practices.
> [Ezekiel 8:13-16; Jeremiah 7:18; Jeremiah 44:25]

The similarities between this festival of Babylon and the Christian Lent-Easter cannot just be coincidental!

11. Mother and Child Worship

Modeled after Semiramis as mother and Tammuz as son, this popular, primitive, and deeply emotional configuration appeared in Egypt as Isis and Horus; in Greece as Aphrodite and Eros; and in Rome as Venus and Cupid.

Lastly, and most influentially, it appeared in Christianity as Mary and Jesus, "the Madonna and Child".

12. Sunday

As each day of the week was named to honor a pagan deity, the first and foremost of days would venerate the 'Sun-deity'; hence the name Sunday. Consecrated in Babylon for the sun deity, Sunday was already 'the Lord's day'.

The supreme god of Babylon, the unconquered 'Sun', who was victorious over all lesser deities, had now conquered the nascent Hebrew Messianic faith, by eliminating the commanded 7th Day Sabbath, substituting in its place, the "Lord's Day" of the Mystery Religion of Babylon.

In this "proud" achievement, the [ephemeral] victory of Babylon, through its transmogrification into Christianity, was now assured.

****

The insatiable ego of man has always been the fertile ground upon which Satan would plant and cultivate the seeds of his masterful and depraved delusions.

Kings, Pharaohs, Emperors, and Popes could not accept the notion that one day they would be rendered powerless, and die. Embracing, like Adam and Eve, the first satanic lie, that "they would not surely die" [Genesis 3:4], they erected pyramids, obelisks, cathedrals, ziggurats, towers, steeples, statues, and icons, all in a futile attempt to secure their place in eternity, so as to live on forever, and be worshipped.

And so it was, that the universal pagan religious doctrine of 'the immortal soul' was easily incorporated into the Christian faith, and figures prominently in its core beliefs. Indeed, the goal of " personal salvation in Jesus Christ" is to wrest this immortal element of man, (the soul), from the evil grasp of Satan and the everlasting torment of the devil's fiery hell, delivering it into the loving embrace of "Christ", where the immortal soul will dwell for eternity in heavenly bliss, in the presence of Jesus!

Of all the teachings of my ancestral Roman Catholic Christian faith, the assurance of the immortality of my soul, and the immortality of the souls of my beloved departed grandparents, ancestors, and friends, who would watch over me, and to whom I would pray as intercessors, was the most comforting and assuring.....and the most difficult to give up.

Was it possible that my prayers were said in vain?

Was it possible that they could not hear me or intercede on my behalf?

Was I taught the Word of Elohim ("God") in the Christian religion, or was I taught the deceptive creed of men, and their primitive and egotistical need to be immortal?

****

The death of my grandparents left an indelible impression on my young life. Witnessing the anguished tears of grown-ups at funerals, I was left anxious, afraid, and horrified of death. Well intentioned adults would try to comfort me by their assurance that the loved ones who had passed away were with the angels in the presence of "God".

But the Scripture plainly teaches that man is mortal.

Only Elohim ("God") and His Son, the Messiah possess immortality!

****

> "For the living know that they shall die: but the dead know not anything, neither have they any more a reward: for the memories of them is forgotten. Also their love, and their hatred, and their envy, is now perished; neither have they anymore portion for ever in anything that is under the sun."
>
> [Ecclesiastes 9:5-6]

Thus, the call of the Sovereign King of the Universe, Yahuweh Elohim, and His Son, the Messiah Yahoshua, as revealed plainly in His Word, made my surrender of these comforting lies not only necessary, but essential!

In truth, the sure hope of life beyond the grave rests not on the lie of the immortality of the soul as taught by the Church, but the certainty of the Resurrection, as revealed in our Messiah's victory over death, and His Word.

> "And as Moses lifted up the serpent in the wilderness, even so must the Son of Man be lifted up; that whoever believes may in Him have eternal life.

For Elohim ("God") so loved the world, that He gave
His only begotten Son, that whoever believes in Him
should not perish but have eternal life."

[John 3:14-16]

"Behold, I tell you a mystery; we shall not all sleep, but
we shall all be changed, in a moment, in the twinkling
of an eye, at the last trumpet; for the trumpet will
sound, and the dead will be raised imperishable, and
we shall be changed.
For this perishable must put on the imperishable, and
this mortal must put on immortality. But when this
perishable will have put on the imperishable, and this
mortal will have put on immortality, then will come
about the saying that is written, "Death is swallowed
up in victory."

[1Corinthians 15:51-54]

"I charge you in the presence of Elohim ("God"), who
gives life to all things and of Messiah Yahoshua, who
testified the good confession before Pontius Pilate,
that you keep the commandment without stain or
reproach until the appearing of Messiah Yahoshua,
which He will bring about at the proper time-He Who
is the blessed and only Sovereign, the King of kings
and "Lord of lords"; Who alone possesses immortality
and dwells in unapproachable light; Whom no man
has seen or can see. To Him be honor and eternal
dominion. Amen."

[1Timothy 6:13-16]

****

Christianity's doctrines, dogmas, and creeds, bear full
witness to the sobering fact that she is the heir of this legacy
of the Mystery Religion of Babylon, a system of belief and
practice that, except for the elect, has led the whole world
astray.

The mark of the beast spoken of in Revelation 13:16-18, the number 6, the number of man, is the mark of Nimrod's legacy to humanity.

The sobering conclusion of history is that the woman clothed in purple and scarlet, adorned with gold and precious stones and pearls, holding a gold cup full of abominations, whose name was "Mystery, Babylon the great, the mother of harlots and of the abominations of the earth" [Revelation 17:5], seen by John when he was carried away in the spirit into a wilderness, can be none other than the Christian Church of Rome, (and the break-away Eastern Churches), and her many daughters of denominational Protestantism.

****

No festival of the Christian Church testifies more persuasively of its origins in Babylon and Sun worship than Christmas.

Search the scriptures as earnestly as you are able, for it is found no where in either of the "Testaments", "Old or New"!

Would it surprise you to learn that the "Christian" Christmas is celebrated very much the same way the ancient [pre-Christian] pagans celebrated their mid-winter festival called "Saturnalia"?

Saturnalia originated in the Babylonian Mystery Religion, which commemorates the birth of Tammuz, the young incarnate sun, who was slain, wept for by his devotees, and then returned back to the people.

It was celebrated at the end of December, around the time of the winter solstice, the shortest and darkest day of the year in the Northern hemisphere. A week of feasting was held in Rome, the city whose former name was Saturnia. As the festival was usually held between December 17-23, it preceded the birth of the sun deity on December 25th, and was a time of drunken revelry and the exchange of gifts in the form of "images".

The winter solstice was also celebrated as the "nativity" or birth of the sun by the followers of Mithra, the Persian sun god.

This common belief permeated the Roman Empire.

With Rome as its center, the Greeks [also] came to embrace this Babylonian Mystery Religion. They too regarded Saturn as a representative of the sun; for at nightfall, the planet Saturn appeared in the sky, as a surrogate for the sun, until the sun returned at daybreak.

****

Sun worship began with King Nimrod and his wife Semiramis in Mesopotamia. The sun god, variously known as Nimrod, Bel, Baal, Adonis, or Ra, would visit a tree and leave gifts for the devotees. These sacred trees were of various species: the Babylonians used the evergreen, the Druids used the oak, the Egyptians used the palm, and the Romans used the fir tree.

And in order to make the tree even more attractive, it was customary to decorate it. [Jeremiah 10:3-5]

The Yule log or 'Yuletide' also originated in Babylon. Yule, meaning infant or little child, was celebrated on December 25th, dedicated to Nimrod and Tammuz, and was known as "Yule Day" or "Child's Day".

Adonis'[the sun god's] mother was said to have become a tree when she gave birth.

And yet another heathen myth taught that King Nimrod was 'cut down' by his enemies, and returned to life again as a tree.

Israel, as Elohim's chosen nation, was warned against such practices; as we read in Jeremiah 10:1-5.

"Hear what the LORD says to you, O house of Israel. This is what the LORD says: ' Do not learn the ways of the nations or be terrified by signs in the sky, though they terrify the nations. For the customs of the people are worthless; they cut a tree out of the forest, and a craftsman shapes it with his chisel. They adorn it with silver and gold; they fasten it with hammer and nails so it will not totter. Like a scarecrow in a cucumber field are they, and they cannot speak; they must be carried, because they cannot walk! Do not fear them, for they can do no harm, nor can they do any good."

And in Deuteronomy 4:19, 20:

> "And beware, lest you lift up your eyes to heaven and see the sun and the moon and the stars, all the host of heaven, and be drawn away and worship them and serve them, those which YHWH your 'God' has allotted to all the peoples under the whole heaven. But YHWH has taken you and brought you out of the

iron furnace, from Egypt, to be a people for His own
possession, as today.
and again here, where it is commanded:
"You shall not follow other gods, any of the gods of the
peoples who surround you."

[Deuteronomy 6:14]

[Further warnings are declared in Deuteronomy 11:16, 17:3;
Exodus 22:20; and Job 31:26-28]

****

Faithful and obedient followers of Yahuweh Elohim, His
Torah, and the Messiah of Israel, can find little Scriptural
support for the beliefs, practices, holidays, and traditions
of Christianity.

But coming out of this religious system comes with a heavy
price.

The cost of such a decision may be exceedingly high; indeed
many will be rejected by their families, their church, and
their peers, because they will have abandoned the world's
familiar customs and beliefs for the Truth of Elohim, as it
is found in His Word.

Indeed, the world's rejection of the true disciples of the
Messiah should not come as a surprise.

Consider the words of Yahoshua Himself:

"Do not think that I came to bring peace on the earth;
I did not come to bring peace, but a sword."

[Matthew 10:34]

> "And He said to them, 'Truly I say to you, there is no
> one who has left house or wife or brothers or parents
> or children, for the sake of the Kingdom of 'God', who
> shall not receive many times as much at this time and
> in the age to come, eternal life.'"
>
> [Luke 18:29,30]

In order to truly know our Father in Heaven and His Son,
our Messiah-Redeemer Yahoshua, we must study His
whole Word, [that means the Torah, Prophets, Writings,
and Messianic Scriptures!] diligently, seeking Him and
His Truth with all of our heart, all of our strength, and all
of our life.

> "All Scripture* is inspired by Elohim ['God'] and
> profitable for teaching, for reproof, for correction, for
> training in righteousness; that the man of 'God' may
> be adequate, equipped for every good work."
>
> [2Timothy 3:16,17]

(*The Scripture referred to here is the Torah, the Prophets, and the Writings, since
the Messianic Scriptures ("New Testament") were not yet compiled nor canonized
as "Holy Writ".)

In doing so, as a called-out, peculiar, and set-apart ['holy']
people, we will realize that we must inevitably separate
ourselves from the rest of the world and its religious system,
the Christian Church.

After all is said and done, only in taking on the yoke of the
Kingdom of Heaven, can we experience the true blessings
of discipleship.

And then we will realize that it is indeed worth the cost.

"For whoever does the will of My Father Who is in
Heaven, he is My brother and sister and mother."
[Matthew 12:50]

This is the wonderful inheritance of an obedient faith,
founded on Scripture, assuring those who run the good
race, and endure until the end, a place in the Eternal Family
of the Messiah and our Father in Heaven.

Like Abram, and like Ruth, who came from out of the
nations,

I have heard the call,

I have listened,

and I have obeyed,

for "He has given me ears to hear".

I have followed "The Light in the Wilderness".

NEW BEGINNINGS

[The Testimony of Angela Mary Parisi]

As a child, I loved anything that had to do with religion. I would stop and listen to the church bells as they rang, thinking they were singing to the Almighty in heaven. Actually, anything that had to do with Scriptural stories, would capture my interest and my heart... I would desperately want to find out more about them and the people who were so special to the Almighty. I often wished I were one of them.

Being raised Roman Catholic, my thoughts and actions revolved around the prayers I was taught, and the holidays we as a family observed and celebrated together. I taught my children prayers that I recited as a child, and introduced them to the way I celebrated Christmas, Lent, Easter, Halloween, and other church days of recognition. There was much too much comfort, security and joy to doubt, or suspect, even for a brief moment, that the church may be teaching doctrine contrary to the Scriptures (Bible). From the very beginning, my family was Catholic, and so was I.

But the Almighty had other plans for me.

I began to question what I had been taught.

Was the Church teaching the Eternals' word, or were they teaching their own version of the Scriptures?

It has now taken almost 27 years for me to discover what I have come to know as the Truth; and it is this: Truth is derived from Torah, the Word of our Father and His Redeemer Messiah, and not written and created by man so as to fulfill his own selfish ego.

Mine has been a journey filled with persecution from family and friends who have not been called, and therefore do not understand my response to His revelation. But it has also been filled with the love and support of my Mother and daughter who have come to embrace the truth as I have.

It has also been a journey of blessing, privilege, and honor, bringing me to the land of Israel, where I have walked in Bethlehem, Jericho, Tiberias, Nazareth, the Galilee, and Jerusalem. Of all of these, my most memorable experience happened at the waters of the Jordan River, north of the Sea of Galilee, where I was baptized in the Name of Yahoshua, the Messiah of Israel.

Finally, it has been a journey ordained and appointed in heaven, surely even before the foundations of creation itself. Two people, a Jew and a Gentile, the author and myself, from different cultures and religions, have been brought together for one unique Messiah centered purpose: to study the Torah, and to learn the Truth from the Word of Elohim.

> "But now in Messiah Yahoshua you who were formerly
> far off have been brought near by the blood of Messiah.
> For He Himself is our peace, who made both groups

into one, and broke down the barrier of the dividing wall...."

[Ephesians 2:13,14]

****

This then, is the story of how it all started; but the journey will surely continue, until I reach His Eternal Kingdom, the New Jerusalem, for it is only by leaving Babylon, and not looking back, that one may truly have, "New Beginnings"!

****

"And many peoples will come and say, "Come, let us go up to the mountain of Yahuweh, to the house of the Elohay ['God'] of Jacob; that He may teach us concerning His ways, and that we may walk in His paths."
For the TORAH [Law] will go forth from Zion,
And the WORD of Yahuweh from Jerusalem."

[Isaiah 2:3]

AFTERWORD

"The Messiah of Israel":

[The MAN Almost No One Knows]

A little over 20 centuries ago, a child born of a Jewish mother in Bethlehem, Israel, grew up to be a rabbi and a carpenter. He learned his craft from his adopted father, Joseph, studied with rabbis in the Temple in Jerusalem, never married, bore no children, and lived only 33 years. Considered a revolutionary by some, a prophet by others, His destiny was His identity.

For He was both a revolutionary, and a prophet; but He was also the Messiah of Israel, the "God-Man" [eesh-Elohim in Hebrew], the Saviour, the Word incarnate, spoken of in the Torah, the Prophets, and the Writings [Psalms], and attested to by hundreds of eyewitnesses.

****

It is an amazing fact of history, that within just a few short years of His life on earth, an apostasy, a falling away from the Truth, seized and captivated the hearts and minds of most of the masses, just while the small flock of His true disciples began to disappear.

The Jewish Messiah from Nazareth, Israel became the victim of history's greatest"Identity Theft", bringing about a change of His Name and Person, so as to render Him and His Atoning Work, if it were possible, powerless and purposeless.

The brains behind this masterful conspiracy of unprecedented deception was [and is] heaven's adversary, the spirit personality we know as Satan. The muscle for this ignominious project was the powerful Roman Empire. The instrument that orchestrated this whole symphony of sanctified discordant propositions and assertions was the Gentile religious establishment which assumed its role as "the vicar of truth", and came to be known as the Roman Catholic (and) Christian Church.

Through this majestic and muscular church-state alliance, a broad road of compromise and concession was paved with the crumbling stones of the ancient and pervasive Mystery Religion of Babylon, and held together with the mortar of syncretism.

Of all of the Church's notable successes, none of her achievements was more significant and consequential than the Identity Theft of the 'Jewish Messiah Yahoshua' by the 'Christian Christ Jesus'. And for twenty centuries, this transmogrified Yahoshua [Joshua] the Moshiach [Messiah] into "Jesus Christ" has been presented to the world as the Saviour.

****

While the credentials and pedigree of the authentic and true Messiah are revealed throughout the Hebrew Scriptures, [Torah, Prophets, and Writings], a prophetic portrait of the Saviour is proclaimed in its most stunning accuracy in Zechariah [2:10-3:10].

In this wondrous account of the promise of Redemption fulfilled, Yahuweh will come and dwell in the midst of Zion, and many [Gentile] nations will join themselves to Him and become His people. Judah will become His portion, and He will choose again Jerusalem.

Beginning in Chapter 3, Zechariah is given a vision of Joshua, the High Priest, standing before the angel of Yahuweh, with Satan at his right hand to accuse him.

But Satan is rebuked by Yahuweh, and Joshua is reckoned as a man plucked out of the fire, a man clothed with filthy garments, from whom iniquity is removed. He is to be clothed with royal robes, and a crown, assured by the angel of Yahuweh that, if he walks in His ways, and performs His service, He will govern Yahuweh's house, be judge in His courts, and have free access to all among those who are standing here.

But all of these men, including Joshua, are a symbol, for Yahuweh will bring forth His Servant, the Branch, before Whom is a seven faceted engraved Stone, a Stone with seven eyes, and the iniquity of the land will be removed in one day, a day when every man shall sit as neighbors under the vine and the fig tree!

The accusing Satan, the adversary, is silenced. As father of lies, iniquity, and sin, he is undone and finished by the sudden and complete work of the Branch, Joshua, when iniquity, the chief cause of sorrow and suffering, is removed.

[A similar and complementary vision of the Redeemer, whose Name will be called, "Yahuweh our Righteousness", is given to the prophet Jeremiah in (Jeremiah 23:5,6)]

The portrait of Joshua as Suffering Servant, Sin Bearer, High Priest, Judge, Ruler, and Royal King is complete in this prophetic portrayal of Israel's Redeemer.

The Name of the Messiah-Redeemer would be Yahoshua (Joshua); and His Name will be called, Yahuweh Tzidkeinu, Yahuweh our Righteousness.

The Messiah Yahoshua, Who will remove iniquity from the land in one day, is Yahuweh!

****

Nevertheless, despite all of this, Israel as a nation remains, according to Yahuweh's plan, through the Mystery of the Kingdom, largely in stupor regarding the identity of the Jewish Messiah [Romans 11:7-16], and the Gentile Christian Church has essentially ignored and rejected the Apostle Paul's admonition to them in Romans 11:17-36 and 2Thessalonian 2:3-5, 8,9,10.

The Christian religion of the Gentile nations, in their arrogance toward Israel, the Torah [the Law], the Sabbath, and all things Jewish, have gone so far as to replace the rich root and natural branch of this olive tree with their own wild, uncultivated beliefs and traditions, proclaiming "Jesus Christ" as saviour of the world, casting away Yahoshua [Joshua], the Messiah of Israel, as He is poignantly and powerfully portrayed in this prophecy of Zechariah.

The rebuke of Yahuweh against Satan did not diminish or eliminate his [Satan's] mission to lead the whole world astray.

On the contrary, it would appear that it caused him to redouble his efforts to deceive.

Yet, warnings against this strong delusion abound throughout the Messianic Scriptures. Among them are:

Matthew 7:13

Matthew 24:23

2Corinthians 11:3,4, 13-15

Galatians 1:6,7

1Timothy 6:21

and most especially in 2Thessalonians 2:9-15, where we read:

> "that is, the one who is coming is in accord with the activity of Satan, with all power and signs and false wonders, and with all the deception of wickedness for those who perish, because they did not receive the love of the Truth so as to be saved. And for this reason, Elohim ['God'] will send upon them a deluding influence so that they might believe what is false, in order that they all may be judged who did not believe the Truth, but took pleasure in wickedness.
> But we should always give thanks to Elohim for you, brethren beloved by Yahuweh, because Elohim has

chosen you from the beginning for salvation through
sanctification by the Spirit and faith in the Truth.
And it was for this He called you through our gospel,
that you may gain the esteem of our Yahuweh,
Yahoshua, the Messiah.
So then, brothers, stand firm, and hold to the
traditions which you were taught, whether by word
of mouth or by letter from us."

Through misinterpretation, deficient exegesis, faulty
hermeneutics, error-ridden teaching, and ignorance
of the Hebrew Torah, Prophets, and Writings, the
Church remains consciously unaware of her role in the
dissemination of this powerful delusion.

"But the weapons we fight with are not of the flesh,
but mighty in Elohim for overthrowing strongholds,
overthrowing arguments, and every high thing that
exalts itself against the knowledge of Elohim, taking
captive every thought to make it obedient to the
`Messiah, and being ready to punish all disobedience
when your obedience is complete."
                                        [2Corinthians 10:4-6]

The Redeemer Himself proclaimed to the Samaritan
woman at the well,

"You worship that which you do not know; we worship
that which we know, for salvation is from the Jews."
                                        [John 4:22]

****

"Jesus Christ" is not just another name for the True
Messiah of Israel.

In the name of Jesus Christ:

pagan holidays are celebrated,

Christmas is recognized as his birth date,

Good Friday as the day of his death,

Easter as the day of his resurrection,

the trinity of the 'Godhead' is proclaimed,

Sunday is sanctified,

graven images are wrought,

Scripturally unclean meats, seafood, and fowl are eaten,

the teaching and commandments of Yahuweh and His Torah are done away with, (nailed, as it were, to the cross),

and the Christian Church is titled and founded.

Jesus Christ is the central figure, and object of worship of Christianity, but it is not his pierced hands or scarred body that moves history, affects atonement, and gives us our redemption.

Jesus Christ is a pretender to heaven's throne, a cosmic imposter, a counterfeit messiah.

> "But I am afraid, lest as the serpent deceived Eve by his craftiness, your minds should be led astray from the simplicity and purity of devotion to Messiah. For if one comes and preaches another Yahoshua whom

we have not preached, or you receive a different
spirit which you have not received, or a different
gospel which you have not accepted, you bear this
beautifully."

[2Corinthians 11:3,4]

"For such men are false apostles, deceitful workers,
disguising themselves as apostles of Messiah. And
no wonder, for even Satan disguises himself as an
angel of light. Therefore, it is not surprising if his
servants also disguise themselves as servants of
righteousness; whose end shall be according to their
deeds."

[2Corinthians 11:13-15]

Jesus Christ is 'the man of lawlessness'; for the Law of
which we speak is the Law of Elohim, revealing the will
of Messiah's Father in heaven, the Torah!

"So then you will know them by their fruits.
Not everyone who says to Me, Lord, Lord, will enter
the kingdom of heaven; but he who does the will of
My Father who is in heaven.
Many will say to Me on that day, Lord, Lord, did
we not prophesy in Your Name, and in Your Name
cast out demons, and in Your Name perform many
miracles?
And then I will declare to them, 'I never knew you;
DEPART FROM ME, YOU WHO PRACTICE
LAWLESSNESS!'"

[Matthew 7:20-23]

"Do not think that I came to abolish the Torah or the
Prophets; I did not come to abolish, but to fulfill. For
truly I say to you, until heaven and earth pass away,
not the smallest letter or stroke shall pass away from

the Torah, until all is accomplished. Whoever then annuls one of the least of these commandments, and teaches others to do so, shall be called least in the Kingdom of Heaven; but whoever keeps and teaches them, he shall be called great in the Kingdom of Heaven."

[Matthew 5:17-19]

"He who believes in the Son has eternal life; but he who does not obey the Son shall not see life, but the wrath of Elohim abides on him."

[John 3:36]

"For I am Yahuweh, I shall not change, and you, O sons of Jacob shall not come to an end."

[Malachi 3:6]

The Church has triumphed in her witness for Jesus Christ for almost 2000 years, and counts billions of souls as her faithful Christian disciples. But her place in the history of the world is not forever assured.

Indeed, a time is soon coming when the identity of Jesus Christ, as the man of lawlessness, in whose name the Christian religion was founded, and by whom, the whole world was led astray, will be revealed.

The Church will then ask:

"For what reason has Yahuweh declared all this great calamity against us? And what is our iniquity, or what is our sin which we have committed against Yahuweh Elohim (Elohaynu)?

Then you are to say to them, 'It is because your forefathers have forsaken Me', declares Yahuweh, and have followed other gods and served them, and bowed down to them; but Me they have forsaken and have not kept My Torah [Law]." [Jeremiah 16:10,11]

"O Yahuweh, my strength and my stronghold, and
my refuge in the day of distress,
To Thee the nations will come from the ends of the
earth and say,
"Our fathers have inherited nothing but lies,
Futility and things of no profit."
Can man make gods for himself,
Yet they are not gods!
Therefore, behold, I am going to make them know-
this time I will make them know My power and My
might;
And they shall know that My Name is Yahuweh."
[Jeremiah 16:19-21]

****

All predictions and fulfilled Jewish prophecies that have been mis-applied to Jesus Christ, rightfully belong to

YAHOSHUA the Messiah.

He is the faithful and obedient commandment keeping Saviour, Who lives in the faithful and obedient lives of His disciples, for those who love Him obey His Commandments. [John 14:15]

He always ate kosher food and observed the 7th day Sabbath, and every special day ordained by His Father.

He is the Son of Man and Son of Elohim['God'],

He is the First and the Last.

He is the Creator and Revealer, empowered by the Spirit of His Father.

He is the Hope of Israel and the true Saviour of the world.

He is the Word become flesh, the Living Torah.

He was slain as the Passover sacrifice on Passover.

He rose from the grave three days later, on the Sabbath.

He is Emanu-El, El ['God'] with us, the "God-Man".

He is the Resurrection and the Life.

He is the Way, the Truth, and the Life.

In conclusion, Yahoshua, (NOT Jesus Christ), is the Only True and Authentic Historical Sinless Redeemer-Messiah Yahuweh Yahoshua of Israel.

****

In the wilderness of Sinai, Moses led the children of Israel for forty years, but the moment of their actual departure from the Mountain begins like this:

"And they set forward from the Mount of Yahuweh three days journey; and the ark of the covenant of Yahuweh went before them in the three days journey, to seek out a resting place for them. And the cloud of Yahuweh was over them by day, when they set forward from the camp.

And it came to pass, when the ark set forward, that Moses said:

'Rise up, O Yahuweh, and let Thine enemies be scattered; and let them that hate Thee flee before Thee.'

And when it rested, he said:

> 'Return, O Yahuweh, unto the ten thousands of the families of Israel.'
> [Numbers 10:33-36]

(The 35th and 36th verses proclaim that Yahuweh will "Rise up" before His enemies, and Yahuweh will "Return" to the families of Israel. These two verses are bracketed in the actual Hebrew Scriptures with the inverted Hebrew letter 'nun'. Rabbinic commentaries on this unique configuration in Torah generally reflect the belief that the verses are not in their original place, or are taken from another source.

However, inverted 'nun's are not just parentheses. Every jot, and every tittle in Scripture is there for a purpose, His purpose.

The letter 'nun' is the first letter of the Hebrew word "neefal", which means, 'to be raised up', 'to be lifted up', 'to be redeemed'.

The proclamation of Moses in the wilderness is an invocation of faith, gladness, and ultimate triumph in the Hope of Israel's redemption.

Might not the word "neefal", conveying all of this, be the real reason for the appearance of two 'nuns' in the Scripture?]

****

Except for the will of Heaven and the Plan of Election, the Messiah of Israel would have disappeared from history [His Story] "without a trace", (and the strong delusion of the man of lawlessness and false religion might have triumphed).

But in Yahuweh's perfect wisdom, through the preservation of Israel, faithful and obedient believers, His Torah, and the Messianic Scriptures, the sublime vision of a world redeemed will surely take place. And in that new heaven and new earth, at its center, in the New Jerusalem, will be the Rightful and Righteous Saviour and King.

YAHOSHUA THE MESSIAH,

"The Light in the Wilderness."

****

We are all on a journey in the wilderness from Mount Sinai, the mountain of Yahuweh.

As Moses proclaimed presently and prophetically, the Ark, the Presence of the Almighty Himself, which went before the nation on this special occasion, must rise up, and has risen up, in the resurrection of Yahuweh Yahoshua, the Living Presence, the Messiah of Israel.

And when the Ark will rest, on that eternal Sabbath, Yahuweh Yahoshua, the Messiah of Israel will return.

> "And [so] Yahuweh will be
> King over all the earth;
> in that day, Yahuweh will be the only One,
> and His Name, the only One."
> [Zechariah 14:9]

About the Author

Norman Martin Wolk, M.D. is a graduate of the University of Southern California School of Medicine and University of Colorado Medical Center, and has been a family physician since 1977.

For as long as he can remember, religion and revelation has held a special fascination for him, believing that man's wholeness and health cannot be separated from the "holiness", consecration, and purpose he is called to in obedient faith by the Author of Scripture Himself.

At the age of 29, Norman had a life changing "Damascus road experience", leading him to the Messiah of Israel, Who is "The Light in the Wilderness".

This is a wondrous journey of faith, courage, hope, and discovery. It will change the way you see not only this world and its religions, but the Kingdom of the Redeemer and 'the world to come'.

Printed in the United States
129729LV00001B/213/A

9 781425 957926